# DIGITAL DRAMA

## Teaching and Learning Art and Media in Tanzania

# Paula Uimonen

Routledge
Taylor & Francis Group

NEW YORK AND LONDON

First published 2012
by Routledge
711 Third Avenue, New York, NY 10017

Simultaneously published in the UK
by Routledge
2 Park Square, Milton Park, Abingdon, Oxon OX14 4RN

*Routledge is an imprint of the Taylor & Francis Group, an informa business*

© 2012 Taylor & Francis

*Library of Congress Cataloging in Publication Data*
Uimonen, Paula.
Digital drama : teaching and learning art and media in Tanzania /
Paula Uimonen.
    p. cm. – (Innovative ethnographies)
1. Arts–Study and teaching–Tanzania. 2. Digital media–Tanzania.
I. Title.
NX388.9.T3U36 2011
700.7109678–dc23                                            2011041156

ISBN: 978-0-415-89410-4 (hbk)
ISBN: 978-0-415-89411-1 (pbk)
ISBN: 978-0-203-12258-7 (ebk)

Typeset in Adobe Caslon
by Cenveo Publisher Services

SFI Certified Sourcing
www.sfiprogram.org
SFI-00453

Printed and bound in the United States of America
by Edwards Brothers, Inc.

*In loving memory of*
*Jouko Uimonen (1966–2003)*
*Vilho Uimonen (1935–2010)*
*Godwin Kaduma (1938–2007)*

*I dedicate this book to Simbo Ntiro (1961–2008)*

www.innovativeethnographies.net/digitaldrama

Please visit the book's website for access to additional ethnographic material including multimodal essays, digital audio documentaries, and photographs, as well as maps, links, and Google Earth Street View access to many of the sites described here. Readers of the electronic version of books in this series will be able to make use of hyperlinks embedded throughout the text. Readers of the traditional, print-based version of books in this series can access the same web pages by referring to the URLs and directions given in footnotes. Hyperlinks can be activated by clicking on the words preceding the following symbols:

indicates a *photograph*;

indicates an interactive Google *map*/Google Earth link;

indicates an external *web link*;

indicates a *video*;

indicates music or another type of *audio* file;

indicates a bonus *multimodal essay*;

indicates an interactive *dialogue* platform such as a blog;

indicates additional information such as a bonus text-based *essay*;

indicates drawings, sketches, graphics, or other *visual art* displays.

# Contents

CONTENTS

# ILLUSTRATIONS

# ACKNOWLEDGMENTS

Like all scholarly work, this book is very much a joint effort and many people deserve to be acknowledged for their individual and collective contributions to *Digital Drama*.

Let me start by thanking Helena Wulff and Ulf Hannerz for their unswerving support in seeing this project through. Helena's encouraging enthusiasm, scholarly dexterity and warm friendship have gotten me through many ups and downs over the years. An Africanist at heart, Ulf's careful reading of the whole manuscript gave me the confidence to complete it. I recognize the Tanzanian custom of lifelong gratitude to teachers as a humble way of expressing my respect for my intellectual mentor.

I would also like to extend my thanks to the reviewers who offered insightful comments throughout the project's various forms: Catherine Preston of Kansas University, Paul Stoller of West Chester University, and Christopher Kelty of University of California, Los Angeles.

Colleagues and students at the Department of Social Anthropology at Stockholm University have provided intellectual support for which I am grateful. A special thanks to all postgraduate students for your insightful contributions during courses on visual culture and digital anthropology and the many PhD students whose work I have been able to follow while teaching at the department.

I would also like to thank my new colleagues at the Department of Computer and Systems Sciences at Stockholm University. Since I took over the Swedish Program for ICT in Developing Regions (Spider) in January 2011, I have had the pleasure of discovering a remarkably dynamic, creative, and multidisciplinary environment. Special thanks to Love Ekenberg for appreciating digital anthropology and the Spider team for supporting my academic and managerial endeavors.

If it had not been for the virtual presence of my Facebook friends, the writing of this book would have been quite solitary and a lot more boring. Thank you for sharing the experience. Special thanks to Susanne Andersson, Åse Bjurholm, Fredrik Bertilsson, Tommy Dahlén, Paolo Favero, Sverker Finnström, Raoul Galli, Keith Hart, Anne-Lise Langoy, Katja Sarajeva, and Oliver Thalén for posting encouraging words, analytical hints, and stimulating reading.

This project was supported by a research grant from the Swedish International Development Cooperation Agency (Sida/SAREC) for which I am grateful. I would also like to thank the Tanzania Commission for Science and Technology (COSTECH) for the research permit that made my fieldwork possible.

Phillip Vannini, editor of the *Innovative Ethnographies* series for Routledge, has been a pillar of encouragement and inspiration since we first connected. Jonathan Taggart and Paul Ripley created the website for *Digital Drama*. Jonathan has patiently revised the site, for which I am grateful. I would also like to thank Anna Carroll for her careful copy-editing. Last but not least I thank Routledge for publishing this innovative series.

To all my Tanzanian and *mzungu* friends and research collaborators: *asanteni sana*! Whether or not you appear in *Digital Drama*, I can but hope that this book can repay some of your generosity, kindness, and hospitality. *Tukopamoja*! Special thanks to my Tanzanian mother Mama Kaduma and brother Sixmund Begashe, for your love and care. I also wish to thank John Sagatti, Hussein Masimbi, and Vitali Maembe for reading and encouraging my writing, David Estomihi for visual illustrations, and Julia Salmi for sharing *sisu* and *pamoja*. *Nashukuru* Mzee Rashid Masimbi for reading the entire manuscript and sharing your insightful and encouraging comments. Mzee Theophilus Mlaki thank you for acknowledging that this project grew into something much bigger than you had expected. Hopefully this book is worthy of the Father of Internet Social Networking in Tanzania it is dedicated to.

I am indebted to all of you, but only I can be blamed for any shortcomings in this text.

# ABBREVIATIONS

| | |
|---|---|
| AU | African Union |
| BAWA | Bagamoyo Women Artists |
| BCA | Bagamoyo College of Arts |
| COSTECH | Tanzania Commission for Science and Technology |
| DANIDA | Danish International Development Agency |
| DFID | Department for International Development (UK) |
| EAC | East African Community |
| EAP | Executive Agencies Programme |
| EASSy | Eastern Africa Submarine Cable System |
| FMI | Financial Management Initiative |
| GTZ | Deutsche Gesellschaft für Technische Zusammenarbeit |
| HKU | Utrecht School of the Arts |
| ICDL | International Computer Driving Licence |
| IDI | ICT Development Index |
| LFA | logical framework approach |
| MoEVT | Ministry of Education and Vocational Training |
| NACTE | National Council for Technical Education |
| Norad | Norwegian Agency for Development Cooperation |
| NOTA | Norway–Tanzania (project) |
| OAU | Organization of African Unity |
| OUT | Open University of Tanzania |
| PSRP | Public Service Reform Programme |

| Sida | Swedish International Development Cooperation Agency |
| TAMWA | Tanzanian Media Women's Association |
| TaSUBa | Taasisi ya Sanaa na Utamaduni Bagamoyo |
| TEA | Tanzania Education Authority |
| TLSB | Tanzania Library Services Board |
| TTCL | Tanzania Telecommunications Company Ltd |
| UDSM | University of Dar es Salaam |
| UPS | uninterruptable power supply |
| VSO | Volunteer Services Overseas |
| WAN | wide area network |
| WSIS | World Summit on the Information Society |
| ZIFF | Zanzibar International Film Festival |

# PART I
## MISE-EN-SCÈNE

# 1
## INTRODUCTION

*Tuwaenzi Wakongwe*[1]

The musicians look solemn as they beat their *ngoma*[2] (drum), while the slideshow slowly rolls on, projecting honorary text against the wall behind them. Maulid Mohammed is seated at the front of the group of drummers, dressed up for the occasion in a blue shirt with decorative stripes and matching trousers. His rhythmic drumming appears effortless, but after a while he breaks out in a sweat, as he speedily moves his long thin arms to beat the *ngoma*, one fastened between his legs, the other one on the floor next to him. Seated on simple wooden chairs, the handful of musicians are surrounded by a dozen drums of varying sizes, all handmade and decorated with strips of animal hide, in shades of white, brown, and black. Following customary practice, the drums have been tuned over an open fire to get the sound right, and they are played by hand, to accompany the dancers on stage. Master Musician Digalo is seated a few chairs down from Maulid. Both of them have been teaching traditional instruments for decades, and while they lack advanced formal education, their mastery of traditional music is unmistakable. One need not be an expert to appreciate the magic sound Maulid creates when striking the *ngoma*, while his missing front teeth and agile movements make for a lasting visual impression.

Hussein Masimbi stands behind his teachers, rhythmically beating the drum between his legs, his lips tightly sealed in concentration. The special event he has organized is finally coming together and judging from the positive response of the audience, everything seems to be falling into place.

*Tuwaenzi Wakongwe* (let us honor the legends) is the title of this special commemorative event, organized in tribute to deceased teachers at Taasisi ya Sanaa na Utamaduni Bagamoyo (TaSUBa)[3] ▨, formerly known as Chuo Cha Sanaa Bagamoyo or Bagamoyo College of Arts (BCA). The art college was established in 1981 by the government of Tanzania and remains the only institute for practical arts training in East Africa. The college offers a three-year diploma program in dance, drama, music, fine art, or stage technology, and short courses of varying duration. In 2007, the college was transformed into an executive agency, hence the name TaSUBa, which does not have an English equivalent, but translates into "Institute of Arts and Culture Bagamoyo." Following the ideals of neoliberal public sector reform, TaSUBa is expected to be more business oriented, managed at an arm's length from its parent ministry, Wizara ya Habari, Utamaduni na Michezo (Ministry of Information, Culture, and Sports). In theory, executive agencies are supposed to deliver public services in a more efficient and effective manner. In practice, the process of institutional transformation tends to be highly problematic. In the case of TaSUBa, it is wreaking havoc with the cultural essence of *sanaa* (art).

Tonight digital media interlace with traditional *ngoma*, beaten with bare hands to honor the legacy of past teachers, including the visionary *mwalimu* (teacher) Julius Nyerere, Tanzania's first president who sought to build the spirit of the nation in the hybrid form of *ujamaa*, African socialism. In this postcolonial state, cultural hybridity is a defining feature of the very process of *maendeleo* (development), along with Pan-Africanism and cosmopolitanism. When taking a closer look at artistic production and training at TaSUBa, through the life histories of its students, alumni, and teachers, we will find an incredible mix of cultural elements, a complex blend of cultures past and present, near and far. And to make sense of this cultural richness, along with the chaos, confusion, and crisis framing artistic production in Tanzania, we will rethink one of the classic concepts in anthropology—liminality—while exploring a new form of statehood—the state of creolization.

At TaSUBa, the contradictory forces of global capitalism accentuate a hybrid condition of permanent liminality, a sense of life that is always in between, a *state of creolization*. From the perspective of Tanzanian artists, *sanaa* serves as a mirror of society. It resides in a space of in between, occupying a liminal position in the social world. But liminality is not just a condition of betwixt and between, *neither here nor there*, as Victor Turner defined it in his classical anthropological work; it can also be viewed as a condition of being *both here and there*, then and now. This becomes evident when appraising TaSUBa's position in the state apparatus. By virtue of being a government agency, TaSUBa is both part of and apart from the state. I propose the term "state of creolization" to capture the complexities of an institutional framework that is as multifaceted as it is dynamic, blending different cultural strands in the context of asymmetric center–periphery relations. Linkages between culture and power in world society are intrinsic to anthropological uses of the concept of creolization, as exemplified in the work of Ulf Hannerz. And since anthropology is a discipline that is very much about the power of the between, as Paul Stoller so eloquently argues, it offers valuable insights into the complexities of cultural hybridity. This book takes cultural hybridity as its starting point, rather than conclusion, to nuance our understanding of globalization and cultural digitization. Having thus spelled out the theoretical gist of this book, let us return to the legends being honored through the power of drums, dance, and digital media.

Hussein got the idea to arrange this special event after the sudden death of Mzee Bazil Mbata on 13 October 2010. The late Mzee Mbata, a Master Musician[4] at the college, was only a few years away from retirement when he unexpectedly passed away. In addition to being a Master Drummer, Mbata was skilled in making and playing traditional instruments and composing music. Like most teachers at the college, Mbata originated from another part of the country, in his case one of the Makonde tribes in the south, his wife from the coastal region. They had six children, including Shabani Mbata, a recent graduate from the college, who drums together with Maulid, Digalo, and Hussein on this special evening of 17 December 2010. To honor his late father, Shabani is wearing a dark t-shirt, with a hand-painted image of a drum and the name Mbata written on the front.

Hussein Masimbi,[5] 🔊 a professional drummer and teacher at the college, is one of the many people Mbata trained and inspired during his almost three decades of work at the college. Now in his early thirties, Hussein spent the better part of his childhood and adolescence at the college, as the son of the first principal of Chuo Cha Sanaa, Mzee (honorary title for elders) Rashid Masimbi. At the time, the family lived in a simple house on campus, near the college canteen. Hussein became friends with many students who passed by his home and the artistic environment inspired him to pursue a career in arts, despite his father's misgivings about future income and employment opportunities. Hussein was particularly interested in music and learned to play the traditional *ngoma* as well as the modern drum kit. After graduating from the college with a diploma in arts, Hussein spent some time in Norway, following which he was recruited as a temporary teacher at the college, in dance and choreography. Softly spoken and diplomatic, with a handsome face and gentle smile, Hussein is known and liked by many people. His fluency in English and cultural suaveness are also appreciated by his many European friends and colleagues, making him a cultural broker par excellence. As for his artistic outlook, Hussein's understanding of *sanaa* builds on the embodied experience of having spent most of his life at the college, a sense of community that he feels has gotten lost over the last few years, although he is unsure why.

Like many students, alumni, and colleagues, Hussein was deeply touched by Mbata's sudden departure, so he wanted to organize a special event to mark the 40 days of his death, thus following the cultural practice of ending the customary 40-day mourning period with a celebratory event. But Hussein did not manage to do so on time. His colleagues from the dance department were also keen to organize something; hence they decided to prepare a bigger event, in honor of all departed teachers. Despite the cultural significance of mourning rituals in Tanzania, this kind of performance had never been organized at the college before. If successful, the event would be repeated annually, thus following the Tanzanian custom of organizing annual memorials for people who have passed away, in celebration of the lives they have led and the people they have touched.

In Tanzania, art is very much part of social life, and as such it is also positioned between life and death, embedded in social relations that extend to people who are no longer alive. The *Tuwaenzi Wakongwe* event was a way of re-establishing a translocal arts community in the spirit of *sanaa*, honoring past legends, while reasserting social ties between present and past artists within the social context of the surrounding community. In English the event was called a concert, but far from being a celebration of art for art's sake, it was inspired by a local understanding of art for society's sake, a truly social musical event.

Hussein and his colleagues prepared an evening of performances in a style they were all too familiar with, relying on the ethos of *pamoja* (togetherness). Hussein contacted some music groups he knew in Dar es Salaam and Bagamoyo, some of which he had performed with on past occasions. Even though they would not get paid, artists welcomed the opportunity to pay tribute to Mbata and other past teachers from the college. Some of the groups from Dar es Salaam were led by artists who had graduated from the college. Local groups had been inspired by the college in general, and many young artists had been trained by students at the college. Whether or not they had studied there, all groups were thus connected to the college, in one way or another. Teachers and students at the college were equally enthusiastic, especially those who specialized in traditional dance and music. Management remained rather aloof throughout the preparations, but allowed the organizers and performers to use the splendid facilities of the reconstructed TaSUBa Theater.

### Digital Tributes

The slideshow[6] 🎥 projected against the wall above the drummers is entitled *TUNAOWAENZI KUMBUKIZI* (let us honor the legends, in another version), with the subtitle *MUNGU AMETOA, NA MUNGU AMETWAA* (God gives, and God takes). The words are in capital letters, as is customary for headings written in Kiswahili. The honorary title and religious statement are followed by three slides with bulleted lists of names: Basil Mbata, Dr Hukwe Zawose, Ms Luiza Maganga, Martin Buriani, Thomas Umila, Kazaura Menard, Godwin Z. Kaduma, Lubeleje Chiuta, John Kyando, Kisaka A. Kisaka, Mbota Nyangi, Lugwisha Christian, Frank Makulugo. The slideshow runs in auto-mated mode, the names appearing one at a time, thus accentuating each individual teacher, before listing them in groups of four or five. The effect is spectacular; combining digitally produced textual tributes with the sights and sounds of drummers and dancers on stage, thus connecting past and present individuals within the context of a vibrant community. The slideshow is running from a laptop placed on a simple desk below the stage, next to it another desk with the projector. It is a makeshift arrangement, accentuating TaSUBa's peripheral position in the global network society, far from the metropolitan centers of the global art world. Yet the creative combination of digital media and traditional art forms reminds us that the digitization of culture is a dynamic process, one that builds upon and blends with preexisting cultural forms in innovative ways. In the state of creolization, cultural digitization tends to be low tech, yet high impact.

From time to time, David Estomihi runs over to restart the slide-show. In his mid-twenties, David is one of the youngest teachers at the college. He graduated from TaSUBa in 2009, with a major in fine arts and minor in stage technology. Talented, bright, and hard working, David was awarded "Best student in academics" upon graduation. He was retained at the college as a teacher assistant in fine arts, and to assist in the information and communication technology (ICT) build-ing, which is how I know him. David is a very softly spoken young man, with a slender physical build and gentle demeanor. He is from the *wachagga* tribe, born in the Kilimanjaro region, which is where his mother lives, working as a secondary school teacher. When he was a student, David was very good at drawing and painting, so he figured it might hold a future for him. He heard of the Bagamoyo College of Arts from a friend of the family who was studying at the University of Dar es Salaam (UDSM). David consulted his grandfather and they agreed that since he had a talent in arts, he should apply. In 2006, David took a short course at the college, and then he enrolled in the three-year diploma program. Since he majored in fine arts, David followed a curriculum that included a graphic design course in his third year and he also got the opportunity to attend extracurricular classes in computer animation led by Dutch students from the Utrecht School of the Arts (HKU). Having shown great talent in computer-mediated art work, and a general interest in technical matters, David got to work as an assistant in the ICT building after his graduation, helping out with ICT classes, technical troubleshooting, and website maintenance. Thanks to this position, he has regular access to computers, allowing him to create new forms of art work, which he often posts in Facebook. David likes to combine handmade and computer-based techniques, thus exploring the traditional–modern hybrid genre that distinguishes the more innovative forms of art production at TaSUBa.

The ICT building[7] where David works has been the main hub on campus for my fieldwork (2009), and before that, the main product of my years of engagement at the college as an ICT consultant (2004–2007), contracted by the Swedish International Development Cooperation Agency (Sida). I like to think of the ICT building as my baby, especially the room that students call the Internet room, the only place on campus where they can access the Internet. It was only in 2004 that Chuo Cha Sanaa got Internet access, a milestone in the college's history corresponding to local aspirations for membership of an interconnected world of arts. Most students have not used the Internet before joining the college, but once they enroll in the diploma program, they take ICT classes every semester, now a compulsory subject in the curriculum.

In a country like Tanzania, digital inclusion is a question of partial inclusion. At TaSUBa, 120 students share the meager facilities of a poorly equipped computer room. In 2010 management finally got around to investing some resources into the computer room, bringing the total number of computers to ten, instead of three to five.

It was in Facebook that I learned of Mbata's tragic death, through the postings of John Sagatti who at the time was in South Africa but in close contact with his friends at TaSUBa. Sagatti worked as a temporary teacher at the college for a few years before he went to Johannesburg in 2010 for an MA in drama. Word of Mbata's sudden departure spread rapidly, TaSUBa students, teachers, and alumni expressing their sadness on their Facebook walls, while supporting each other in their loss. Months later, when I posted a photo of Sagatti playing the keyboard at the *Tuwaenzi Wakongwe* event, he responded with a feeling shared by many people performing at the event:

> It made us feel good playing for people who worked so hard to give us what they had, it was an honor playing for them … I hope there will be next time … where we can join our hands and play again … I like the idea … Thanks Bacco [nickname for Hussein]!

A few days before the event, on 13 December 2010, David uploads a promotional poster in Facebook[8] that he has designed on a computer, thus making it visible to his network of more than 250 online friends. He adds almost 50 tags to the image, linking it to students, teachers and alumni from TaSUBa. The tagging highlights the event in his friends' profiles, thus spreading the news through online networks, while serving as an invitation to attend. David adds the comment "A TRIBUTE TO THE MASTERS!! DO NOT MISS" to the image and over the next few days he receives eight positive comments in reply, along with six "likes." Some of his friends will attend, others regret being too far away.

The *Tuwaenzi Wakongwe* poster is bilingual, offering details like *wasanii watakaokuwepo*/performing artists, *tarehe*/date, and *mahali*/ venue in Kiswahili as well as English. But the event itself is performed in Kiswahili, the national language Tanzanians are so proud of. It is also the language that Tanzanians prefer to use, especially in oral communication, and happily teach to visiting *mzungu* (white person, plural *wazungu*). At TaSUBa, English is supposed to be the language of instruction, but teachers tend to conduct their classes in Kiswahili, sometimes mixed with English. In Tanzania, even language use reflects the liminality of a state of creolization, combining international (English), national (Kiswahili), and local (tribal) languages in different contexts, a cultural hybrid of colonial and postcolonial modes of communication.

The poster is printed and posted in different places around Bagamoyo town, as well as on the TaSUBa notice board, thus spreading news of the event through more well established channels. The notice board hangs on the wall of the administration building, next to a public payphone that no longer works. It is framed by a wooden cabinet with locked glass doors, the key for which is kept in a nearby office, along with keys for other campus facilities. Schedules of classes and exams are posted on the board, as well as administrative information, social announcements, and promotional posters for performances and other cultural events. Students and faculty are expected to check the notice board every day, to keep abreast of what is happening at TaSUBa. Information is also passed on through more informal channels, not least as gossip and rumors. Tanzanians love to talk, and they love to gossip, which is one of the most important sources of information in everyday life.

Not surprisingly, it is above all through the poster and word of mouth that the audience of some 500 people is attracted to the commemorative event at TaSUBa. As is often the case, the audience is primarily local, composed of the TaSUBa community, Bagamoyo residents, and the occasional *mzungu*. The entrance fee is low, only TSH 1,000 (USD 0.80) for *wakubwa*/adults and TSH 500 for *wadogo*/ children, and no distinction is made between residents and non-residents. Hussein notes happily that they manage to collect over TSH 200,000, money that will be given to Mbata's family. But almost half the audience enters for free. Even TSH 1,000 is more than many locals can pay in this poverty-stricken town on the Swahili coast, yet on this particular evening, lack of cash is no obstacle to the consumption of art and culture.

The TaSUBa Theater is a magnificent venue for artistic perform-ances, and a key actor in *Digital Drama*. With an auditorium that seats 1,500 people, the theater is promoted as the largest performing arts venue in East Africa. It is a modern construction in concrete with white walls, wooden window frames and shutters, and a roof of corrugated iron. The main stage has a wooden floor, elegantly framed by long green drapes in batik and large wooden sliding doors. An international-standard sound and light system accentuates the per-formances on the spacious main stage, while concert-quality speakers mediate a soundscape that can be heard at quite some distance away.

This modern construction replaced the majestic African-style theater that dramatically burned down in 2002, thus initiating the digital drama of executive transformation that this book is about.

The audience is scattered throughout the large auditorium, most of them sitting in groups of family and friends. The concrete steps that serve as seats feel quite hard after a while, but since the auditorium is not packed, people can stretch their limbs from time to time and even move in and out of the auditorium without too much trouble. A handful of plastic chairs are placed below the mixing board in the middle of the auditorium, but they remain empty throughout the evening, a silent reminder of the absence of VIP guests. *Tuwaenzi Wakongwe* holds no political value, but its cultural significance is unmistakable, as evidenced in the startlingly numerous audience. The spectators express their appreciation through loud applause, punctuated by whistling and shrieking when exceptional artists perform on stage. In Tanzania, staged performances tend to be highly interactive, characterized by social proximity rather than distance between performers and audience.

The performances are documented with digital cameras and video cameras, as well as mobile phones. Throughout the evening, people (myself included) walk up to the stage to take close-up shots of the performers, while others capture the stage acts from afar. Most people in the audience do not possess cameras, but some have advanced mobile phones, thus enabling them to capture the performances on camera or video. Unlike more formal TaSUBa events, especially the annual arts festival, there is no designated staff documenting the event, but some of the faculty and students use their private equipment to record the performances.

It is quite impossible, however, to record the atmosphere in the theater, a sense of sadness mixed with vibrant creativity, feelings of loss muddled with joy and festivity. It is a very special evening indeed, the depths of which cannot be digitally recorded or documented, only experienced, through mind, body, and soul.

### Performing for the Legends

Mary Chibwana, Neema Mirambo, and Elizabeth Buriani suddenly enter the stage, just after a dance performance by a group of third-year

**Figure 1.1** TaSUBa students performing in honor of their teachers. Photograph by author

**Figure 1.2** Audience at *Tuwaenzi Wakongwe* event. Photograph by author

TaSUBa students. The drummers accompany their movements, as they slowly dance to the front of the stage, gently sweeping their arms and hands above the floor. Mama Neema and Mama Buriani have tied *khanga* (printed cloth) around their waists; Mama Mary is wearing a long tunica over her dark tights, with a matching glittering scarf tied around her waist. The women bend down on their knees at the front of the stage, while continuing their dramatic sweeping movements, as if cleaning the earth where their beloved ones are buried. Inspired by their improvised dance, Maulid stands up without missing a beat, bending his knees to hold the *ngoma* between his legs. The women complete their improvised tribute[9] 📷 by lowering their heads to kiss the floor and touch it with their cheeks, before rhythmically dancing off the stage. TaSUBa's senior dance tutors have paid their respects to their departed teachers and colleagues, and in the case of Mama Buriani, her late husband. With lifelong careers of serving their nation through cultural performances, initially through the National Dance Troupe, then as students and teachers at Chuo Cha Sanaa, these stunningly beautiful women were among the first female professional dancers in Tanzania. Tonight they honor the legends they have performed with in the past through an improvised dance that expresses the very spirit of the nation, embodied in the staged performance of traditional art and culture.

On this special evening, TaSUBa is honored by the presence of family members of the late Zawose, Kaduma, Luiza, and Mbata. Their attendance is acknowledged by the Master of Ceremony, Timothy T.C. Chelula, a TaSUBa student who also works as a record producer at Studio 69 in Dar es Salaam. T.C. is dressed up for the occasion in black trousers, a white long-sleeved shirt and a necktie, with a black ribbon tied around his sleeve, a global symbol of mourning. From time to time, T.C. announces the presence of family members of the departed teachers, and at one point he asks them to stand up and make themselves known to the audience. Mama Kaduma, who rarely attends performances at the college, despite living next to the campus, is dressed up for the occasion in a beautiful yellow dress, with a thin gold-embroidered white scarf wrapped around her torso and a matching scarf tied around her hair, her earlobes adorned with gold jewellery.

I sit next to her for a while, my beloved Tanzanian mother, who readily adopted me as her daughter after the passing of her late husband, who was like a father to me. Mama Kaduma enjoys the performances, but she later tells me that upon hearing the name Godwin Kaduma she felt a lump in her throat. It is even more unusual that the Zawose family is seen at TaSUBa. The late Dr Zawose was one of Tanzania's most famous musicians, hand-picked by Nyerere and internationally recognized by the likes of Peter Gabriel, with whom he performed. Zawose also taught at Chuo Cha Sanaa for a while, but his family has felt neglected by the college for a long time. Tonight they are present, appreciating that people at the college remember their late father.

Traditional dance, acrobatics, and music are the main ingredients of the program, performed by TaSUBa teachers and students as well as outside artists. John Mponda, senior dance teacher and choreographer, leads a group of students in a dance[10] 📷 they have practiced only for a few days. Among the students is Julia Salmi, a young woman from Finland who is taking the diploma program at TaSUBa, majoring in dance, with drama as minor. It takes a while before I spot Julia on stage, her characteristic blond dreadlocks hidden under a black headscarf. Not used to wearing a costume, Julia keeps readjusting the scarf tied around her waist, but she dances in perfect synchrony with her fellow students. A group of acrobats[11] 📷, trained by one of the teachers at TaSUBa, performs several numbers. Their brightly patterned, full body costumes are visually pleasing and some of their more daring stunts, like three people standing on top of each other, are well received by the audience. Acrobatics has been part of the repertoire of national culture since the 1960s, a gift from China during the heydays of *ujamaa*. For many years it was a compulsory subject at Chuo Cha Sanaa, but in the specialized TaSUBa curriculum, acrobatics is only taught to dance and drama students.

When Master Musician Werema Chacha[12] 📷 performs a solo number on stage, the audience responds with loud enthusiasm. Seated on a low stool, Chacha strings his *litungu*,[13] 📷 a traditional instrument from the Mara region. It is a harp-like instrument with eight strings fastened to a wooden frame and a round body of animal hide. The muffled sound of the *litungu* is amplified by a microphone, which also captures the sound of bells fastened to a long wooden stick that Chacha masters with his toes to beat the rhythm. When Chacha retired from Chuo Cha Sanaa a few years ago, the art of *litungu* playing retired along with him. I miss Master Musician Matitu on stage, and the beautiful sound of his *marimba* (xylophone), but I am told he is out of town. He has also retired from the college, but he has been called back to teach as a consultant, he tells me excitedly when I meet him later on. With both Maulid and Matitu back at the college, traditional music may stand a chance after all.

Well into the evening, it is time for Vitali Maembe to perform, a graduate from Chuo Cha Sanaa, now a professional artist. Earlier in the evening Maembe has been drumming along with Maulid, Hussein, and Digalo. He starts off with a song that Mbata taught him, to remind the audience that he was a teacher. "He taught me this song," Maembe explains to the audience, "and he still had so many things to give us, but he left. He also encouraged us, we don't have to worry so much, because this is also how the *aliunyelu* (insect/bee) is doing it." He proceeds with the song about the *aliunyelu* in Mbata's tribal language:

> *Aliunyelu mwanja* (The bee is leaving)
> *Kuleka mapemba gangacha* (Left the seed, but it is not yet ready for harvesting)
> *Aliunyelu mwakutenda, aliunyelu mwakutenda* (This is how the bee is doing it x 2)

It is a song that is related to Mbata's death, which was very sudden. The *aliunyelu* is very important, because it makes something happen, by fertilizing flowers (*mapemba*). So the bee comes and gives something good to the plant, but then it leaves, without waiting to see if the plant is ready. Mbata had indeed fertilized many plants, at the college as well as in private. Maembe was one of them and the Master Drummer treated him like a son. Mbata never asked Maembe for payment after their private classes, instead he would occasionally ask him to buy him a drink or contribute something if and when needed, and only if Maembe had money to spare. Mbata was a man who did not like quarrels; he was very open and responsible to people around him, Maembe recollects.

Maembe proceeds with *Leo* (today), a song of his own that celebrates traditional dance (*ngoma*), which he performs in an improvised connection with his ancestors. As he sings he calls his ancestors: Zawose, Kaduma, Mwendapole, Mbata, and Nyerere. He also includes lyrics by Zawose and Mwendapole in his song. Maembe has not planned to make this connection; it just comes to him on stage, he later tells me. As he sings, he feels that he is communicating straight with those people. People he has never met, like Mwendapole, people who have advised him on his music, like Kaduma, or people with whose families there has been mutual respect, like Zawose. He just mentions all those people who are there with him, including his late father as well as the father of the nation, Nyerere. "Let us call our ancestors[14] 📷 to bless our day," and they come.

During his third and final act, Maembe sings *Mwali Selina*[15] 🎸 (little girl Selina), another cheerful song praising dance, which inspires many friends to dance with him on stage. When Maembe takes off his guitar, young men from the audience jump up on stage to dance along with him. Even T.C. gets inspired, and they perform a double act. Suddenly Shabani Mbata joins the band, excitedly beating his *ngoma*, while Hussein Masimbi masters the drum kit that is hoisted on a wooden platform on the side of the stage. John Sagatti towers over the keyboard. As more and more people flock to the stage, Maembe casually walks off to briefly watch them from the auditorium. The people sitting next to him are busy recording the performance on their mobile phones. Maembe returns to the stage and joins the dance, rhythmically moving his strong, lean body in unison with his friends on stage.

"*Sanaa* is back at TaSUBa!" I marvel, as I experience this special evening of performances, executed with so much feeling, creativity, improvisation, and humor. Tonight I can feel the heart of TaSUBa beating new life into the culture of Tanzania and its ethos of *pamoja*.

"This is how *Digital Drama* should end," I think to myself, because this is what TaSUBa is all about, a place for *sanaa*. But the story does not end here. So let me use the rest of this book to explain how TaSUBa lost sight of *sanaa*, and with it the spirit of the nation.

## Outline of the Book

*Tuwaenzi Wakongwe* takes place when I am at TaSUBa to go through my draft manuscript with the people who appear in this book. I spend three weeks in Bagamoyo in December 2010, carefully reviewing passages with the individuals who appear in them, correcting minor mistakes in the text. I have several meetings with the Chief Executive and the Academic Director to discuss the manuscript. With the help of John Sagatti I also organize group meetings with teachers and students. I meet with Rashid Masimbi in Dar es Salaam on two occasions, the second time to go through the entire manuscript. The Chief Executive Juma Bakari gives his comments on the draft while I am in Bagamoyo and sends the comments of his colleagues in the management group via email after my return to Sweden. I consult the Europeans I write about via email prior to my travel to Tanzania, and after my return I receive a long critical commentary from the NOTA project representatives. Meanwhile, my manuscript is being scrutinized by the reviewers appointed by the publisher. Only a year has passed since I completed my fieldwork and *Digital Drama* is nearing completion. I spend the next few months revising the text and hopefully you now find it readable.

The aim of this book is to describe and explain the changing circumstances of art production and training at TaSUBa, with an emphasis on digital media and intercultural interaction. A related aim is to provide a critical analysis of how the neoliberal culture complex is performed in the peripheries of the global network society, in the context of postcolonial, postsocialist Tanzania. Since the analysis deals with questions of nationalism, Pan-Africanism, and cosmopolitanism, along with the social processes of creolization, digitization, and cultural brokering, the book also aims to build upon and contribute to anthropological theory building on globalization. A final purpose of this book is to explore more innovative ways of writing and presenting ethnography.

The title *Digital Drama* draws on the concept of *social drama* (Turner 1996 [1957], 1987), to underline this book's anthropological orientation. Turner (1987, 74) defined social dramas as "units of aharmonic or disharmonic social process, arising in conflict situations," with four main phases of public action: breach, crisis, redressive action, and restoration. I use the term "digital drama" to capture a social drama of considerable complexity, the institutional transformation of a government arts college (BCA) into an executive agency (TaSUBa). The introduction of the Internet in 2004 forms part of these institutional transformations, aimed at introducing more neoliberal forms of governance and a more business-oriented mode of cultural production. The word "digital" in the title signals this book's disciplinary lineage in digital anthropology. As one of the pioneers of this emerging research field, I use this opportunity to explore how digital media can be studied ethnographically and, more importantly, how anthropological knowledge can be used to describe and explain cultural digitization in an African setting.

As suggested in the subtitle, I focus on digital media in the context of teaching and learning at an arts institute that is historically and culturally linked to *the* teacher of Tanzania, *mwalimu* Julius Nyerere. In addition to looking at how digital media are used in art training and production I investigate their role in historical developments, thus building on the anthropology of art and aesthetics as well as previous research on art, culture, nationalism, and politics in Tanzania. State-making in an African context is of particular relevance for my analysis, along with relations of dependency and inequality in a highly asymmetric world order, issues dealt with in great depth by the scholars I rely on in my analysis.

Having thus introduced the gist of this book, a few words should be said about its accompanying website[16] . You are encouraged to visit the website while reading the book, to get a better feel for the sounds, images, characters, and events described in the text. The site contains about 160 photos and 23 videos, along with links to relevant online resources. Having experimented with various websites related to my research since 1997, I welcome this opportunity to publish a book that takes advantage of the interactive, multimedia nature of the Internet. The website tells the story of *Digital Drama* in the form of a visual, digital narrative that aims to deepen your understanding of the textual narratives in this book. For e-book readers, hyperlinks in the text will guide you to the online material, but the site should also be viewed on its own. Hopefully this print/e-book/website experiment can strengthen the production and presentation of anthropological knowledge. I look forward to your reflections and feedback through the website!

This book is divided into nine chapters, organized into three thematic parts, followed by a postscript. The first part (Mise-en-Scène) introduces TaSUBa, Bagamoyo, and Tanzania, while outlining the theoretical orientation of this research project. The ethnography is presented in Parts II and III, structured into thematic chapters. The second part (Cultural Transformations) introduces the digital drama of executive transformation, discussed and elaborated in relation to arts training and production. The third part (Cultural Dependencies) focuses on intercultural interaction, through cultural exchange and performances, to reach the concluding climax of *Digital Drama*. Each chapter starts with a historical retrospect, followed by analyses of more contemporary events or activities, then concluding with a more focused discussion on cultural digitization. The postscript contains methodological reflections, explaining how the data gathering process was carried out.

The characters in this book appear with their real names and identities, instead of fictitious names and anonymous descriptions. At times I use more anonymous terms, when citing statements that are quite general, or of a more sensitive nature, or in case someone has chosen to withdraw their name. The decision to use real names was largely influenced by the opportunity of having a website accompanying the printed book, the online publication of audiovisual material rendering any concerns about hiding the identities of research collaborators rather meaningless. Moreover, since this is the first ethnography of TaSUBa, it would only seem fair that the people who have contributed to my research also get their place in history. Even so, the analysis aims at drawing theoretical insights that cannot be pinned down to any specific person or event described in this book. So no one who appears in this book should be blamed for the conclusions I make. In recognition of my debt to my research interlocutors, I can but concur with Narayan and George (2001, 828): "In receiving stories from people, we are often receiving gifts of self: it is incumbent on us to handle these gifts with respect as we pass them onward in our scholarly productions." I sincerely hope I manage to do so.

Let me underline that this book intends no harm to anyone. I know that the standard answer to *habari?* (what is new?) is *nzuri* (fine), and I do appreciate this positive spin on everyday life in Tanzania. Yet there is something to be said for the little word that can be placed between how things should be and how things really are: *lakini* (but). Since anthropologists are the "sojourners of 'the between'" (Stoller 2009, 4), the *lakini* is every bit as important as the *nzuri*. For in between things is where we find the social reality we aim to describe and explain: in the dissonances between what people say they do and what they actually do, in the discrepancies between ideals and practices, in the discords between vision and reality. In between things we find the conflicts, tensions, and contradictions that make for interesting ethnography. This is also the stuff that makes for interesting drama, as the *msanii* (artist) knows all too well. And since art and anthropology are linked in different ways, not least as narrators of the in between, this social drama is the stuff of *Digital Drama*.

# 2

# Storyboard of *Digital Drama*

*Karibu TaSUBa!*[1]

Even before you see the campus, you can hear TaSUBa, through the rhythmic sound of *ngoma* and *marimba*. The music guides you across an unpaved sandy road, framed by large trees that give some relief from the blazing hot sun, to a large iron gate marking the campus entrance.[2] The sound of traditional instruments grows louder as you enter the gate and approach its origin, a large mango tree with young music students seated on tree trunks on your left, tutored by *mwalimu* Matitu, a gangly, old Master Musician. On your right you see a one-story building, with a spectacular view over the Indian Ocean. The side is painted with Bagamoyo College of Arts, Internet Café[3] in bold black text, against a blue background, depicting the sea and the sky. This is the ICT building where art students explore and experiment with digital media, creating hybrid fusion art, while communicating and interacting with their friends and the world at large on the Internet. *Karibu TaSUBa!* Welcome to TaSUBa![4]

If you arrive at night, the brightly lit theater building will greet you from afar, guiding your way through the dusky town of Bagamoyo. Most evenings, the campus is quiet, enveloped in the gentle sounds of cicadas and crickets, with dogs barking or howling in the distance.

Occasionally the silence is punctuated by the roaring engines of a car or *piki piki* (motorcycle) passing by. In the dormitories across the road from the main gate, students are usually resting after taking their evening meal of *ugali* (maize porridge) or *wali* (rice) in the canteen. If there is an event, the campus gets louder, as Bagamoyo residents and curious visitors come to enjoy music, dance or drama performances by local and visiting artists. The murmurs of chatting voices, shuffling bodies, and ringing mobiles intermingle with the smell of perspiration emanating from warm bodies squeezed together on the hard concrete steps of the auditorium. TaSUBa staff and students scurry around, attending to visiting artists and guests, when not performing on stage themselves.

Welcome to the storyboard for *Digital Drama*, an ethnography about digital media and intercultural interaction at TaSUBa, animated with Tanzanian sounds, sights, and sentiments. *Digital Drama* tells the stories of young students who aspire to become artists to serve as mirrors of society, and teachers with lifelong careers in art who have performed worldwide, recontextualizing traditional art and culture in modern settings. It also tells the stories of European teachers and students, who come to Tanzania to pass on their modern skills and to learn more about traditional African art and culture. And there is a story to be told of TaSUBa itself, the origins of which can be traced back to the early days of independence and the urge to preserve and promote traditional culture to craft a national identity, as envisaged by Julius Nyerere, one of the most radical of Africa's early leaders. Entangled in the neoliberal paradigms of global capitalism, the institute is now performing a new role, mediated by digital technology, scripted through executive plans, dramatized through power struggles, and with signs and symbols of modernity as props. The cast is segmented, struggling to make sense of a world that is changing at a pace they cannot keep up with, let alone comprehend, nostalgic for the lost visions of their past.

To most people, TaSUBa is still known as Chuo Cha Sanaa, a bastion of traditional culture since its foundation in 1981, but word is slowly spreading of the many changes taking place due to institutional transformations. While the insistence on a Kiswahili name—Taasisi ya

Sanaa na Utamaduni Bagamoyo—was a deliberate decision to promote the national language, the institute is gradually becoming further and further removed from its cultural roots. Indeed the transformation into an executive agency in 2007 has revealed some of the cracks in a state apparatus that has never placed particular emphasis on culture, despite official rhetoric to the contrary. And in these cracks we find the digital drama of executive transformation that this monograph is concerned with, a conceptual space of liminality, an in-between place that beckons us to recast the mirror image of the state in terms of a state of creolization.

TaSUBa enjoys a beautiful, tranquil location, the spacious campus leading down to a beach lined with palm trees, where traditional *dhow* (sail boats) slowly pass by. Next to the beach is a conglomeration of one-story buildings: three classrooms, a library, and administrative offices. This part of campus is green and luscious, with sprinkler-watered parcels of grass and leafy trees. In front of the administration building is a cabinet-like structure, with glass doors and a small corrugated iron roof. The cabinet displays the Master Plan, posters with computer-generated images outlining plans for infrastructure development. The first phase of the Master Plan is manifested in the nearby theater and flexible hall, large modern constructions in concrete, with white painted walls and wooden window frames and shutters. Hidden behind a corrugated iron fence is another part of this phase, a modern two-story beach house, divided into the Principal's house and a small guesthouse. Near the entrance gate is the Mwembe (mango) theater, a small concrete stage and an open-air auditorium, framed by large mango trees.

The ocean breeze that rustles the trees by the beach subsides as you walk into the interior, where the campus stretches through a large, mostly underdeveloped area, with some derelict buildings used by the music and fine arts departments. Above these buildings is the recently renovated campus canteen, with a large dining hall and a roofed outdoor eating area that doubles as a classroom. Large trees provide shaded areas for art practice and social interaction in front of the canteen. Behind the canteen is the road, across it student dormitories. Most dormitories are run down, offering cramped accommodation

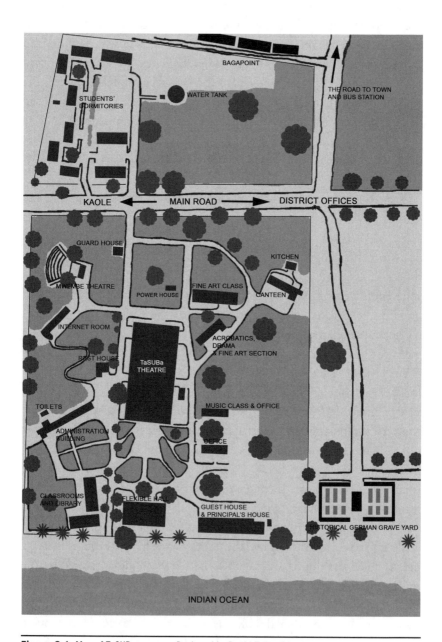

**Figure 2.1** Map of TaSUBa campus. Designed by David Estomihi

in fanless rooms shared by two to four students. Although the planned renovation of the old dormitories was neglected in the first phase of the Master Plan, the construction of some new dormitories was completed, offering more spacious accommodation, for those who can afford it.

South of the campus is Beach Bora Resort and a few hundred meters down, the exclusive Millennium Hotel. While the low-cost resort is quiet most of the time, the hotel is often busy, hosting conferences and workshops for different organizations from Dar es Salaam, mostly government agencies. On top of the hill, across the sandy road leading to the hotels, is the private residence of the late Mzee Kaduma, with a small private theater he constructed prior to his untimely death, a lasting testimony to his lifelong career as actor, playwright, and Director of Culture. On the edge of the residence, some small buildings are rented by local shopkeepers, offering food items, refreshments and snacks to customers, mostly from TaSUBa, the police station and the nearby residential area as well as *mzungu* volunteers and tourists. North of the campus is the German Cemetery, with tombstones of former colonial rulers facing the ocean, and next to it, the Badeco Beach Hotel, with its white triangular monument and black sign denoting the "place where the German colonialists used to hang to death revolutionary Africans who were opposing their oppressive rule." A small pathway leads up the hill from the cemetery, past Mwanamakuka primary school located behind the college canteen. The school derives its name from another nearby cemetery where abandoned tombstones designate the burial site of the black Swahili ruler Mwanamakuka, a local leader predating the German colonialists.

On the other side of the road, next to the student dormitories, is an area known as Bagapoint with some shops selling tourist art and cafeterias serving *wali*, *ugali* and *chips* (deep-fried potato). Popular among TaSUBa teachers and students, foreign volunteers and local rastas, the cafeterias stay open until late evening, serving cold beer to the sound of loud music. An unpaved road leads past Bagapoint into Bagamoyo town, passing a large football ground, a primary school and a post office, before intersecting with the main road leading to Dar es Salaam and a road leading to the local bus station. Returning to TaSUBa, the

road leading to the college continues south to Kaole, a historical trading post predating Bagamoyo, and north to historical sites, passing
local government offices, a fish market, and tourist hotels.

Bagamoyo[5] 🔱 is a small town some 75 kilometers north of Dar es
Salaam, across the fabled island of Zanzibar. Located on the Swahili
coast, it has a history of intercultural engagement, from Arabic and
Indian traders to Christian missionaries and German colonial administrators (Mercer 2007). In the first half of the nineteenth century,
Bagamoyo became an important trade post for slaves, ivory and other
commodities. As coastal trade shifted from Kilwa in the south to
Zanzibar, Bagamoyo prospered accordingly, becoming the island's
main connection on the mainland and a hub in the slave route leading
to the interior of Tanganyika. By then Kaole had stagnated and today
only some ruins remain of this former trading post. Over time,
Bagamoyo has evolved into a town of some fame, not least due to its
cultural history. The name Bagamoyo, from *bwaga* (lay down) and
*moyo* (heart) is generally associated with the slave trade of the past,
alluding to the despair of slaves upon landing in this coastal town for
shipment to the slave markets in Zanzibar.

Although predominantly Muslim, Bagamoyo served as the landing
point for the first Christian missionaries in East Africa, and the
Catholic mission is still one of the most influential religious actors in
town, maintaining its only museum. Bagamoyo was also the place
where Arab and Western explorers ventured inland, John Hanning
Speke passing the town in his search for the source of the Nile, Henry
Morton Stanley in his search for David Livingstone, and although
Livingstone himself chose a different route for his explorations, his
remains passed through Bagamoyo, temporarily resting at the chapel of
the Bagamoyo Mission, before being shipped onward to Zanzibar and
England. For a short period, between 1886 and 1891, Bagamoyo was
the headquarters of German East Africa, a German colony that lasted
from the 1880s to World War I, and included what is now Burundi,
Rwanda, and Tanganyika. In the *Encyclopædia Britannica* of 1911,
early communication and transportation linkages are recognized:
"Bagamoyo is in telegraphic communication with Zanzibar and
with the other coast towns of German East Africa, and has regular

steamship communication with Zanzibar." From 1922 until self-rule in 1961, Tanganyika was a British mandate. Today, Bagamoyo is the district town of Bagamoyo district, with an estimated population of more than 80,000 people.

Before the road connecting Bagamoyo to Dar es Salaam was paved in 2002, it was a quiet, sleepy Swahili town, with fishing and agriculture serving as main sources of income. The tarmac road has brought a faster pace of development and a greater degree of mobility, the journey to Dar es Salaam taking only one to two hours as opposed to the better part of a day. Rapid urban development has also brought Bagamoyo physically closer to the commercial capital of Tanzania, as the outskirts of Dar es Salaam have expanded considerably. The bustling bus station in Bagamoyo, constructed a few years ago with assistance from Sweden, has evolved into a main transportation hub serving the whole district. Although tourism is still relatively small, Bagamoyo attracts a growing number of international as well as domestic visitors, and it is a favorite destination for workshops and similar events for public servants. Despite its economic growth, Bagamoyo remains relatively poor, offering few income opportunities, especially for youth. In the middle-class residential area near TaSUBa a fair number of modern housing complexes are being constructed. But most housing in Bagamoyo is of far more modest means, ranging from clay to unpainted brick walls. The town has a vibrant market area, within walking distance from the bus station, and a growing number of small shops, beauty salons, and eating places. There are quite a few shops selling mobile phones and phone accessories and a few Internet cafes, some even air conditioned, catering to local residents as well as visitors.

### Tutors, Students, and *Mzungu*

"This was all a big forest, even the place where I stay now was forest," Mary Chibwana recollects as she recounts her arrival in Bagamoyo in the early 1980s. Only 16 years old when she was recruited by the National Dance Troupe, Mary spent a few years in Dar es Salaam, staying in the urban area of Ilala, where she worked with girls from different regions. During the mornings they had rehearsals and in the evenings classes, to go through secondary education. When Bagamoyo College of Arts was established, she and a few other young women got a chance to go there for further study so they could become teachers at the college. Unhappy to be in a forest, a dark place with no disco, Mary initially wanted to return to Dar es Salaam, but decided to stay on after all. Now in her mid-forties, Mary has spent most of her professional career teaching traditional dance, and she notes that "students are happy with me as *mwalimu*." She also enjoys giving courses to Europeans, to teach people with "no rhythm or movement," as she puts it. Mary is, however, frustrated by the college's new curriculum which doesn't allow her "to go deep in teaching," and even more perturbed by the state of traditional culture, especially dance, which is "going down."

Since her first journey abroad, the destination for which was an African Festival in Nigeria in 1977, Mary has performed in different parts of the world. All the travelling here and there has made her feel "well known in the world." She also runs a small guesthouse, catering to Western tourists. Originally she set up the guesthouse for *mzungu* who were coming to study *ngoma* at the college. But nowadays Mary's Nice Place caters to everyone, a welcoming guesthouse within walking distance from the college. At TaSUBa, Mary is part of the theater management group, exploring more commercial venues for artistic production, her life history thus continuing to be interwoven with the institute's social trajectory. Whenever she gets a chance, she encourages performances in traditional dance, organizing events like *Usiku wa Ngoma* (Dance Night) with local dance groups. And she often gets on stage herself, whether to perform an improvised promotional pitch, a traditional dance, or to honor her deceased colleagues, as was the case at the *Tuwaenzi Wakongwe* commemorative event she starred in.

Mary recalls with great pride that one of the reasons she was selected for the National Dance Troupe was her "beautiful appearance" and three decades later she remains strikingly attractive. Now a full-figured *mama* (honorary title for women), Mary's feminine features accentuate a woman of great beauty, who carries herself with great confidence. Mary is always stylish, often wearing tailored skirts or dresses, sometimes trousers with a tunica on top, with colorful accessories matching her outfit, along with different hair styles, straight, curly or pleated, naturally black or with colored streaks. Something of a drama queen, Mary is rather theatrical in her everyday behavior, often using vivid gestures to underline her equally dramatic words and expressions, sometimes clicking her tongue for emphasis. Mary is quite fluent in English, but she prefers to communicate in Kiswahili.

Like Mary, most teachers at TaSUBa have several, overlapping professional identities, as artists and performers, as teachers or tutors as they prefer to call themselves, and as government employees. In everyday professional life, these identities are expressed in a variety of ways. In the morning, teachers sign in at the administrative office in government ledgers that track their working hours. Their teaching schedules are neatly posted on the official notice board, along with a detailed schedule of the whole academic year. Teaching duties are interspersed with performances, at TaSUBa and elsewhere. The prestigious Bagamoyo Players are composed of some of the most senior teaching staff, with a long track record of performances in different parts of Tanzania and abroad. In their everyday interaction, the artistic disposition of the teaching staff is evident in their humorous and often dramatic modes of communication, with expressive body language and animated story telling. Their dress code is that of creative artists rather than state employees, with colorful batiks, tailored outfits of their own design, and t-shirts from past performances or projects. Only the Chief Executive and some male staff members sometimes wear suits, a government dress code that most of the faculty ignores, despite the institute's new executive agency status.

In terms of social organization, TaSUBa can be categorized into three, hierarchically structured social groups: management/administration, teachers/tutors, and students. Each group is internally stratified: management/administration is subdivided into the Chief Executive and the management group, which directs the work of the administrative staff. The teaching staff, which numbers between 40 and 50, consists mainly of senior tutors, who are middle aged or near retirement and a handful of junior tutors in their twenties or thirties. The students, now 120 in total, are categorized according to their year of study and collectively represented by a student union, which has a small office in one of the art buildings. In terms of social class, most staff and students belong to a relatively privileged social stratum, the minority of Tanzanians who have completed secondary education. By virtue of holding permanent positions in the civil service, teachers can be categorized as middle class, although their artistic position sets them apart from the urban, professional elite. BCA used to attract students based on talent rather than resources, but the higher tuition fees charged by TaSUBa are translating into a more elitist student body. When it comes to gender, women are in a minority, constituting only 20–25 percent of the student body and faculty.

Reflecting the cultural hybridity of Tanzanian nationalism, TaSUBa is ethnically diverse, constituting a translocal arts community (Uimonen 2009a). Officially the country has some 124 ethnic groups, or tribes, as they are locally known. In everyday life, tribal identity is mainly expressed through ethnic stereotyping and intertribal joking relations. Tribal culture is also embedded in the various art forms taught at TaSUBa, especially traditional dance and music, which are linked to their tribal origin. In Tanzania, tribal identities are, however, secondary to the overriding national identity. Indeed, the translocal character of Tanzanian nationalism, which has always been decidedly transtribal (Geiger 1997), needs to be emphasized. In Tanzania, unlike most countries in Sub-Saharan Africa, ethnic identity is subsumed under an overriding national identity, not just in political rhetoric but in everyday life. People marry across tribal groupings, people move across tribal areas, and people speak in tribal as well as non-tribal languages, many mastering several local languages: the languages of their parents, their spouse, and the area where they live.

This sense of national identity, so deeply embedded in the Tanzanian sense of self and society, is most clearly articulated through the national language, Kiswahili. Disassociated from tribalism or colonialism, Kiswahili solidifies national unity, regardless of citizens' tribal origins. Tanzanians take great pride in their national language and their country is considered the origin of this African language spoken by more than 100 million people on the continent. Like the French, Tanzanians can discuss their language at great length, and opinions often differ about phrasing and spelling.[6] Tanzanians never seem to tire in their efforts to teach visiting *mzungu* at least a few words of Kiswahili, and they like to greet the rest of the world in their national language, as exemplified by the default language of the bilingual (Kiswahili/English) website of Chuo Cha Sanaa (Uimonen 2009a). Even so, reflecting its colonial legacy and continued dependence on donor aid, as well as aspirations to be part of world society, English is the official language of higher education (from secondary school) and the higher courts. This emphasis on English does not correlate with people's language skills or everyday practices. Most Tanzanians are far from fluent in English and many feel shy to speak it. Even in situations where they have to write in English (e.g. the classroom), people tend to speak in Kiswahili. This code switching is evident at TaSUBa, where textbooks, assignments, and exams are in English but classroom instruction tends to be in Kiswahili.

Religious identities are equally diverse and the TaSUBa community is made up of both Muslims and Christians. Staff and students regularly attend religious services in local mosques and churches; sometimes religious events are organized on campus. In everyday speech, plans and predictions tend to be followed by statements like "God willing" or "*inshallah*," illustrating how human action is considered to be determined by higher powers, including of course more traditional forms of spiritual power, like witchcraft, for which Bagamoyo is quite famous throughout Tanzania.

TaSUBa is also culturally diverse—*mzungu* visitors and collaborators are regularly seen on campus, along with the occasional international student. The college is featured in travel guides to Tanzania as one of Bagamoyo's worthwhile sites to visit, especially during the annual arts festival. Transnational connections with cultural others form part of TaSUBa's history, embodied in collaborative relations with artists and art institutes from around the world. The college has also been supported by donor agencies, especially the Norwegian Agency for Development Cooperation (Norad) and the Swedish International Development Cooperation Agency (Sida), and it has worked together with institutes like Deutsche Gesellschaft für Technische Zusammenarbeit (GTZ), Danish International

Development Agency (DANIDA), and the British Council, as well as some UN agencies.

### The Script of Digital Anthropology[7]

You can assess the number of people inside the Internet room from the amount of shoes scattered outside the entrance door.[8] This room is one of the few places on campus with a wall-to-wall carpet, a thin, burgundy-colored floor covering, kept clean with a modern vacuum cleaner and the custom of removing one's shoes before entering a private space. This is of course not a private space, quite the opposite; it is one of the most popular places on campus, at least for students. During ICT classes, as many as 15 pairs of shoes clutter outside the closed door, a motley assembly of sandals, sneakers, and slippers. Between ICT classes, the number of shoes varies from a few to over a dozen pairs. Students drift in and out of the room, work on assignments, check their email accounts, log into Facebook, or search for information online. They tend to sit together, two or three at each computer, chatting with each other, while taking notes on paper or saving information on flash disks (USB memory sticks). At night and on weekends, the room is dark and quiet, secured with a sturdy iron gate locked with heavy padlocks.

The number of shoes outside is in stark contrast to the number of computers inside. Two rows of wooden tables crafted by a local artisan, meticulously marked with serial letters and numbers denoting their institutional ownership hold some seven to eight computers, typically only three to five of them working. The 15-inch flat screens convey a flashy high-tech image that is somewhat counteracted by the slow speed of the computers, their processing speed dating back to 2004, when they were first procured. In Europe, the computers would probably have been replaced after three or four years, but this is Africa where machines get fixed well past due date. At the back of the room, a stack of discarded computers, keyboards, printers and a small photocopying machine, equipment that may or may not get repaired one day. Three ceiling fans shift the hot and humid air around, although not fast enough to keep the mosquitoes at bay when you sit down on one of the wooden chairs.

**Figure 2.2** TaSUBa ICT building. Photograph by author

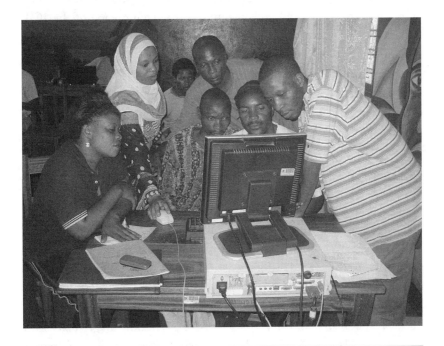

**Figure 2.3** ICT class. Photograph by author

The Internet room[9] 📷 in the ICT building is the only place on campus where students can access the Internet.[10] The computers are connected through a local area network (LAN), through a main router in the adjacent ICT management room that also connects the office next to it, used for video editing and video documentation. The building is also connected through a wireless network, which when it is working is used by a small number of staff and students who have laptops of their own. Internet connectivity is at the speed of 128 kbps, through a dedicated line from Tanzania Telecommunications Company Ltd (TTCL), former state monopoly. The speed is not too slow by Tanzanian standards, although a far cry from the broadband enjoyed in Europe, and not always quite fast enough for multimedia applications like YouTube. Internet services are regularly interrupted, for a few hours, days and sometimes weeks, due to technical failure, overdue payments, absent signatories for invoices, or heavy downloads consuming the monthly allotment of data transfer. Did I mention the frequent power failures that regularly interrupt all ICT activity? The mechanical beeping sound of uninterruptible power supply (UPS) units for computers is a regular feature of the soundscape of the ICT building.

I am elaborating on the Internet room at TaSUBa to give you an ethnographic introduction to the emerging subdiscipline of *digital anthropology*. A decade and a half after Escobar's (1994) writings about cyberculture, this branch of anthropology is still in formation. Despite a number of influential studies, there is neither a theoretical canon guiding this field of inquiry, nor is there an established definition of the subdiscipline itself.[11] Scholars have used the terms "virtual ethnography" (Hine 2000), "Internet ethnography" (Kelty 2008, Miller and Slater 2000, Uimonen 2001), and "virtual anthropology" (Boellstorff 2008) to denote anthropological inquiries into digital media.

By way of a working definition, I would suggest that digital anthropology focuses on the development and use of digital media and communication technologies in different social and cultural contexts. By digital I refer to technologies that build on the process of digitization, the conversion of data of various sorts (e.g. sound, image, text) into binary code (1s and 0s). This cluster of technologies is also referred to as information and communication technology (ICT), the most significant examples of which are the Internet, now used by an estimated 2 billion people, and mobile telephony, used by some 5.3 billion people worldwide.[12] Over the last few years, we have witnessed an intensified convergence between digital technologies, contributing to their ubiquity in everyday life. This convergence has been accompanied by a shift toward a more embedded understanding of digital technology, as illustrated by the concept of digital media. From an anthropological perspective, the word "media" refers to all communicative technologies that mediate social interaction regardless of physical proximity, mass media and non-mass media, writing and print, thus constituting cultural technologies or machineries of meaning (Hannerz 1992b, 1996).

Digital anthropology offers the means to investigate a variety of topics of interest to anthropologists in relation to the development and use of digital media. The actual development of digital technology is a field of inquiry in its own right, as exemplified by anthropological investigations into Internet development (Kelty 2008, Uimonen 2001). The use of digital media has proven to be of even greater interest and anthropologists have investigated Internet and mobile phone use in a variety of social contexts, especially non-Western ones (e.g. Barendregt 2008, Garsten and Wulff 2003, Horst and Miller 2006, Miller and Slater 2000, Tenhunen 2008). Boellstorff (2008) should be recognized for the first in-depth ethnography of the online virtual world Second Life, based on fieldwork carried out solely online, while Kelty (2008) should be credited for publishing his entire monograph online,[13] for free modulation. Anthropologists are also paying attention to popular multimedia applications like YouTube, for investigation as well as innovative forms of presentation (Wesch 2007,[14] 2008[15] ), and social networking sites like Facebook (Gershon 2010, Miller 2010, 2011). More commonly, digital media have formed part of anthropological investigations into specific social groups or social phenomena, rather than the primary focus of inquiry (for an overview, see Coleman 2010). I would not categorize most of these studies as digital anthropology, but they certainly contribute to our understanding of cultural digitization.

To make a contribution to this body of scholarly work, this project looks at digital media and intercultural interaction in the institutional context of TaSUBa. In many ways, the investigation follows a rather traditional ethnographic approach, focusing more on the social and cultural embeddedness of digital technology (Hine 2000, Miller and Slater 2000) than virtual culture and cybersociality (Boellstorff 2008). My approach is informed by theoretical interests and methodological choices. Since my first encounter with TaSUBa in 2002 (then Bagamoyo College of Arts), I have appreciated this institute as a site for cultural production worth investigating in its own right, especially given its role in postcolonial national development in Tanzania. With my background in the Internet, modernization, and globalization (Uimonen 2001, 2003a), I have also been interested in TaSUBa's positioning in national, regional, and global networks of interaction and exchange. The Internet offers a window to these developments and their multilayered interlinkages.

Located near the main entrance and overlooking the administrative building, library and classrooms, the ICT building offers a bird's eye view of the campus, a material node in socially distributed networks of cultural production, interaction, and transformation. And it is this cultural complexity that I am primarily concerned with, including the very buildings in which it is performed.

These days digital media form part of what can be described as the neoliberal culture complex (Hannerz 2010), the global spread of which is having a profound impact on the world we live in. My study shows in ethnographic detail how this cultural complex is spreading "across continents," and how it "takes somewhat different shapes in different settings, as it interacts with what was already in place" (ibid., 8). Yet there is something to be said for global similarities as well. We will find that faculty and students at TaSUBa are struggling with existential questions that are similar to the ones anthropologists face at their home institutions, trying to make sense of and accommodate recurrent keywords such as accountability, transparency, privatization, auditing, and excellence (ibid.). Hopefully my ethnography of an arts college in Tanzania can contribute to a greater understanding of these social phenomena and "perhaps it will eventually—I hope sooner rather than later—be understood that universities cannot be run quite like businesses," since "their multifaceted cultural roles demand some particular care" (ibid.).

In order to appreciate this cultural complexity, I approach digital media by way of classical anthropological theory, especially network theory. Although it was a sociologist rather than anthropologist who rose to the task of developing the most elaborate social theories on the *network society* (Castells 1996, 1997, 1998, 2004), network theory has a long history within anthropology, not least in the early anthropology of Africa (Kapferer 1973, Mitchell 1969). Networks of social relations form the basis of anthropological empiricism, which route connections through persons (Strathern 1995). In network theory, these connections are often traced through cultural brokers. Hannerz (1980, 190–191) describes the broker as "a person with a particular kind of network range," who "facilitates contacts among persons, groups or institutions who are otherwise not within easy reach of one another."[16] With its long history in anthropology (e.g. Geertz 1960, Wolf 1956), the cultural broker is well recognized in contemporary studies of transnational mobility (e.g. Lindquist 2010). Whether composed of individual or institutional social actors, cultural brokers play an important mediatory role in cultural digitization.

I am particularly fond of anthropological network theory because it has preceded the Internet—the network of networks—while capturing its essence. Well before the Internet became public, Hannerz conceptualized the city (1980) and later on the world, or global ecumene (1992a), as a network of networks, to capture the social distribution of culture in complex societies. When tracing its early developments in developing countries, I analyzed the Internet in terms of a culture of networking, based on the cultural visions and social practices of the Internet pioneers (Uimonen 2001). So I have been thinking with networks for quite some time.

### Partial Inclusion in the Global Network Society

A satellite image of the African continent at night[17] ▶ shows a dark continent, with some lights in urban settlements along coastal areas, but vast stretches of unlit territory. It is a huge continent with a total population of more than one billion people. The dark tracts are the rural areas where the great majority of Africans still reside, without electricity, let alone Internet connectivity, albeit a surprising number do have mobile phones. Mobile telephony has been identified as one of the three motors of change in contemporary Africa, along with Chinese investments and the emergence of a new African middle class (Dowden 2009, 516). Rather than portraying a black hole of informational capitalism (Castells 1998, 161–165), the satellite image shows how global trends do not always flow but they can also *hop*, skipping over much of what lies between (Ferguson 2006, 38). From an African perspective, this lack of digital infrastructure is often perceived as "*lack of modernity*," locally understood not in terms of cultural inferiority, but as a matter of political–economic inequality (ibid., 33, emphasis in original).

As exemplified by this visual image of digital stratification, Tanzania is located in the global shadows, a place-in-the-world that should be understood as "both a location in space and a rank in a system of social categories" (Ferguson 2006, 6). It is important to underline the relationality of Africa's place-in-the-world, which has to do with likeness, an "inseparable other-who-is-also-oneself to whom one is bound" (ibid., 17). The interrelatedness of centers and peripheries becomes all too evident when assessed in terms of digital inequalities.

The Internet is quite a marginal, albeit not insignificant, actor in the rapidly expanding Tanzanian landscape of modernity (Appadurai 1996). In 2009, Internet subscription rates covered a mere 1.55 percent of the population.[18] By contrast, mobile phone subscriptions are estimated at 17 million people, or approximately 40 percent of the population. At TaSUBa, Internet access is still limited to specific places, but whereas some students did not own mobile phones a few years ago (Uimonen 2006), these days all of them have mobile phones. Tanzanians tend to have the smartest model they can possibly afford, an important means of daily communication and a highly valued status symbol (cf. Barendregt 2008, Horst and Miller 2006). In Africa, radio and to a lesser extent television are still far more pervasive than the Internet. In 2006 Tanzania had 47 radio stations and 29 television stations, while many viewers also have access to satellite TV.[19] At TaSUBa, there is a TV set in the Internet room, which is switched off pending the purchase of a TV antenna, but for a while the college subscribed to satellite TV through DStv.[20] There are no cinemas in Bagamoyo, but a few bars show movies and television shows, while cheap Asian-made copies of Western movies and television series can be bought in town. Some students have radio sets or CD players, which they listen to in the dormitories. Tutors often read newspapers, which are available at low cost, and the glossy journal *Si Mchezo*, freely distributed by Femina Hip, is widely circulated at the college.[21]

My own material confirms Ekström's (2010, 87) conclusion that there is a "widespread view that Tanzanian culture is changing because of the rapidly expanding, and increasingly globalised media culture." TaSUBa tutors are quite aware and to some extent concerned that Tanzanian youth are increasingly influenced by global media flows, not least global popular culture. Like young women in Dar es Salaam, the cultural identities of TaSUBa students are influenced by different cultures, including mediated ones (ibid., cf. Fuglesang 1994, Weiss 2002). Indeed, like in other parts of the world, Tanzanian mediascapes are increasingly shaping people's understanding of a plurality of imagined worlds (Appadurai 1996).

In Tanzania, cultural identities and imaginations are not only influenced by the mediated sounds and images of other cultures, but also the ways in which the media are imagined. I have argued elsewhere that "the Internet is doing to cosmopolitanism what print media did for nationalism," offering a sense of belonging to a global imagined community (Uimonen 2001, 77). This explains the positive expectations of Internet access at BCA when it was first connected in 2004, expressing desires to be part of an interconnected art world (Uimonen 2009a). Nonetheless, digital media continue to be embedded in social and material realities of a more localized kind. Five years down the road, TaSUBa students still appreciate the ability to communicate and interact with the rest of the world, but they also express their frustration about the *scarcity* of computers and related facilities, demonstrating that they have yet to realize their imagined place in the world (Uimonen 2011).

At TaSUBa, Internet access is limited to the ICT building and the administrative building, while the theater management group has its own connection, in the new theater. Originally, the idea was to connect the whole campus through a wide area network (WAN), but this plan never got realized. The college pays TSH 450,000 per month (approximately USD 350) for its data allotment of 40 GB, which is more costly than the combined monthly salary of two ICT teachers.[22]

The ICT facilities are managed by a small team of staff, housed in a small, cluttered office in the ICT building. The ICT manager, Brighton Maganga, is a senior fine art teacher in his early fifties, married with five children. Originally from Tabora region, he has a BA in fine and performing arts and a postgraduate diploma in scientific computing, from UDSM. He came to teach at BCA in 2001 and in 2008 he was given the position of ICT manager, to "administer the ICT section," as he describes it. The ICT tutor, Rehema Nzige, is 30 years old, married with one child. Before joining BCA in 2006, she was working at the Kasulu Teacher Training College in Kigoma, in a remote corner of Tanzania. Rehema has a diploma in education, a certificate in computing, and a certificate in the International Computer Driving Licence (ICDL). In addition to teaching ICT classes at TaSUBa, Rehema is taking a BA degree in business administration at the Open University of Tanzania (OUT). TaSUBa used to have an ICT technician, Thomas Emmanuel, who also doubled as ICT tutor, but he left for a position at OUT in 2009. As mentioned earlier, David Estomihi, a recent graduate from the college, assists with ICT facilities and training, while maintaining the TaSUBa website.

Limited as it may be, the fact that TaSUBa has Internet access begs for a more nuanced appraisal of digital stratification, not least to account for patterns of partial inclusion (cf. Uimonen 2011). In the global network society, Tanzania occupies a peripheral position, often thought of in terms of digital divide or digital exclusion.[23] In the ICT Development Index (IDI) for 2010, Tanzania ranks 138th out of 152, neighboring Kenya ranks 115th, and Uganda 140th (ITU 2011). By comparison, Sweden comes second, while Norway ranks 11th, the United Kingdom 10th, and the United States 17th. Heavily influenced by binary logic of digitization, Castells (2004, 23) postulates that "the network society works on the basis of a binary logic of inclusion/exclusion." He recognizes that fragmentation is a "structural feature of the network society," which he rightly sees as "a dynamic structure" that is "highly malleable to social forces" (ibid.), yet his insistence on the binary logic of inclusion/exclusion does not fully account for variations in access. TaSUBa has Internet access, but it still plays a marginal role in the transnational flows of culture, which continue to be dominated by metropolitan centers acting as cultural switchboards (Hannerz 1992a, 51). Thus, rather than looking at Internet access in Africa in terms of digital exclusion, it is worth exploring connectivity in terms of partial inclusion, to capture global interconnections as well as asymmetries.

### Art for Society's Sake *Sanaa*

Painted by fine arts students, the interior of the Internet room is artistically decorated with murals depicting African art and global connectivity. These paintings show the cultural identities of Tanzanian art students and their sense of belonging to an interconnected world of art, culture, and peaceful coexistence (Uimonen 2011). They also express culturally informed expectations of digitally mediated cultural interaction, visual displays of imagined futures in a cosmopolitan world.

The Internet room has two large framed photographs on the walls, one depicting the *Baba wa Taifa* (Father of the Nation) Julius Nyerere and the other the current president, Jakaya Kikwete. It is no coincidence that Kikwete is dressed in a dark business suit, crisp white shirt, and discreet burgundy tie, a visual embodiment of the capitalist orientation of contemporary Tanzania, aspiring to be part of the global market economy. Nyerere on the other hand is depicted as a gentle old man, a wise *mzee*, whose socialist visions appear to belong to a bygone era, along with his modest suit. These framed photographs of past and current political leaders visualize the government identity of TaSUBa, its ongoing role in national development, and its entanglements in the transformations from socialism and traditionalism to structural adjustment and neoliberalism. TaSUBa can thus be conceptualized as an artistic field contained within a field of power, hierarchically positioned in complementary and contradictory relations of domination and dominance within the social structure of the state (Bourdieu 1993).

Depicting the epicenter of *Digital Drama*—the TaSUBa Theater[24] —the innermost wall of the Internet room is covered with a colorful portrayal of a *makuti-* (thatched-) roofed theater, majestically set against the Indian Ocean. A landmark in the East African art world, this is the theater that was ravaged by a fire on 31 January 2002. Six years later, the management proudly inaugurated a reconstructed theater, with a fire-proof corrugated iron roof, heavy iron gates, and fire extinguishers. By then, Bagamoyo College of Arts had become Taasisi ya Sanaa na Utamaduni Bagamoyo, and, the Kiswahili name notwithstanding, more firmly entrenched in the global forces of capitalism.

Unlike Western ideals of *art for art's sake*, the Tanzanian artistic field can be defined in terms of *art for society's sake*, thus reflecting emic understandings of art and creativity. In an African context, art is very much part of society, embedded in a social-relational matrix with its own aesthetic system (Born 2010, Gell 1998). As exemplified by the *Tuwaenzi Wakongwe* commemorative event, art is performed in close interaction with the community, serving as a cultural expression of social relations, which are maintained even after people pass away, since ancestors are an integral part of the social fabric. Indeed, Chernoff (1979, 154) could have written about *Tuwaenzi Wakongwe* when he described how at musical events "the values of African traditional wisdom are integrated into a style of communication which is both musical and social." This social function encompasses all art forms.

The Swahili word for art is *sanaa*, which makes for a telling play on words. The adverb *sana* means very, very much or extremely, as in *karibu sana* (you are very welcome), *asante sana* (thank you very much), or *pole sana* (extremely sorry). When I was taught the word *sanaa* during one of my first visits to TaSUBa, it was explained to me with a humorous reference to the connection between *sana* and *sanaa*, suggesting that art is but an extreme version of life itself, a commentary, critique, or reflection on human existence, in an exaggerated form. When I discussed the meaning of art with TaSUBa tutors during more recent fieldwork, they concurred with this view, underlining that art is an extension of as well as reflection on reality or life, something created to be a representation of your thoughts and emotions, an expression of humankind's struggle to understand its surroundings. In Africa, they explained to me, art is close to life.

The most common understanding of *sanaa* is *art as a mirror of society*, underlining how art functions as a moral corrective, thus performing a critical, reflexive role in social processes. Like *sanaa*, the local notion of aesthetics, *ujumi*, underscores morality. A value-laden concept denoting something of high quality, *ujumi* is not restricted to beauty. To clarify, one of the tutors explained that a woman is not merely appreciated for her physical beauty, but also her character, way of life, attitude, and understanding.

Art has a long history in Tanzania. During our group discussion, TaSUBa tutors elaborate on the many traditional art forms in Tanzania, dating back to day one, when society was born. Traditional arts include performing arts as well as art objects: music, dance, rituals, story telling, recitation, initiation ceremonies, sculptures, carvings, cloth making, knitting, bark cloth, cave paintings, henna decorations, skin scarring, tooth cutting, tooth sharpening, weaving, pottery, etc. For something to be defined as art, it has to be something extra, something exaggerated, even magic. Art is also created to be beautiful to attract people, although the tutors quickly add that beauty is in the eye of the beholder, and that even things that may appear ugly, like some Makonde wood carvings, can posses a form of beauty. The tutors bring art into the realm of social relations, using joking relationships between tribes as an example of creativity in social interaction. Humor is indeed an important aspect of art and people even joke with dead people, to release sorrow and to console. And as much as art is used to educate people, it is also used to entertain them.

"Art is life," Vitali Maembe explains to me as he recalls his life history, adding "I was doing art as a child but I did not think of it as art, it was just life." Like many other students at the college, Maembe started painting when he was a little boy. He was born in 1976 in Rukwa, Sumbawanga, home to the *wafipa* tribe, but he grew up in Dar es Salaam, where his father worked as a customs officer. Maembe enrolled at the college in 1998 to develop his skills in fine art, but discovered that he also had talent in dance and music, which he eventually majored and minored in. He wanted to become a professional artist so that people would listen to his message. When Maembe performs on stage, he puts on an artistic show that demonstrates his multi-talented artistic formation, combining music and dance in a unique style of his own design. His deep voice articulates poetic lyrics in Kiswahili, his warm smile taking the edge off his delivery, softening critical messages on social issues like corruption.

Art has given Maembe "a voice," a "mirror," which he uses to express things that people try to conceal, social issues like drugs, HIV/AIDS or corruption. Maembe is driven by a desire to "make something good for society" and to nurture "artists with ability to say something in society." He needs money to realize his vision, "but I don't want to abuse art or myself," and although he recognizes that he is "not living in a good life," he feels that "my heart is at peace." With over 1,000 friends in Facebook, Maembe is not alone in his passionate conviction of art for society's sake.

Let us now turn to TaSUBa's position in the social structure of the state apparatus, to explore the liminality of art, a key concept in this book. Just like technology, art is a transformative process, which in its most abstract sense occupies a space between nature and culture, an in-between space that is socially constituted through mediation, translation, and networks (Latour 1993, 37). In the case of TaSUBa, this space is demonstrated by the institute's positioning as a social actor in the field of power, an artistic field within the state apparatus. This in-between space is accentuated by the role and function of art in Tanzanian society, *sanaa* serving as a mirror of society, close enough to portray society, distant enough to provide a reflection of it. When it comes to its social position, TaSUBa can thus be conceptualized in terms of liminality, a state of betwixt and between (Turner 1969).

Liminality can be approached as being *neither here nor there*, but it can also be analyzed in terms of being *both here and there*, *then and now*, thus offering a juncture from which to assess the complexity of the digital drama that this ethnography is concerned with, epitomized in the state of creolization. My reconceptualization of liminality builds upon anthropological analyses of the in between (Friedson 2009,

Stoller 2009). Based on his work on the musical experience so integral to ritual life of the Ewe in Ghana, Friedson (2009, 189) concludes that "within this musical field, things are neither far nor near, here nor there, but always-already profoundly in-between." He locates musical experience at "the crossroads where paths intersect and intertwine" (ibid., 188), constituting a way of being-in-the-world that is always in between, both here and there. Similarly, reflecting on his lifetime on the "anthropological path through the between," whether among Songhay sorcerers in Niger or African art dealers in New York, Stoller (2009, 114) underlines that "the intercourse of universes of meaning and intent that fills the spaces of the between" are characterized by "cultural hybridity." "This hybridity," he notes, "makes the ethnographic enterprise exceedingly difficult." Let us now turn to the concept of creolization to make better sense of the cultural complexities of hybridity.

### Liminality, Cultural Hybridity, and Creolization[25]

I am standing near the security booth at the TaSUBa entrance with my camera when Nina Stanley walks over to greet me. Rather than just waving to me from the Mwembe theater she is passing, which is considered rather impolite in Tanzania but somewhat typical of *mzungu*, she walks over to customarily inquire how I am doing and how my research is going. Nina is a first-year student at TaSUBa, majoring in fine arts, with a minor in drama. Born in Moshi, Kilimanjaro region, she belongs to the *wachagga* tribe. Nina caught my attention during her interview for the auditions in June 2009. As I listened to her elaborate on the role of art in society, I was struck by her eloquence and intrigued by her confident, tomboyish appearance. We became friends and research collaborators, Nina sending me updates via Facebook between my fieldwork periods, while assisting me through various forms of data gathering on site. As we are standing by the security booth, I explain to Nina that I am fascinated by the new poster at the entrance. "Yeah, we get a lot of entertainment here," she responds. We chat for a while, before Nina proceeds to her class and I continue taking photographs, until I head for a cold soda at a nearby cafeteria. In the evening I note that this brief encounter under the scorching sun has burnt my skin, despite weeks of exposure, while Nina's comment about entertainment lingers on in my mind.

The plastic poster for Bagamoyo Kamambe Nights[26] was set up in November 2009, replacing a wooden board painted with Wizara ya Habari, Utamaduni na Michezo, Chuo Cha Sanaa Bagamoyo (Ministry of Information, Culture and Sports, Bagamoyo College of Arts) and the PO box, telephone, and fax numbers of the college. The assembly took several days, as the poster was meticulously readjusted to its frame, while a blackboard was fastened below it, with the weekly program drawn in chalk, and to complete the process, the poster was crowned with an electronic lamp. Meanwhile, the old sign was placed upside down,[27] its long supporting shafts leaning against the corrugated iron roof of the security booth. It was not the replacement of telephone and fax numbers with a web address that caught my attention, or the substitution of a wooden sign with a plastic poster. These details were of course significant, as was the visual display of African exotica replacing factual bureaucratic text, not to mention the shift in language, and the addition of electric light. What struck me was the realization that I was observing the very process of institutional transformation, embodied in the change of entrance signs for TaSUBa.

The replacement of signs denoting the very identity of TaSUBa was a visual expression of the multifaceted character of liminality. While the computer-designed poster replaced the hand-printed old sign, the new official sign for TaSUBa remained hidden under a mango tree some distance from the entrance, marking the location of the envisaged entrance of the future.[28] The liminality of institutional transformation could not have been more explicit, positioning TaSUBa both here and there (local and global), and now and then (existing and future entrance), in an intricate melange of cultural elements that were tied to global power structures.

The Bagamoyo Kamambe Nights program was initiated with the help of a collaborative program between Norway and Tanzania. The poster was designed by a Norwegian adviser, placed at TaSUBa through Fredskorpset, a collaborative partner of the NOTA project.[29]

Dating back to 1999, the NOTA project was started by a Norwegian music teacher, Hanne Maeland, and Mzee Peter Nyambasi, at the time principal of BCA, focusing on "development and building up professional competence in the field of modern music."[30] Over time, it has been broadened to "organizational development," changing "from being an aid project to being a cooperation project." Today, the project describes itself as a mutual, intercultural collaboration promotion network involving Taasisi ya Sanaa na Utamaduni Bagamoyo (TaSUBa), the Stavanger School of Culture (SSC), and the University of Stavanger (UiS).[31] The NOTA project is but one instance of globalization at TaSUBa, a process of cultural interconnectedness materialized through interactions, relationships, and networks between people and places (Hannerz 1996).

The change of entrance signs is an example of cultural creolization, a highly dynamic and malleable process in which hybrid cultural forms are produced (Hannerz 1987, 1996, 2006). Although the concept of creole originates in the Caribbean, it has been more widely adapted in anthropology, often in reference to matters relating to transnational cultural interconnectedness (Hannerz 2006). Far from being just another way of denoting cultural blending, creolization captures a process of cultural transformation that takes place in a highly asymmetric world order, a *creole continuum* that reflects the political economy of center–periphery relations (Hannerz 1996, 67). Creolization is thus closely related to different degrees of symmetry and asymmetry in the social organization of global culture (Hannerz 1992a).

Tanzanian statehood offers an impressive example of cultural creolization, which is why I define it in terms of a *state of creolization*, a highly unstable structure, constructed through a melange of cultural fragments that also reflect the asymmetric structure of the world order. Bayart's (2009, 28) suggestion that creolization is intrinsic to the historicity of African societies is particularly applicable to Tanzania, where early forms of statehood built on the hybrid ideology of African socialism, *ujamaa*, as formulated in the famous Arusha Declaration of 1967. It was a form of statehood that sought to combine traditional community values with the demands of modernization in an ever-changing world. Indeed from the outset, the Tanzanian state was a state of creolization, the complexities of which have intensified over time.

## Mungu Ibariki Afrika

As indicated by the title of its national anthem, *Mungu Ibariki Afrika* (God bless Africa),[32] ▭ ♫ Tanzania is a country that blends nationalism and Pan-Africanism with spirituality and modernity. It is a country where the supposedly linear paths of history tend to coexist, in a motley blend of postcolonialism, postsocialism, and neoliberalism, and where a deep-seated sense of national unity coexists with a cosmopolitan appreciation of being part of the world at large that can be traced to precolonial times. Life in Tanzania is very much about being here and there, then and now, in a permanent state of liminality, in a state of creolization.

These days, digitally mediated globalization is affecting African statehood, in many ways reaffirming the rather shaky foundations of postcolonial society. In his authoritative account of the African way of politics, or politics of the belly, Bayart (2009, xliv) notes that the ongoing privatization of the state does not really constitute a retreat or collapse of the state, but rather its recomposition. Contrary to the claims of donor-driven public sector reforms, the phase of economic liberalization, including the privatization of public enterprises, offers more continuity than change in state formation. This is a characteristic of African state-building since colonial times, whereby sovereignty is exercised through the creation and management of *dependence* (ibid., xxvi).

The experience of Tanzania both concurs with and differs from scholarly readings of state-crafting in Africa. It is not for nothing that in the many accounts of corruption, big man politics, lawlessness, warfare, armed conflict, and ethnic strife, so common in discussions of the postcolonial African state, Tanzania is largely absent. This is not a country where the grotesque and the obscene have characterized a postcolonial regime of domination, as has been the case in Cameroon (Mbembe 2001, 103). Nor has the Tanzanian one-party system, replaced with a multiparty system in the mid-1990s, constituted the kind of decentralized despotism observed in Togo (Piot 2010, 7).

Using the violent exploitation of a mining company in Zaïre as an example of Mobutu's excessive accumulation and abuse of power, Bayart (2009, 239) notes that the division of spoils has been less cruel in some African countries (Senegal, Ivory Coast, Gabon, and Tanzania). This is not to say that Tanzania has been immune to African way of politics, but it has enjoyed some layers of insulation.

Unlike its neighboring countries, Tanzania continues to enjoy national unity, peace and stability, indicating that the foundations of statehood rest on more solid ground than many other African nations. Many of the principles of *ujamaa*,[33] which means familyhood in Kiswahili, are built on local community values, thus having wide popular appeal. As Ferguson (2006, 75–76) notes, it was a political doctrine that combined the "rhetoric of international socialism" with "central moral oppositions that would be familiar to any ethnographer of the region: selfishness versus sociality, sharing versus exploitation, benevolence versus malevolence." Indeed, with the extended family as its foundation, the hybrid ideology of *ujamaa* sought to anchor socialism as well as democracy in the traditional roots of African society (Havnevik 2010). The unifying sense of familyhood extended beyond the tribe, the community, the nation, and even the continent, to "embrace the whole society of mankind" (ibid., 35). Hence, *ujamaa* was a cultural hybrid of traditionalism, nationalism, socialism, Pan-Africanism, and cosmopolitanism. No wonder that Tanzania welcomed progressive radicals from around the world, from Malcolm X to Che Guevara.

As demonstrated in the title of its national anthem, postcolonial Tanzania was led by a devoted Pan-Africanist. Julius Nyerere[34] may not have played the role of Kwame Nkrumah of Ghana, Ahmed Sékou Touré of Guinea, and William Tubman of Liberia, forerunners in the creation of the Organization of African Unity (OAU), later the African Union (AU). But he made sure Tanganyika signed up as a member from the outset, on 25 May 1963. And even before Tanganyika gained her independence on 9 December 1961, Nyerere articulated his vision of African unity and liberation:

> We will light a candle on Mount Kilimanjaro
> which will shine beyond our borders,

giving hope where there is despair,
love where there is hate,
and dignity where before there was only humiliation.

(Nyerere 1959, cited in Mwakikagile 2006: 27)

Nyerere's words were not just empty rhetoric as Tanganyika, Tanzania after the union with Zanzibar in 1964, played an active role in liberation struggles throughout the African continent, as exemplified by South Africa. When Nelson Mandela first travelled abroad in early 1962, he passed through Tanganyika. Upon landing in Mbeya, Mandela noticed something he had never experienced before. The local hotel where he was staying had no color bar, but blacks and whites were sitting together talking with one another. As he recalls, "I then realized that I was in a country ruled by Africans. For the first time in my life, I was a free man" (Mandela 1995, 345). When Mandela met Nyerere in Dar es Salaam on the following day, he noted that his house was far from grand and that he drove a simple car, a small Austin. "This impressed me, for it suggested that he was a man of the people. Class, Nyerere always insisted, was alien to Africa; socialism was indigenous" (ibid.).

Nyerere was a teacher, *mwalimu*, which was the title he himself preferred, as opposed to that of *Baba wa Taifa*, Father of the Nation. His professional training made him unique among African leaders, and it helps explain his humility and commitment to the improvement of others. He studied and later taught at a government secondary school in Tabora, which remains one of Tanzania's top educational institutes. After studying for a teaching diploma at Makerere University in Kampala, Nyerere got a government scholarship to attend the University of Edinburgh, making him the first Tanganyikan to study at a British university, graduating with an MA degree in economics and history in 1952. It was during his stay in Edinburgh that Nyerere started exploring the ideas of socialism, which he then adjusted to African circumstances, not least by incorporating religion and spirituality, along with cultural traditions, which he actively tried to decolonize.

Even so, much of Nyerere's version of socialism built on his own tribal background in the Zanaki village of Butiama, Musoma. In the traditional Zanaki social order, individual status was social rather than political, reciprocal generosity was a core value, and local leadership was in the hands of wise and charismatic elders (Havnevik 2010, 45). This is why Nyerere himself figured that he "grew up in a perfectly democratic and egalitarian society" (ibid.). Meanwhile, Nyerere's insistence on social equality set him apart from the Western emphasis on individual liberty, while his vision of self-reliance made for a problematic integration in world society. The state of creolization was indeed set for an alternative development path (ibid.).

It is only by recognizing Nyerere's role in early state formation that Tanzania's historical trajectory of postcolonialism and postsocialism can be fully understood in the age of millennial capitalism (Comaroff and Comaroff 2000).[35] Here the "perceptible nostalgia for the security of past regimes" is not a matter of seeking solace in a repressive past (ibid., 299). Rather, it is nostalgia for a past that in fundamental ways is reconstructed as something better than the present, "a time when the government 'genuinely' cared for its people" (Kamat 2008, 364). This is why Tanzania is not a place like Togo, a zone of unstable sovereignties where the state has been replaced by NGOs and churches, a place that people wish to escape through exile or salvation (Piot 2010). Even though life is hard, Tanzanians are rooted in a place that they love, a nation once led by an African statesman, now in a state of moral crisis where the idioms of hunger and eating serve as cultural critique of social transformations that value selfishness as opposed to togetherness.

### Professional, Personal, and Political Engagements

If I were to pick a date of particular significance in my years of working with BCA/TaSUBa it would be 12 July 2004.[36] This was the day when BCA first got connected to the Internet, the celebratory tone of which was conveyed in an email sent to me the following day:

> Dear Dr. Uimonen!
> CONGRATULATIONS!!
> I have the pleasure to inform you that BCA has officially been connected to the Internet on 12th July 2004 at around 10.00am. I would like to take this opportunity to congratulate you for the

big success for the ICT project at BCA. I believe, this connection will open a new chapter in the history of the college and contribute tremendously in the process of transforming BCA into a dynamic arts training centre in East Africa.

Most of my ethnographic engagements have perhaps not been as spectacular, but they do cover an eventful period in the history of BCA/TaSUBa, from 2002 to 2009. I first visited BCA in October 2002 as part of a study tour in preparation for an ICT4D Strategy for Sida (Uimonen 2003b). At the time, I got a lift with Ambassador Sten Rylander, who drove his car to Bagamoyo to attend a meeting. On the road he said something that has stuck with me: "It is easy to find problems in Africa. The challenge is to find solutions." From 2004 to 2007 I was engaged as an ICT consultant at BCA, contracted by Sida and the Embassy of Sweden in Dar es Salaam to initiate and later monitor what came to be known as the ICT project. My services were offered in response to BCA's request for sponsorship for ICT facilities and training. The ICT project covered the establishment of Internet access and ICT facilities, recruitment and training of technical staff, and development of a website. With time it also involved the production of a multimedia theater performance, *Once Upon a Dotcom*, for the World Summit on the Information Society (WSIS) in Tunis in 2005 and an ICT user study (Uimonen 2006, 2009a). In October and November 2008 I returned to the institute, now TaSUBa, to prepare for ethnographic fieldwork, which I carried out from April to August and November to December 2009.

In between these professional engagements I have visited BCA/TaSUBa on numerous occasions in my private capacity, having forged friendships and family ties with people involved with the institute in various roles. Early on I made a habit of paying a visit to Mzee Kaduma whose house overlooked the college and whose life stories I cherished. With time Mzee Kaduma became like a father to me and after his unfortunate death on 27 September 2007 his widow Mama Kaduma took over his parental role. I was unable to fly to Tanzania to attend Mzee Kaduma's funeral, but my Tanzanian brother Sixmund Begashe ensured my participation via email and texting. I have also stayed friends with many BCA teachers, students, and alumni.

My professional and personal experiences in Tanzania extend beyond Bagamoyo, centering on the late Simbo Ntiro. Between 2005 and 2008, I worked as an ICT advisor with other clients and projects in Tanzania, including the Tanzania Commission for Science and Technology (COSTECH) and the Ministry of Education and Vocational Training, former parent Ministry of BCA (MoEVT 2007). During this period, I was living with Simbo Ntiro in Dar es Salaam, a relationship that deepened my understanding of Tanzania in so many ways. In addition to our friendship and romantic relationship, we shared the same line of work and collaborated professionally at various levels (e.g. Ntiro and Uimonen 2006). Simbo's untimely death in a car accident on 13 July 2008 opened my heart to Tanzanian values, especially the true meanings of *mungu tusaidia* (God helps us) and *tukopamoja* (we are together), while plunging me into the intricacies of chagga traditions. Simbo was an East African, with a Ugandan mother, Dr Sarah Ntiro, the first woman university graduate in East and Central Africa, and a Tanzanian father, Professor Sam Ntiro, the country's first High Commissioner to the UK and a Commissioner of Culture. Simbo's brother Joseph Ntiro lives in Kampala. Simbo was also a cosmopolitan, described himself as a netizen, with many *mzungu* friends, some of whom flew all the way from the UK to attend his burial in Kilimanjaro. But above all, Simbo was a Tanzanian. In tribute to his selfless efforts, the local ICT community awarded Simbo the posthumous title *Father of Internet Social Networking in Tanzania*.[37] During my fieldwork at TaSUBa I was immersed in an artistic environment that we both had cherished, and to which Simbo was indirectly linked through his late father, one of Tanzania's greatest painters.[38] Whenever I pass the fine art building at TaSUBa, with its painting of Mount Kilimanjaro, I am reminded of Sam and Simbo Ntiro, now resting in their family house on the slopes of the white mountain of the *wachagga*, with its *Uhuru* (freedom) Peak reaching the heights of the world's Seven Summits.

As for my engagements as an anthropologist, while I agree with the need to blur the distinction between academic and applied anthropology (Pink 2006, Kedia and van Willigen 2005), a division rarely made by African anthropologists (Ntarangwi 2006), I tend to separate my work into two parts, as ICT consultant and as academic. The mate-rial I have gathered in my two roles represents different forms of knowledge production. As an ICT consultant, I collected data that were of immediate use for my assignment, rather than for the sake of research, which has entailed broader and more systematic data gather-ing. Similarly, the notes I took and the reports I wrote were produced for very different purposes, free of academic jargon and theorizing, full of development-speak. Even so, my anthropological gaze was always broader than my terms of reference, so my engagements with BCA/TaSUBa have always constituted an anthropological field (cf. Pink 2006).

It is clear that my earlier engagements as ICT consultant were entangled in the asymmetric donor–recipient relations of so called development partnership (Dahl 2001). The world of development is problematic in anthropology, often dividing those involved in "development anthropology (the practice of development)" and those concerned with "the anthropology of development (the study of devel-opment)" (Little 2005, 35). The latter tend to be more vocal within the discipline, generating critical insights into the power and politics of development. In Tanzania, development can quite easily be interpreted as a hegemonic form of representation, with national policy represent-ing a depoliticized mode of technocratic governance, dominated by a transnational policy elite (Escobar 1995, Ferguson 1994, Gould and Ojanen 2003). But in order to appreciate how Tanzanians make sense of *maendeleo* (development), it is worth keeping in mind that the myth of modernization serves as a cosmological blueprint shaping people's understanding of the world (Ferguson 1999, 13–14).

Having now recast myself as an academic, I am not insulated from politics or asymmetric power relations, quite the opposite. I tend to agree with the notion that "there is no anthropology outside politicised institutional settings, and that what we do as ethnographers and as anthropologists is always part of some sort of political agenda" (Green 2006, 125). In writing this monograph I take on a more political role than when I advised TaSUBa management on the ICT project, trained ICT staff, or negotiated with donors for funding. This is the first ethnography of TaSUBa, and as the management group reflected when they formally accepted my research request, while the institute has been written about in evaluation, status and progress reports, it has not been written about in an academic report. This is not to say that Bagamoyo College of Arts has not figured in other academic accounts (e.g. Askew 2004, Edmondson 2007, Lange 2002), but not as the primary focus of inquiry, or the subject of an ethnography in its own right.

Having spent the last few years commuting between Sweden and Tanzania, I have become acutely aware of the differences between how Africans view themselves and how they are viewed by others. Western media portrayals tend to be dominated by a regional storyline of Afro-pessimism, with a penchant for stories on ethnic conflict, despots, victims, AIDS, chaos, and gloom (Hannerz 2004, 117–130). In Sweden, with its history of five decades of development cooperation with Tanzania, the image of Africa is equally distorted. Textbooks for school children tend to focus on poverty and underdevelopment, thus portraying a continent without culture (Palmberg 2001). Meanwhile, in their quest for cultural authenticity and otherness, many anthropologists have stayed away from critical analyses of modernization in African communities and societies, focusing on traditional rural life, or local forms of cultural resistance, rather than aspirations to and imitations of global modernity (Ferguson 2006, 157–161). No wonder that the skewed portrayal of Tanzania in the so-called documentary film *Darwin's Nightmare* was so popular among Western intellectuals, despite its many factual and analytical errors (Molony et al. 2007),[39] confirming stereotypical notions of Africans as helpless victims of global power.

In writing this monograph I cannot avoid engaging in the politics of portraying Africa. Not the Africa expressed in the poster of a dictator, sculpture of violent beheading, or painting of military gunfire with which my colleague Sverker Finnström used to decorate his part of our shared office (Finnström 2008). But the Africa of a colorful poster for an arts festival, a poster for a multimedia theater performance, and a batik painting of Mount Kilimanjaro displayed in my part of the office. Africa is diverse, *kabisa (*absolutely)! Still there is something to be gleaned from the Pan-African identity shared by youth in war-stricken northern Uganda and students at an arts college on the Swahili coast, cultural expressions of "ordinary Africans actively shaping their own lives" that media audiences rarely get a glimpse of, to cite the *mzee* whose former office Sverker and I used to share (Hannerz 2004, 142). Perhaps the world got a flavor of these Pan-African sentiments during the World Cup in South Africa in 2010. One of my Tanzanian friends posted his version of African unity in Facebook following Ghana's victory over the United States: "UNITED STATES OF AFRICA WAMEMFUNGA [defeat] UNITED STATES OF AMERICA … Nomaa [fantastic]." So there is much to be said for the interconnectedness that Africans feel toward one another and the world at large, in cultural, political, economic, and perhaps most importantly, in moral terms.

If Western anthropologists are to play a meaningful role in contemporary Africa, it is perhaps by using our privileges to tell these stories of diversity, complexity, and interrelatedness, hopefully with at least some of the warmth, creativity, and humor that frame everyday life in a place like TaSUBa. *Karibu Tanzania! Karibu Afrika! Tukopamoja!*

# PART II

## CULTURAL TRANSFORMATIONS

# DIGITAL DRAMA OF EXECUTIVE TRANSFORMATION

### Nyerere, National Troupes, and Cultural Brokers

"This is our first president, Mr. Julius Nyerere," Nina says, adding "You can see his statue, it is very well done," as she runs the video camera up and down the full-sized sculpture of Nyerere.[1] We are walking with video through campus and among the places Nina has selected to record[2] is the statue of Julius Nyerere in front of the administration building (see Chapter 9 for discussion of walking with video as a research method). It was made by a student in the late 1990s, using cement and grey color paint, depicting a young Nyerere holding a torch, which is toured through the country annually to mobilize the population, staff explain to me. Hussein, who also captures it on video, figures this is the finest sculpture of Nyerere in all of Tanzania and explains that the student who made it, a good friend of his, paid for the materials to complete it out of his own pocket. The sculptor was Paul Ndunguru, a famous Tanzanian artist, who performed with the Wahapahapa Band at the *Tuwaenzi Wakongwe*, to honor his departed teachers. As Nina and I continue our walk to the Internet room she wants to record next, I ask her if Nyerere was a good president. "Yes, I think he was all right as a president, because I wasn't around when he was president. But what I've heard from people, he was a good president. And he was very, very famous, not only in Tanzania, but in Africa and the whole world. Because when he died, there were lots of people from outside of Tanzania who were mourning for him, and it was really sad that day." What year was that? I ask her. "It was in 1999. I was in Grade 6. I remember we didn't have to go to school that day because of that. And we had like a week of mourning. It was some sort of like a short holiday, but a sad one." We continue our walk. "We are approaching the school Internet cafe," Nina narrates. "We're going up the hill." It is past 5 pm, and the computer room is closed so we cannot film inside. But I am reminded that the room holds a framed photo of Nyerere, similar to the one hanging in the TaSUBa Chief Executive's office.

As illustrated by Nina's choice to film his statue, Julius Nyerere remains a powerful icon of Tanzanian nationalism, remembered with deep-seated respect. Popular understandings of Nyerere are above all anchored in his nationalism and Pan-Africanism, deeply rooted Tanzanian cultural identities. This is why the reverence many Tanzanians feel for Nyerere is genuine, unlike the artificially constructed personality cult and narcissistic self-gratification of many political leaders in Africa (Mbembe 2001, 120–123). These days, Tanzanians within and outside the country use digital media to preserve and promote Nyerere's legacy; recordings of his speeches are available on YouTube and Facebook has Nyerere groups.

Thus it is no surprise that Nina pays homage to *mwalimu* Nyerere. Wearing a bright red t-shirt with the Coca Cola logo in Thai script, trousers, and sandals, her hair worn in funky braids, fingers and ears adorned with silver jewelry, Nina looks like the embodiment of global popular culture. Yet, her cultural roots are firmly anchored in Tanzania, a country she is proud of. While much has changed since Nyerere's rule, the first president is part of Nina's life history, and she remembers his death with sadness, a sense of loss shared with the nation and the world at large. Exemplifying the emotional attachment of nationalism (Anderson 1991, 141), Nina's grief shows that "nationalism 'works' in Tanzania," providing "a sense of social cohesion [that] continues to make the country stand apart" (Edmondson 2007, 13).

I am introducing *mwalimu* Nyerere as one of the lead actors in the digital drama of executive transformation, because his nationalist visions and aspirations form essential parts of the history of TaSUBa. Under the leadership of President Julius Nyerere and Prime Minister Rashid Kawawa, art and culture were placed on the national agenda, and the postcolonial state became a cultural actor, along with its other roles in the nation-building process. The complex linkages between performing arts, culture policy, nation-building and state-making in Tanzania have been well documented by American and European researchers, who have also taken courses or taught at Bagamoyo College of Arts during their fieldwork (Askew 2002, 2004, Edmondson 2007, Lange 2002). These scholars situate the college in the cultural realm of the state, as a bastion of cultural nationalism (Edmondson 2007, 68) or as one of the principal performers of the state aesthetic (Askew 2004, 318).

In its official historical narratives, the origins of BCA are traced to Nyerere, who within a year of Tanganyika's independence in 1961 established a Ministry for Culture. His vision was vast:

> I have ... set up an entirely new Ministry: the Ministry of National Culture and Youth ... because I believe that its *culture is the essence and spirit of any nation.* A country which lacks its own culture is no more than a collection of people without the spirit which makes them a nation. Of all the crimes of colonialism there is none worse than the attempt to make us believe we had no indigenous culture of our own; or that what we did have was worthless ... So I have set up this new Ministry to help us regain our pride in our own culture. I want it to seek out the best of traditions and customs of all the tribes and make them part of our national culture.
>
> (Nyerere 1962, cited in Askew 2004, 306, emphasis added)

To develop the cultural essence of the nation, the Government relied on various constellations of cultural brokers in the construction of an imagined political community (Anderson 1991). Both German and British colonial administrations had been carried out through indirect rule, mediated by local chiefs. Nationalists saw these traditional chiefs as pawns of the colonial state, and one of the first acts of the independent government was to abolish chiefship (Spear 2004). Having thus gotten rid of the guardians of traditional culture, who were not in a position to redefine their cultural middleman role in the new political order (Geertz 1960, 248–249), the state created its own cultural brokers.

In 1963, the Government established a National Dance Troupe, followed by a National Acrobatics Troupe, and a decade later a National Drama Troupe, later reconfigured as the National Performing Arts Company. The concept of national troupes was not unique to Tanzania, which engaged in cultural exchanges with national troupes from other countries, for example Guinea, Zambia and China (Askew 2004, 306). The National Troupes served as pilgrim functionaries, travelling around the country and the world to perform the unifying rites of nationalism (Anderson 1991, 54–65). Through their cultural perform-ances, they also played the role of cultural broker groups, mediating between different levels of integration in society (Wolf 1956, 1076). In 1974 the Ministry of National Culture and Youth issued a pamphlet entitled "Cultural Revolution in Tanzania," encouraging the creation of cultural troupes throughout the country, to further educate and mobi-lize the population (Lange 2002, 58).[3]

Cultural hybridity was a key element in the production of national culture. Like Touré in Guinea, Nyerere's program of cultural national-ism sought to "recover 'authentic' African culture," while encouraging artists to "build innovatively on older traditions" (Dave 2009, 459). While espousing traditionalism, both national leaders encouraged hybrid cultural production: in Guinea the focus was on music with Cuba as a source of inspiration (ibid.); in Tanzania cultural exchange with China brought acrobatics into the national culture repertoire. Nyerere himself encouraged cultural borrowing, stating that "a nation which refuses to learn from foreign cultures is nothing but a nation of idiots and lunatics" (cited in Askew 2002, 191).

Mzee Rashid Masimbi, who served as the first principal of Chuo Cha Sanaa from 1981 to 1996, was an influential broker of national culture, actively translating culture policy into cultural practice. Forming part of the intelligentsia, the new priesthood of the nation

(Smith 1988 [1986], 157), Masimbi was an unusually highly educated man in the early years of independence. Born in Tabora in 1945, he acquired a university degree in education, literature, and theater from UDSM. After some years of teaching literature and languages in secondary schools, he was shifted to the ministry responsible for culture in 1974, to set up the National Drama Troupe. Masimbi remained at Ministry headquarters, as head of the theater section and later as coordinator of the culture program. In 1979 he returned to UDSM for a Master's degree in theater, following which he was appointed to establish Bagamoyo College of Arts. In 1996, he was transferred back to the headquarters. Having now retired from government service, Masimbi heads the Tanzania Theatre Centre, which is housed around the corner from the National Arts Council where the arts college he once led was first set up.

As I listen to Masimbi's eloquent story, I feel transported to a time of grand vision, while his sparsely furnished office and rusty old air-conditioning unit reminds me of a more humble material reality. Seated in a small office, Masimbi punctuates his carefully chosen words with vivid gestures, waving his long, thin arms, while his eyes sparkle with concentration and inspiration. The theatrical delivery of his historical narrative reminds me of his artistic talents as a stage actor, while the content of his recollections and reflections speak the language of morality rather than ideology, culture rather than politics, wrapped in a deep-seated love and concern for his country. In telling me about the background of BCA, starting with the establishment of the Ministry for National Culture and Youth in 1962, Masimbi elaborates on the Government's rationale:

> One of the major responsibilities was to *revive, preserve, promote* and *develop* Tanzanian culture. This was very clear; it was the main function. In the performing arts, they thought that one of the instruments for revival, preservation, promotion, and development was to establish specific groups, which would be directly employed by the government … So here we have what we call the National Performing Arts Company, with acrobatics, traditional dance and music, and drama. The working procedure of the Company must involve a lot of travelling, to show to the

people what they were doing. Promotion actually meant doing performances all over, development implied a bit of research and some creative ideas to see how dances could be brought up to the current environment. Especially in dance, we were moving from participatory to audience performance arrangements. When you perform on stage it's a bit different, because now people are going to be watching you, instead of actually participating in the dance. So this is development, to show how you are doing, so others can also do it.

(Masimbi, July 2009)

It took more financial resources than the state could muster to realize the objectives of national culture production, which was one of the main reasons why BCA was established in 1981. No matter how much artists may have rallied behind the Government's ambitious cultural program, whether willingly or not (Lange 2002, 57–62), the integration of culture in the state apparatus remained incomplete, not least due to a lack of material resources (Askew 2002, 184–191). As a result of economic hardships, by the end of the 1970s the National Troupes were more stationary than mobile, unable to perform their nationalist pilgrimages. Meanwhile, the Government had cultivated other cultural brokers to achieve the spatial encompassment and verticality of the state (Ferguson and Gupta 2002). For instance, the Army, Prisons Service, and National Service established their own performing groups, as did parastatals like the Textile Company, the Tanzania Railways Corporation, and the Tanzanian Shoe Company, thus covering national security as well as economic production, while district culture officers were dispersed in administrative offices throughout the country. What was missing, Masimbi notes, was a training program to supply these groups and to train cultural administrators. Thus the idea of setting up a school, initially at the National Arts Council in Dar es Salaam where the National Performing Arts Company was housed, but soon enough it was shifted to Bagamoyo, to have more space for expansion and to maintain a more rural connection, closer to traditional culture.

Within a decade of its establishment, BCA felt the squeeze of structural adjustment, with fewer opportunities for state employment for graduates. The culture sector was struggling to maintain some form of representation in the state apparatus, where it had been shifted around between different ministries (Askew 2004, 310–313). In Dar es Salaam, commercial cultural troupes started to be established in 1979, reaching a staggering number of over 50 groups by the mid-1980s (Lange 2002, 65–67). Some of these troupes drew on the talent of former members of National Troupes and BCA staff or graduates. Nonetheless, throughout the 1990s, the groups kept diminishing, and by 2001, various musical genres had exceeded the popularity of variety shows performed by local theater groups (Edmondson 2007, 136–137). Meanwhile, with the introduction of a multiparty political system in the mid-1990s, the spread of media, especially television, contributed to the development of new cultural forms like popular drama (Lange 2002), while radio gave a major push to local music production (Ekström 2010), not least the digital genre hip hop, and its local version *bongo flava* (Perullo 2005). Instead of working as civil servants, most BCA graduates had to establish themselves on the commercial market, performing in local bars or other public venues, or sell their services to the burgeoning civil society sector of NGOs, often sponsored by donor agencies.

### Theater in Flames and Crisis of Governance[4]

By October 2002, when I first visited BCA, the college had stagnated, the burned remnants of the theater building accentuating a general sense of deterioration, marking the first phases of the digital drama of executive transformation. The fire that destroyed the theater building[5] was a symbolic transgression, a breach of social relations and normative frameworks that led to the eruption of a crisis (Turner 1987, 74–76). As with the social drama of the Ndembu of Turner's study, individual aspirations for power and status were at play. But what erupted after the fire was above all a *crisis of governance*, revealing ideological paradigm shifts of considerable proportion. While Masimbi had carried out some market-oriented reforms, especially a revision of the curriculum in 1996 to achieve a greater degree of specialization, his administration reflected a crumbling state apparatus. The leadership of Masimbi's successor, Mzee Peter Nyambasi, was indicative of the continuing marginalization of culture in the public sector from 1997 to 2002. After the fire, Nyambasi was replaced with Mzee Juma Bakari, whose skills in maneuvering the crisis undoubtedly benefitted from his lifelong career in drama and public service. Having been a member of the National Drama Troupe, Bakari joined BCA in 1985. By 2002, he had reached the position of coordinator of studies, had an MA degree in theatre studies from Leeds University, and an impressive repertoire of international performances. This professional background and international exposure proved very handy in Bakari's dealings with ministry headquarters and donor agencies, all keen on solving the crisis, focusing on management and institutional set-up.

The crisis was followed by a phase of redressive action, a process in which the reconstitution of governance in the spirit of *neoliberal public sector reform* was carried out as a judicial process, with strong liminal features and a pronounced degree of reflexivity (ibid., 75–76). The legal redressive machinery was set in motion by Tanzanian authorities who undertook an investigation of the causes of the fire, while Sida, which had sponsored the construction of the theater in 1990, requested a review of the college's capacity building needs, thus initiating a process of reflexive scrutiny.[6] While recognizing BCA's critical role in the national culture sector, the review was explicitly aimed at enhancing the college's regional and international position, with a view to developing it into a regional centre of excellence, as per standards set by the East African Community (EAC). The review, conducted by a Danish consultancy company, concluded that the overall impression of BCA was mixed (COWI 2002). While BCA's positive impact on the preservation of cultural heritage and development of arts in Tanzania was widely acknowledged, there was a widespread view that the College performed at a minimum. The management structure and institutional set-up was identified to be a major obstacle to BCA's "huge potential" for being a "dynamic, creative and professionally managed centre of excellence for the East African region" (ibid., 3). While underlining the need for greater transparency, more marketing and a stronger focus on the individual training needs of staff and students, the consultants recommended a "step-by-step process towards autonomy" (ibid., 4).

The phase of redressive action culminated in the transformation of BCA into TaSUBa, a process we will soon scrutinize in greater detail, after placing Internet development in this context of institutional change. Although an inanimate actor in this digital drama, the Internet embodied in the ICT building[7] 📷 mediated institutional transformations aimed at reconfiguring BCA as an executive agency. The COWI report had specifically mentioned Internet access as a prerequisite for institutional improvement, the demand for which was restated in BCA's *Strategic Plan for 2003–2006* (MoEC/BCA 2003). Following a request to Sida, BCA received some support for ICT facilities, starting with the formulation of an ICT Strategy (Uimonen 2004). With the stated vision "BCA aspires to use state of the art information and communication technology (ICT) to become a dynamic, creative, innovative and transparent Institution for high quality training, research and professionalism in the Arts," the ICT Strategy built on the Strategic Plan, while identifying concrete areas for ICT integration, through a phased approach scheduled for 2004 to 2007 and onwards (ibid., 12). In parallel, BCA was registered with the National Council for Technical Education (NACTE) and a new curriculum was developed, along with a Master Plan for infrastructure development,[8] 📷 supported by Sida, Norad, and the government of Tanzania.

### Thatcher, TaSUBa, and Audit Culture

It may be useful as background to note that the Tanzania Executive Agency Concept is similar to the British Government's 'Next Steps Initiative' which itself was part of a broader programme called the Financial Management Initiative (FMI). This began in the early 1980s after Margaret Thatcher's Government reviewed the state of public sector management performance, concluding that major improvements were required ... The British Government's policy is that executive activities should be undertaken by the private sector wherever possible. Otherwise, in line with the main recommendation of the Next Steps report, the work should be carried out by Agencies within a policy and resources framework set by the parent Ministry.

The Government of Tanzania has been through a number of similar reviews over the last few years and, unsurprisingly perhaps, has reached the same conclusions and has decided to adopt a similar approach. It has examined its non-core functions to see which can be better undertaken either outside Government altogether, or in semi-autonomous Executive Agencies. Accordingly, the Government has established the Executive Agencies Programme (EAP) as an essential component of its Public Service Reform Programme (PSRP).

(PO–PSM 2006, 4)

When I first read these passages during fieldwork, in an electronic version emailed to me by the consultant who had overseen BCA's transformation into an executive agency, I was taken aback by the references to the British government, Margaret Thatcher, and the 1980s, thus explicitly pinpointing the origins of what anthropologists refer to as audit culture, along with its core values of management and performance through public sector reform (Shore and Wright 1999, 2000, Strathern 2000). As I continued reading the *Implementation Workbook* produced by the President's Office–Public Service Management (PO–PSM), which oversees the Public Service Reform Programme (PSRP), I realized that I had stumbled across an almost ideal type of audit culture, an exemplary case of the global spread of neoliberal forms of governance in institutes of higher learning (Wright and Rabo 2010). The *Implementation Workbook* provided an overall framework for the *TaSUBa Framework Document* and the *TaSUBa Strategic Plan (2008–2011)* I had received from management at the beginning of my fieldwork, and in my folders I found a predecessor, the draft *Business Analysis Report*, which I had myself been involved in revising, at the time focusing on ICT integration. From an anthropological perspective, these policy documents represent normative cultural texts, models of society offering analytical keys into the architecture of modern power relations (Shore and Wright 1997, 7–12). From the perspective of *Digital Drama*, they offer scripts for the redressive phase of legal action, bringing BCA into the folds of the neoliberal culture complex.

TaSUBa was one of 24 executive agencies launched or strengthened during the first phase of the Public Service Reform Programme (PSRP), which was implemented from 2000 to 2007, building on the Executive Agency Act of 1997, formulated with support from the UK Department for International Development (DFID) (Caulfield 2002). The main thrust of this phase was "Instituting Performance Management Systems" to "improve MDAs service delivery and regulatory functions through a more efficient Public Service" (PO–PSM 2008, v). Within this context of public sector reform, the aim of the Executive Agencies Programme was "to deliver public services more effectively and efficiently, within available resources and for the benefit of customers, taxpayers and staff" through "discrete management units (Agencies), with responsibility for conducting some of the executive functions of Government" (PO–PSM 2006, 4). Some key features of an executive agency are: clear lines of accountability, responsibility, and authority; the use of modern business planning and management methods; and, individual tailoring of the organization to match the needs of the services to be provided, as specified in a framework document implemented by a chief executive who is personally and publicly accountable for the delivery of results (ibid., 5). In summary, the executive agency is a semi-autonomous, not independent, government organization, managed by a chief executive at arm's length from government, business-like in operation, customer focused, and publicly accountable (ibid., 6).

These documents are laden with the policy keywords that anthropologists associate with audit culture, a global phenomenon that has been interpreted in terms of an epochal change in governance, centered on accountability (Strathern 2000). The very concept executive agency is expressive of the neoliberal underpinnings of new managerialism in which audit technologies serve as instruments for new forms of governance and power (Shore and Wright 2000, 59–60). The making of TaSUBa clearly builds on the idea of reinventing institutes of higher learning as enterprises, using free market norms as an organizing principle of state activities, a process defined through keywords of new managerialism, such as efficiency, effectiveness, and performance (ibid.). If anything, the very aim of the first phase of the Public Service Reform Programme rests on the foundations of audit culture, which are reinforced even further in Phase II, the thrust of which is "enhanced performance and accountability" (PO–PSM 2008, v).

In reality, however, audit culture is an ongoing process, subject to cultural remodelling. No matter how dominant the acceptable forms of audit culture may seem, or the extent to which audit practices coalesce into a distinct cultural artifact, the global spread of which has the momentum of a cultural movement (Strathern 2000, 1–4), audit culture is far more complex than concealed political ideology writ large, while its global distribution is far messier than the rise to dominance of neoliberalism. I am not challenging the neoliberal thrust of the executive agency concept in Tanzania, the ideological underpinnings of which are quite explicit in the cultural keywords used to define it. Nor am I questioning the appropriateness of the term "audit culture" to understand and critique dominant forms of governance. But since we are dealing with culture, we should not lose sight of the fact that audit culture is, like all complex forms of culture, an instance of cultural flow, socially distributed as a network of perspectives (Hannerz 1992b).[9] And since audit culture is socially organized as a network, we can more clearly appraise the role of cultural brokers, whose strategic positioning in wide-reaching networks of contacts and influence allows them to perform the translation and mediation of audit culture (cf. Boyer and Rata 2010).

I am insisting on this processual, actor-oriented concept of culture as a flow of meaning to explain and make sense of audit culture at TaSUBa. The ways in which individual and institutional social actors have interpreted, modified, and improvised the executive agency concept at BCA points to the inherent complexities of audit culture, which is performed in a multitude of ways. To appreciate this diversity, I agree that audit culture should be studied ethnographically in different social contexts, paying close attention to the interrelations as well as discrepancies between discourses and practices, thus allowing for an appraisal of audit cultures in the plural (Kipnis 2008, 285–286). Nonetheless, while audit cultures come in many different forms, the ideological thrust is decidedly neoliberal. Of course neoliberalism in Tanzania is just as much of a cultural hybrid as African socialism, which is why postcolonial, postsocialist contexts offer interesting insights into the cultural variations of "governmentality" (Foucault 1991).

Before turning to a more detailed investigation of the production of these cultural texts, a few words are in place to clarify the value of an anthropological approach to the executive agency transformation process. In her critical evaluation of what she defines as the agencification process in Tanzania, Caulfield (2002, 210) points to the mismatch between "a highly centralized core bureaucracy and political system, and a reform programme inspired by a liberal, market type doctrine of decentralized authority and fragmented bureaucracy." Rather than problematizing the cultural origins or political rationale of such reform efforts, or the international power relations at play, she points to their perverse outcomes in the Tanzanian context. While this detailed analysis of agencification is interesting and accurate in many ways, it fails to appreciate that what may come across as mismatch or perverse outcomes reflects the complexities of African state-building. As Bayart (2009, 262–263) reminds us, while the sub-Saharan postcolonial state clearly diverts from Weber's bureaucratic ideal, these state formations "should not be labeled as pathological."[10] If anything, an anthropological appreciation of the state in postcolonial cultural contexts can demonstrate the provincialism of Western scholarship of the state and its tendency to "universalize a particular cultural construction of 'state-society relations'" (Gupta 1995, 378). It can also bring forth the asymmetric interrelatedness of various state constellations in global governance structures.

### Workshops and Executive Ritual

We are seated around a large table in an air-conditioned room at one of the hotels at Kunduchi Beach, an area just outside Dar es Salaam often used to organize workshops, conferences and other meetings, especially for state agencies. For the beach hotels, such events comprise a significant part of their business, in many cases surpassing the income generated from tourism. For participants, they offer an opportunity to work and stay in a luxurious and relaxing setting, while earning extra income. State employees receive a daily allowance commensurate with their position in the state hierarchy when attending workshops outside their offices. Usually defined as travel allowance or sitting allowance, and sometimes referred to as *bahasha culture*, from the envelopes used for their distribution, these cash payments form a substantial part of the income of civil servants, often exceeding their monthly salary. As of late, non-governmental organizations have argued that allowances represent an emerging form of corruption and some donor agencies feel uncomfortable about paying them.[11] Even so, the practice of allowances is systemic, in Tanzania as well as other African societies. Far from being an indigenous innovation, it is historically rooted in the colonial administrative system, intensified by donor-driven reductions of state expenditure during structural adjustment, and of continued significance in the age of neoliberal reforms where state salaries have yet to match living costs.

This particular workshop is part of the preparatory process for the BCA executive agency transformation, facilitated by a consultant contracted by the PO–PSM, who acts as a cultural broker for policy implementation. The workshop participants are senior staff at BCA, a small team of employees and the Principal, who also functions as a cultural broker, mediating and translating the meaning of the transformation process to his colleagues. Defined as the Agency Implementation Team, the group is composed of teachers in managerial positions as well as financial staff, chosen for their understanding of the business requirements of the executive agency in the making. Following a five-day workshop on how to prepare the documents required for the transformation process, several workshops are organized in Morogoro and Dar es Salaam to prepare and revise the documents before their finalization. The documents are in the form of templates, with predetermined categories that structure the preparatory process. For instance, the *Business Analysis Worksheet* is divided into ten sections, each starting with a box in which data are to be filled in according to a predefined model.

It is by filling out these templates that the team constructs and defines the executive agency. The process is highly formalized, structured through standardized templates, to facilitate the reflexive practices so fundamental to the constitution of modern society (Beck et al. 1994; Ong and Collier 2005). Even so, the participants in this process have their own subjective notions of what an executive agency represents. The consultant facilitating the process is guided by his understanding of the *Implementation Workbook* and other documents, as well as his experiences of how various state agencies have dealt with the transformation process. The Principal of BCA has his ideas of what an executive agency represents for the institute as well as his envisaged position as its chief executive, as do the other members of the team. These perspectives are shaped by individual life trajectories as well as shared experiences and expectations, not to mention positions in the social structure, the horizon of the Principal's perspective both coinciding with and differing from the perspectives of other team members, undoubtedly having more in common with the Dean of Students and the accountant than the storekeeper, while carrying more weight than the rest of the team. The team shares an insider's view of the institute while the facilitator has an external perspective, although all of them share the experience of working within the state apparatus. Their perspectives are also shaped by their interactions with international actors, the facilitator being more experienced with the neoliberal, Anglo-Saxon world views of DFID and the World Bank, key actors in the Executive Agency Programme, while BCA staff are more used to dealing with representatives from Sida and Norad, key actors in the culture sector, whose perspectives are shaped by the Nordic liberal welfare state ideologies, which are gradually becoming more neoliberal.

Although workshops in Tanzania tend to be characterized by vivid discussions and elaborate rhetoric, the workshop format being quite suitable to this cultural context with its strong oral tradition, the BCA team struggles with the process of defining the institute. Far from being a straightforward exercise of filling out the templates, the process proves to be rather cumbersome, as team members struggle to interpret and respond to the instructions they receive. Benefitting from years of experience of similar procedures, the Principal has the strongest grasp of how to proceed, but most team members have a hard time understanding the process. They also struggle with the language. All documents are prepared in English, which few of them command, the contents of which they discuss in Kiswahili. As much as Kiswahili is the official language of Tanzania, government documents tend to be in English. The majority of civil servants are not fluent in English, despite their formal academic accreditation, so they tend to combine spoken Kiswahili with written English, thus using the code switching so common in the state of creolization. As I've noticed in other government contexts in Tanzania, a great deal of attention is paid to the formal structure of the texts, the form being of equal if not greater concern than the content. In many cases, the BCA team simply replicates information. For instance, in the *Business Analysis Report* the customers' needs of central government, an impressive number of 31 ministries and government agencies, are rather loosely defined and in most cases identical, e.g. information, training of their staff, and edutainment, as are the needs of non-governmental organizations (NGOs), community-based organizations (CBOs), and faith-based organizations (FBOs), all of which are identified as needing sensitization programs, consultancy/services, and designers/designs.

This brief ethnographic portrayal of the executive agency preparatory process can hopefully clarify the cultural process of state-making. As Gupta (1995, 335–337, emphasis in original) has pointed out, rather than representing a coherent spatial unit, the state is constituted through a "complex set of *spatially* intersecting representations and practices," in "multiply mediated" contexts. By analyzing these mediated contexts in terms of networks of perspectives, we can trace the social actors involved in the cultural construction and reconstruction of the state, the workshop in Kunduchi being one such context of intersecting perspectives. In addition to being spatially distributed through different levels of the state apparatus, the networks are hierarchically structured. Some perspectives hold greater power in the construction of the state than others, not least depending on their position in the bureaucratic hierarchy. In terms of network theory, strategically positioned social actors can be categorized as programmers, with the power to define the actual constellation of the network (Castells 2004, 32). In this particular instance, it is no surprise that the perspectives of the World Bank and DFID play a dominant role in the Executive Agency Programme, mediated through the PO–PSM, one of the most powerful government institutions in Tanzania. BCA is a rather subaltern actor in this context, a minor government institute trying to maneuver the emerging paradigms of the neoliberal state, while seeking greater autonomy from the state apparatus. BCA is in turn internally stratified, the perspective of its most powerful representative playing a dominant role in the cultural production of the executive agency.

As is often the case in modern state-making, the executive agency transformation process has strong ritual elements, constituting an *executive ritual*. It is a highly reflexive process, a *rite de passage* or rite of transition whereby a state, as in a culturally recognized stable condition, is altered (Turner 1969, 94). Through the executive ritual, a government agency is transformed into an executive agency, to perform the role of the state in a more business-like manner, in order to achieve a more effective and efficient delivery of public services. The process of transformation is carried out in steps, which can be likened to the main phases in rituals: separation, margin (liminality), and aggregation (ibid.). In the first phase, the ritual subject (the agency implementation team) is detached from the larger BCA community. This is followed by the liminal phase, when the characteristics of the ritual subject are ambiguous, subject to reformulation (workshops). During this phase, the team forms a "normative communitas," which mobilizes and organizes resources, with a view to constructing a more enduring social system (ibid., 132). In the final phase, aggregation, the team is reincorporated into the community, but by then its role and position have been changed, since the social structure to which it belongs has been reconfigured (BCA has become TaSUBa).

This executive ritual underlines the cultural dimensions of the executive agency transformation process. When the latter is viewed as a cultural process, it becomes quite clear that not only are we dealing with different cultural meanings, but these meanings are produced and reproduced by a wide range of social actors, loosely organized into a network. The transformation itself is performed as a ritual, the various phases of which are played out through reflexive intersections in different mediated contexts. Seeing that this ritual involves a heterogeneous cast of characters, whose roles and perspectives are shaped by a diversity of social positions, the fluidity of this process should become

quite clear. It is not simply a matter of executing change, but of performing a ritual of uncertainty and unpredictability. The result may not
be what was intended or expected, while the process itself unravels the
complexities of liminality, a condition of considerable ambivalence.

Before proceeding to a discussion of the final phase of the digital
drama in which this executive ritual has played such a decisive role, it
is worth recalling that BCA/TaSUBa is not just any old bureaucracy,
but an institute devoted to the arts. This explains perhaps why
PO–PSM representatives I spoke with in Dar es Salaam likened BCA's
transformation process to that of "pulling out teeth." Their horizons
may not have reached so far as to see the inherent tensions of transforming a bastion of traditional culture, created in the spirit of African
socialism and anticolonialist nationalism, into a free market-oriented
business-like state entity. Neither did the agency implementation team
necessarily foresee that greater autonomy from the Ministry might
weaken rather than strengthen the boundaries of their artistic field.
During the liminal phase, it was quite likely that this normative communitas was already envisaging the material benefits of its future
executive agency status, undoubtedly inspired by the air-conditioned
comforts of the luxury hotels in which it was temporarily suspended.
Meanwhile, trained as artists, these social actors could perform the
formalities expected of them well enough to reach the concluding
phase of the executive ritual, reintegation, under the direction of their
principal, soon to be Chief Executive.

## Executive Power, A/C, and Witchcraft

"You know, staff are afraid to say anything about him [the Chief
Executive], because he is known to have powerful witchcraft," an
informant tells me as we enter a recurring topic of discussion, the
management of TaSUBa. People are afraid that he will harm or destroy
them if they criticize him or speak up against him, he explains to
me as we meander over to Bagapoint for some lunch. I find the
information rather amusing, albeit not surprising. Allegations of
witchcraft are commonplace in Tanzania, forming part of, and even
constituting notions of modernity (Green 2005, Green and Mesaki

2005, Sanders 2003). Bagamoyo itself is famous throughout the country for its *waganga* (witchdoctors/traditional healers) and politicians are known to visit the town during election times to get some extra assistance. In the lead-up to the 2010 elections, local journalists mused on politicians' occult campaigning habits and trips to Bagamoyo, while suggesting that an octopus might be of better service, given Octopus Paul's successful predictions in Germany during the 2010 World Cup in football in South Africa.[12]

Some students call him *Mr A/C* (Mr Air Conditioning), for the Chief Executive of TaSUBa is mostly seen passing by in his air-conditioned, chauffeur-driven car, a spotless, white, four-door Toyota pickup with the TaSUBa logo on the door, or unseen in his air-conditioned office, where semi-closed blinds keep him out of public view. This air-conditioned seclusion is unique at TaSUBa. The Toyota pickup is the only staff vehicle at TaSUBa, exclusively used by the Chief Executive. The only offices that are air-conditioned, apart from the Chief Executive's one, are those of his secretary, the heads of the academic and business departments, the accountant, and the offices used by the theater management. The only classroom with air conditioning is the new music studio in the theater building, which is used for music classes on keyboards and computer-based music production. The library, classrooms, and administrative offices have ceiling fans, as does the ICT building. The dormitories do not have fans, not even the more exclusive ones opened in October 2009, and during the hottest period of the year some students choose to sleep outside. Most of the classes take place in the open air, under the shade of trees or roofs, cooled only by the occasional ocean breeze.

Representing a material and sensory expression of institutional hierarchies and power structures, it is not surprising that students pick up on the air conditioning in their characterization of the Chief Executive. Exemplifying how weather is a medium of perception (Ingold 2005), air conditioning offers a powerful metaphor for asymmetric social relations in a physical environment characterized by material scarcity and unequal distribution of material resources. In this hot, tropical climate, the ability to use modern technology to alter climatic conditions is associated with power and social status, asserting the superior positioning of a privileged few. The concentration of A/C to top management, finance, and the new theater complex is instructive of what activities are prioritized under current management, reflecting power relations and institutional hierarchies, rather than overall mandates or visions of the institute at large. Related to A/C is another expression of power, electricity, which in a Tanzanian context is unreliable as well as costly. Power fluctuations are frequent at TaSUBa, often lasting for a few hours, during which most activities in the ICT building and the administrative offices are suspended. The institute has procured a new generator, powerful enough to serve the whole campus. But it is only connected to the new theater building, the flexible hall, and the recently completed Chief Executive's residence.

This concentration of power, mediated through A/C,[13] stands in sharp contrast to the material neglect of other parts of the campus. A few doors down from the exclusively furnished Chief Executive's office is a teachers' room, the interior of which has not changed much since I first visited the college in 2002. If anything, the wooden desks are even more worn out, the piles of paper taller, and only shreds remain of the batik curtains. Some of the teachers who use the room bring in their personal laptops, but mostly the office remains as computerless as it was when I first entered it. As for the classrooms, teaching and learning facilities are deteriorating steadily, many of the chairs missing back seats, while the blackboards can barely be cleaned after years of layers of chalk. Stored in a run-down building, musical instruments have worn out due to climatic conditions, their life spans shortened by humidity, heat, and salty air, while teachers struggle to procure paint and brushes for fine art classes. The library remains as under-resourced as ever, while the ICT facilities are on the brink of collapse.

"If you visited TaSUBa just for a day, you would get a very good impression," an informant tells me, as we're sitting outside the ICT building, overlooking the campus. He goes on to describe how upon entering the gate, a visitor would see the new theater,[14] and after parking his/her car near the administration building,[15] he/she would sit in the Chief Executive's office. As he talks, my mind fills with images of cars passing by, bringing representatives of state and donor agencies for meetings with TaSUBa management, before returning to Dar es Salaam. I am also reminded of my own movements around campus, back when I was an ICT consultant. He is right, I think to myself. Most official visitors would really be impressed, for all they would see would be the newly constructed theater complex, the exclusively furnished office, and the well kept lawn in front of the administration building, with the Master Plan in its cabinet. They might also catch a glimpse of the newly renovated canteen near the road, or the new dormitories erected in front of the entrance gate, and probably the exterior of the ICT building. But this is all they would see; the signs and symbols of modernity, material embodiments of progress, and visual expressions of executive management. And based on these impressions, the visitors would be able to report on the positive developments at TaSUBa, and attribute them to its Chief Executive. What a clever use of the front region as a dramaturgical technique for impression management, facilitated by an ever so tactful audience (Goffman 1990 [1959])!

By now you have probably understood that in practice the management of TaSUBa has little to do with the formal dictates of audit culture and its emphasis on new managerialism, but is viewed from quite different perspectives from within. When I returned to TaSUBa in 2009 to carry out fieldwork, I was keen to learn how the transformation process had played out. To my great surprise, I found that many staff and students were highly critical of the institute's administration and management. Rather than representing an improvement in service delivery, it appeared that the transformation process had led to a general deterioration in academic standards, training facilities, and working conditions. Students were complaining about the high tuition fees and lack of learning facilities, the shortage of computers being one major source of frustration (Uimonen 2011). Teachers were feeling neglected by management, which did not seem to pay much attention to their recurring requests for more adequate teaching facilities, or their ideas for how to improve academic performance, while delaying contractual obligations. And as artists, they lamented the lack of high-quality performances, the production of which had earned the institute a high reputation in the past. Indeed the performers in the back region told quite a different story from the performance team in the front region, suggesting a major performative disruption in this carefully staged display of executive power (Goffman 1990 [1959]).

To appreciate this disruption in the performance of executive power, it is worth revisiting the possible outcomes of social dramas, the final stage of which can be "a reestablishment of viable relations between the contending parties" or "a public recognition of irreparable schism" (Turner 1987, 92). In the case of TaSUBa, we are dealing with a social drama that has resulted in both. At the institutional level, TaSUBa has been reconfigured according to the dictates of neoliberal public sector reform, reaffirming relations with government agencies and external partners. But there is a growing rupture between state ideology and bureaucratic practice as well as between artistic production and cultural practice. The transformation into an executive agency has not translated into a more efficient and effective delivery of public services, nor has it led to greater autonomy for the artistic field. Meanwhile, the new social structure is quite unstable, with segmented social relations and latent social conflicts simmering under the polished surface of executive management.

Since the actors of a social drama have to make sense of their altered reality, it is no wonder that witchcraft and A/C become idioms of executive power. The allocation of A/C reaffirms TaSUBa's external relations with modern institutions, in the cool Nordic countries as well as the chilled offices in Dar es Salaam and Dodoma, but it also enforces the social hierarchy of internal relations. Only top management enjoys the luxury of cool offices, while subalterns have to deal with the stifling heat of the natural environment. This social distance is accentuated through physical seclusion. Contrary to the ideals of transparency and accountability, A/C-mediated executive management is best performed behind closed doors. Since the execution of power is thus hidden from public view, it gets interpreted from different perspectives, the notion of witchcraft reflecting a common understanding of power and social inequality.[16] But perhaps witchcraft also says something about the occult economies of millennial capitalism, and the ways in which business and management are supposed to magically transform the delivery of public services by an ever-diminishing state (Comaroff and Comaroff 2000).[17]

### Online Liminality in a State of Creolization[18]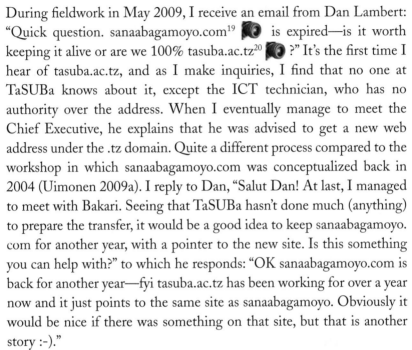

During fieldwork in May 2009, I receive an email from Dan Lambert: "Quick question. sanaabagamoyo.com[19] is expired—is it worth keeping it alive or are we 100% tasuba.ac.tz[20] ?" It's the first time I hear of tasuba.ac.tz, and as I make inquiries, I find that no one at TaSUBa knows about it, except the ICT technician, who has no authority over the address. When I eventually manage to meet the Chief Executive, he explains that he was advised to get a new web address under the .tz domain. Quite a different process compared to the workshop in which sanaabagamoyo.com was conceptualized back in 2004 (Uimonen 2009a). I reply to Dan, "Salut Dan! At last, I managed to meet with Bakari. Seeing that TaSUBa hasn't done much (anything) to prepare the transfer, it would be a good idea to keep sanaabagamoyo. com for another year, with a pointer to the new site. Is this something you can help with?" to which he responds: "OK sanaabagamoyo.com is back for another year—fyi tasuba.ac.tz has been working for over a year now and it just points to the same site as sanaabagamoyo. Obviously it would be nice if there was something on that site, but that is another story :-)."

Dan has served as a technical broker for BCA/TaSUBa since he worked as a multimedia volunteer at the college in 2004/2005, through the UK-based Volunteer Service Overseas (VSO). Having designed BCA's first website, which was launched at the annual arts festival in 2004, Dan has continued assisting the college's web masters from a distance. He has also helped out with domain name registration and maintenance, which would have been hard to do otherwise since no one at TaSUBa has a credit card to make online payments. During his nine months of volunteer work at BCA, Dan taught some courses in graphic design and he also tutored some students, including Mussa Sango, who has pursued a successful career as a graphic designer in Dar es Salaam (Uimonen 2009b). As Mussa pointed out when giving a speech at Dan's wedding in Collonges, France in July 2010, unlike other volunteers, Dan actually lived like a Tanzanian during his stay in Bagamoyo, eating local food and riding a bicycle. The depth of Dan's cultural immersion into local life made a deep impression on his Tanzanian friends and colleagues, many of whom he still stays in touch with.

The change of TaSUBa's website addresses that Dan inquires about in his email is instructive of the liminal or threshold character of social drama, through which crucial principles of a social structure and their dominance at different points in time can be observed (Turner 1987, 92). On the one hand, the change from a .com to a .tz address signals a more national identity, thus reproducing the rationale of having a Kiswahili name for the institute. This nationalist principle is affirmed by TaSUBa's positioning in the national domain name structure, sub-categorized as .ac to accentuate its academic status. On the other hand, the change of online identity forms part of a process whereby TaSUBa is expected to operate in a more business-like manner, more like a .com, aligned with the principles of neoliberal capitalism. Meanwhile, the formalization and structuring of its academic position as ac.tz notwithstanding, TaSUBa is disentangled from the state apparatus, operating at an arm's length from its parent ministry.

This coexistence of seemingly contradictory dominant principles indicates the multifaceted condition of liminality. Turner (1969, 95–97) focuses on betwixt and between to describe the temporary detachment of liminal entities from the prevailing social order, a transitional phase he describes as a "limbo of statuslessness." I would, however, like to stress another dimension of liminality, namely that the state of betwixt and between can also be a matter of being both here and there, a condition of *multiple social statuses* rather than mere statuslessness. This is exemplified by the temporary coexistence of sanaabagamoyo. com and tasuba.ac.tz, as well as the overlapping social statuses contained within both online identities.

In order to make sense of this multilayered coexistence, let me explore liminality in terms of creolization (Hannerz 1987, 1996). A key concept in anthropological studies of globalization, creolization captures the dynamic interplay between cultures, the diversity of creative combinations and syntheses arising from the interactions between different flows of meaning (Hannerz 1987, 546–548). The reason why I want to look at liminality in terms of creolization is that the notion of betwixt and between captures the networked intersections of global cultural flow. While these intersections or nodal points are neither here nor there, but in a state of constant flux, they are also both here and there, spatially and temporally, since culture is an ongoing process, a perpetual linking of different perspectives, which are always positioned, even multiply positioned, in different configurations of space and time.

I am elaborating on liminality and creolization to explain the cultural composition of TaSUBa, and by extension, the Tanzanian state. Even during periods of relative social stability, this government organization has been constituted through a diversity of cultural forms, shaped by various political ideologies, structural economic conditions, and material circumstances. At any given time in its history, it has drawn on a great variety of cultural strands, which have been interwoven into its social fabric, thus creating unique combinations of statehood. In a sense, this institution has always been in a state of liminality, betwixt and between ideal types, neither here nor there, but somewhere in between. It is an exemplary construction of hybrid statehood.

Far from representing a temporary suspension of social order, this in-between state is actually a nexus of social agency, the liminality of the Tanzanian state illuminating one of the fundamental paradoxes of the modern constitution (Latour 1993). Since modern society is based on the premise of separation, the in-between state of liminality does not exist; it is the "unthinkable, the unconscious of the moderns," yet this is actually where everything happens, by way of mediation, translation, and networks (ibid., 37). This is why Tanzanian state-making is instructive of modernity in general, for the African state, "however distorting it may be, reflects our own political image and has a lot to teach us about the springs of our western modernity" (Bayart 2009, 269). Anthropological research on postcolonial states underlines the constant blurring of ideological, cultural, and social boundaries (Askew 2002, Gupta and Sharma 2006), so it would appear that Latour (1993) may have a valid point in suggesting that we have never been modern in the first place.

What we are dealing with is a *state of creolization*, the word state here referring to both a condition or position and a body politic.[21] Since it is a state of creolization, it is always unstable, constituted as a discontinuous series, a constant coming together and pulling apart of different cultural fragments (Benítez-Rojo 1998, 55).[22] The state of creolization should be understood in temporal as well as spatial terms, for the perpetual reconfiguration of cultural fragments draws on cultural flows from different directions, some of them internal, others external, and from different points in time. This hybrid cultural construct is poignantly exemplified by the political ideology of *ujamaa*, which combined African traditionalism with Western modernism. Perpetual cultural blending makes for a state constituted through daily processes of creolization, where cultural pluralism and political cross-breeding are the order of the day (Bayart 2009, 244). While the complexity of the state of creolization is a source of contradictions, rifts, and suffering, it is also a source of invention and a site for political mediation (ibid.). It is a highly dynamic and creative construct, which brings new meanings to the art of government, underlining coexistence and parallel movement, rather than linear succession, in other words discontinuous series (Benítez-Rojo 1998, 55) rather than solid series (Foucault 1991, 102).

Let me conclude this chapter by portraying the state of creolization in more concrete terms, in the character of the Chief Executive who directed TaSUBa's online transformation. Born during the colonial era in Tanga region, Bakari was educated in a missionary school, where he also learnt English. In addition to being a professional actor and director, he worked as a village manager and community development worker, before joining BCA in 1985. After being appointed principal in 2003, he successfully gained the position of Chief Executive, in competition with other candidates. Bakari is a Muslim, and having done his pilgrimage to Mecca, he has the honorific title of Al-Hajj. He is married with six children, but in 2009 he took a second wife, a polygamous custom still permitted among Muslims, albeit a declining practice among educated, urban Tanzanians, who tend to prefer the hybrid form *nyumba ndogo* (little house).[23] In addition to running two households and an arts institute, Bakari is taking a PhD in cultural tourism at the Open University of Tanzania, which helps explain why he actually tends to spend more time outside than inside his chilled office, managing TaSUBa at an arm's length. Bakari speaks fluent English, with a British accent he articulates with a seductively deep voice. He has a great sense of humor and his MA thesis focused on satire in African drama (Bakari 1998). This brief life history will hopefully give a clearer picture of the creolized nature of state actors in Tanzania. The very actors who mediate the state's executive power have multilayered cultural identities, spanning the historical periods of colonialism and postcolonialism, the political economies and ideologies of socialism and neoliberalism, the religious beliefs of Christianity and Islam, as well as monogamous and polygamous family structures. It takes exceptional creativity to manage such diversity, which is why the story of tasuba.ac.tz offers such a splendid drama of state-crafting.

# 4
## SOCIAL AESTHETICS AND ART TRAINING[1]

### Developing Artists through Practical Mastery

"We are inside the theater here, our main theater hall," Kiswigu Bernad narrates as we walk through the spacious corridor leading up to the stage. After sweeping the camera around the wooden stage, she directs it toward the auditorium. "The audience are sitting there. Sometimes it's crowded, up to two thousand people inside. It's full, full, full house," she adds with theatrical emphasis. "So this is where I perform, we do our productions here. It's our main theater." We walk up the steps of the auditorium so Kiswigu can film the stage from the audience perspective and return to the floor below the stage, our eyes turned toward the auditorium. "So these steps here, it reminds me sometimes years ago, I used to come and do my exercises here. Running up and down, up and down," Kiswigu stresses as she moves the camera accordingly. "That was before this theater was burned, because this theater is new. So it was burned and this is a new one. But these steps, I mean this auditorium, is the same. It's only some few they have added, some steps, but almost everything was the same down here. So it was there from the beginning, these steps were there. Before it was burned, I used to come and do exercises here." An impressive exercise routine, I think to myself, covering 30 concrete steps in each direction. No wonder this lady is so fit, yet she is going on 50! But then again, running up and down steps is but one aspect of the physical dimensions of Kiswigu's social formation as an artist and tutor.

Kiswigu is a drama teacher at TaSUBa who started her artist career as the youngest member of the National Drama Troupe. Born in Kyela district in Mbeya region, Kiswigu liked theater from an early age and performed at churches through local drama clubs. After completing her ordinary certificate in secondary school, Kiswigu joined the newly established National Drama Troupe in Dar es Salaam. Initially her parents were not too fond of her choice of drama as a career. Although they were both doing dances, especially in church where they were very active (Kiswigu describes her father as a man of God), women dancing on stage in front of an audience was considered sinful. But Kiswigu managed to convince her parents that performing was in her heart; it was the only thing she wanted to do. So at the age of 15 or 16, she joined the National Drama Troupe and when it was dismantled she was recruited to Bagamoyo College of Arts, where she has worked ever since, with some short interruptions.

Powerfully energetic and eager to learn and progress, Kiswigu has had to climb many steps in her professional trajectory, not least due to her gender. Not only was she the youngest member of the National Drama Troupe, but Kiswigu was also the only woman, quite exceptional at the time. Even at the college, Kiswigu found that her gender was something of a disadvantage. While some of her male colleagues were given opportunities for further study, Kiswigu felt she was "dormant for a long time," "demoralized" by a system in which "a woman can't go anywhere" and "can't do anything." Nonetheless, through her position at BCA, Kiswigu made contacts for further training and job opportunities, especially in community theater. In 2009, she completed her BA degree at Witwatersrand University in Johannesburg, thus complementing decades of professional advancement with formal accreditation. Kiswigu has traveled a fair amount and over the years she has performed in Scandinavia, Germany, England, and Jordan, as well as Kenya, Uganda, Zambia, and Nigeria.

Rather than merely accepting the patriarchal system, Kiswigu created spaces for female performers, especially through the Bagamoyo

Women Artists (BAWA). Some of her male colleagues were against the idea, but they came to see that it was a good thing, since BAWA's performances proved very popular. Initially the group performed in nearby villages and in addition to addressing issues of concern to women they also broke the Tanzanian tradition that women should not speak in public. Soon enough the group was promoted by the Tanzanian Media Women's Association (TAMWA), which brought them to perform at major events in Dar es Salaam. BAWA also performed in other regions, and Kiswigu notes with pride that she visited Nyerere in Musoma, shortly before he died. The group is also known by the current President Kikwete, who insisted on them performing during his first electoral campaign in Bagamoyo, instructing the reluctant District Commissioner to let them on stage since they were his friends.

As we walk through campus, Kiswigu films all kinds of spaces that she associates with her everyday life at TaSUBa. She starts off with the administrative building where she records the ledger she fills in every morning, then the teachers' room where she does her work, followed by the library where she comes to read books and the classrooms where she teaches community theater. We proceed to the beach, where she used to go swimming every day, but nowadays she has too many things to do, although it remains her "favorite activity." Kiswigu zooms in on some fishing boats anchored near the fish market where she buys fresh fish for her family. Returning through the gate, she films the flexible hall, a new building where they sometimes meet, and the ground in front of it where the Bagamoyo Women Artists group sells things during functions, an activity she describes as their "entrepreneur issue." Passing the grounds where the disco is performed, we enter the theater and she also films the exterior of the extended theater hall when we continue up the incline to the ICT building.

"This is our Internet room. This is where we come to use computers,"[2] Kiswigu narrates, diplomatically adding with a tone of laughter "we thank you Paula so much, [s]he is the one who brought all this." As she shoots the painted sign of the exterior, she adds "It's great for us we have this Internet cafe … We thank so much, otherwise I don't know which world we were heading to. But now we are up to date, because of this Internet cafe. Though it needs more, more, more, to put more energy on it."

Kiswigu's video captures the spatial and temporal materiality of her social formation at the college, illustrating how TaSUBa forms a "social aesthetic field" (MacDougall 1999). It is a constructed community, created as an aesthetic space or sensory structure and it is through this "structure of sense impressions, social relations, and ways of behaving physically" that institutionalized forms of art training and production are imprinted in staff and students at the college (ibid., 9). The socially informed body thus produced expresses the underlying principles of the social word with "all its *senses*," which as Bourdieu (1977, 124, emphasis in original) underscores, entails "not just the traditional five senses," but includes the sense of duty, direction, reality, as well as common sense and sense of humor.

It is this embodied social formation that is expressed in Kiswigu's narrational performance of selfhood (Rapport 1998, 180), visualized through a series of activities associated with different places. Her position in the social hierarchy is expressed by the ease with which she enters the main theater building, while her critical remarks about the Internet room, which she was frequently using from the moment it was set up, not least due to her active involvement in Dramatool, suggest that she is not altogether pleased with current developments.[3] Her narratives are both contemporary and historical, mixing comments on ongoing social activities with reflections on things she used to do or places that used to exist, thus spanning decades of institutional development. Kiswigu is not just a performing artist; she is also an actor in a state of creolization.

When BCA was first established in 1981, the curriculum was broad, covering a variety of art forms: dance, music, drama, and acrobatics, and later fine arts. The idea was to give a well rounded training in arts, especially the performing arts of the former National Troupes, to prepare the students for government employment, which is what the great majority (over 80 per cent) of college graduates pursued, working as district culture officers or directing cultural groups for state organizations, Masimbi recollects. Askew (2004, 305) refers to this training program as "a 'broad-focus' education designed to produce generic *wasanii* ('artists')" or "jacks-of-all-arts." By contrasting it with the artistic ideals of local, private musical bands "to produce *ustadhi* ('experts', 'masters' or 'divas')," she argues that the rationale of the college "included an attempt to thwart the development of unequal status and power relations between experts and novices, a position resonant with socialist egalitarian principles" (ibid., 305–309). While I agree that the training of jacks-of-all-arts was suited for national culture production, I would not go so far as to pinpoint its rationale in terms of socialist principles. Not only were the training procedures of the college far more diverse, fluid, and individualistic than the socialist conformity, discipline, and collective orientation suggested by Askew (ibid., 310), but the rationale for the training program was steered by a complex mix of political ideologies, cultural norms, and material realities, while its implementation was left in the hands of artists whose activities were shaped by their individual mastery of specific art forms as well as their perspectives on the role of art in society (see Chapter 2). If anything, the college was set up to produce cultural workers for the construction of a state that is a multilayered and conflictual ensemble of paradoxical and contradictory processes (Gupta and Sharma 2006, 291–292).

In order to appreciate these variations between cultural policy and practice, it is worth recalling BCA's position as an artistic field within the field of state power. Rather than being a static reproduction of a state aesthetic dominated by socialism (Askew 2002, 318), BCA has from the outset been an indeterminate site in the social structure of the state, a field characterized by ill-defined posts and career paths full of uncertainty (Bourdieu 1993, 43). The college's modus operandi has above all focused on the arts. In the beginning, the college only had a handful of teachers, hand-picked from the National Troupes. The student body was also small and initially the college had problems recruiting female students, as women artists were considered morally questionable in the public eye.[4] The great majority joined the college to develop their artistic skills, rather than to pursue a bureaucratic career. As exemplified by Kiswigu, in many cases the choice of arts as a career was driven by a personal desire that challenged established social norms. Thus, while the training program produced generic artists that could serve in various government functions, it was above all conducted with a view to "develop artists," as Masimbi put it. The idea was not to teach in a theoretical sense, but to carefully facilitate the development of individual talent.

BCA's liminal position in the state structure is evident in its traditional–modern aesthetic design, which reflects the cultural hybridity of the state of creolization. Following MacDougall (1999, 2006), the aesthetic design denotes a field of people, objects, and actions, which in turn are interconnected with other social forces, such as history, economics, and politics. In other words, it is a formative aesthetic system that is interrelated with social, political, and economic dynamics (Born 2010).

Through this hybrid sensory structure traditional art forms are reconfigured and performed within a modern institutional setting, thus conflating as well as reinforcing the division between "tradition" and "modernity." A great deal of cultural invention and improvisation goes into this process. By decontextualizing cultural practices and objects from their original rural setting and recontextualizing them in a semi-urban educational environment, traditional cultural forms are reified and objectified. Ritual dances that always change depending on the setting in which they are performed are standardized, repackaged as a certain type of dance, from a certain tribe, performed in a certain way. The very process of standardization forms part of the process of modernization, bringing traditional culture into the folds of modern bureaucratic practices. By recontextualizing tribal art forms as a national culture repertoire, traditional culture is aligned with the modern state structure, building upon tribal differences, while bridging them through an overarching national identity.

From the outset, BCA's training program relied heavily on sensory immersion and embodied practice. The college was constructed as a boarding school and the ideal of developing artistic talent was realized through a curriculum executed through highly personalized tutoring. For many years, the student–teacher ratio was as high as 1:1, and Masimbi resisted pressures from the Ministry to increase the intake of students, insisting on a small student body of no more than 50 students. Since many of the teachers had very little formal education, they trained students in the form of apprenticeship, which is how they themselves had learned their trade. Thus, while BCA offered an institutionalized form of education, the practical mastery of art revolved around body hexis, with training carried out as a structural apprenticeship reproducing the dialectical relationships between the body and a structured, inhabited space (Bourdieu 1977, 87–89). This embodied practical mastery combined "shared and normative embodied practices" with "open-ended embodied practical mastery," enabling the "cultivation of creativity within a modern bureaucratic organization" (Wilf 2010, 564).

The emphasis on apprenticeship and hands-on tutoring reflected the traditional orientation of BCA's hybrid aesthetic design, with pronounced physical and practical dimensions, placed in a semi-rural setting. The traditional aesthetic was performed through bodily exercise, training, and discipline, which explains Kiswigu's exercise routine of running up and down the steps of the auditorium and her daily swimming. Not only were the different art forms mixed, drama for instance containing a great deal of dance and music, but since the students took all subjects, they needed to be physically strong to perform the training program, not least acrobatics which was a compulsory subject. For many years, auditions included arduous physical exercises, to ensure the corporeal aptitude of prospective students and many senior teachers remain impressively fit, despite their mature age. Initially, the campus had few buildings, and art training was conducted in a large open space behind Bagapoint, which now serves as a football ground. But even when the college got more modern facilities, like the open-air theater constructed in 1990, the auditorium doubled as an exercise area.

In terms of world making, the aesthetic design was an important means of imprinting students with an institutionalized set of ideas and values, thus creating a social body in which the materiality of power operated on the very bodies of individuals (Foucault 1980, 55). In addition to a very practical, performance-oriented training program, which required considerable investment of power in the body (ibid., 56), the aesthetic system was articulated through rigorous bodily discipline. Every morning before the sun rose too high, students cleaned the campus, brushing the sandy walkways, clearing litter, and cutting the lawns by hand. This physical activity underlined the college's rural linkages, reflecting a training program based on traditional cultural forms, while instilling the value of manual labor in students.[5] Bodily discipline was also used to express the constellation of power in the college's social hierarchy, extended to regimented control of students' physical movements off campus, not least to maintain a social boundary between the field of arts and the surrounding Muslim community, which viewed the BCA community with a certain degree of suspicion (Uimonen 2009a).

## Auditioning for Art, Aiming for Diploma

"What are the role and function of art in society?" Nina responds to the question in English:[6]  "Art is like a mirror of society. For example, in a particular society if there is corruption, an artist can sing about it and people can then act on it, so people can change. Another example is prostitution. I have seen in your library, there are lots of magazines about HIV, with cartoons. The cartoons will give people something to think. Art can also bring up the economy; you can make art and sell it. And people are kept busy with art, instead of doing drugs and drinking. Art can also be used for decoration." The role and function of art in society is a compulsory question in individual interviews for prospective students. The interviews take place in the classrooms, with TaSUBa teachers seated at desks in the front of the room, facing the interviewees, one at a time. The applicant is handed a list of six questions, out of which he/she is instructed to pick five, including the compulsory one. The interviews last for five minutes, and the applicant can choose to answer the questions in Kiswahili or English, except the compulsory one which has to be responded to in English, thus reflecting the code-switching practices in the state of creolization. The applicant wears a tag with a number, which serves as the primary means of identification throughout the audition rituals, thus underlining their liminal status. Outside the classrooms, applicants wait for their turn, some chatting, others in silence, some standing under the covered entrance to the library, others sitting on the edge of the concrete aisle. Most of them are quite formally dressed, men wearing business trousers and short-sleeved shirts, women skirts and blouses, with matching accessories.

During the interview, Nina elaborates on her background and interest in art. Tagged number 29, she explains that she was born in Moshi in 1985, were she went to an English-medium primary school and then an international secondary school in Zambia, which is why her Kiswahili is a bit weak, she apologizes, although it will get better, she assures the teachers. Upon her return to Tanzania in 2005, Nina did A levels (advanced certificate) for two years in Moshi. She then took a year out and went to the UK. When she came back in March 2009, she decided to do art. Nina underlines that she has a passion and talent for art, thus her choice of study, which her friends have also encouraged. "I know I can develop art and also develop the talent of others," Nina says with confidence, adding that she hopes to start an art school in the future. Like most other applicants, Nina got information about the college from someone she knew; in this case someone who did fine arts there. She looked for more information on the computer and went to the TaSUBa website. She also visited the college in April/May to look around. In response to the last question Nina picks, she says "If I was given a chance to talk to the President, I would tell him to take art seriously. When I was in UK and also in Zambia, I saw how they take art seriously. So President, please support art!"

The auditions last for a week and the applicants, divided into groups according to their choice of major and minor subjects, get some tutoring from TaSUBa teachers to prepare an exhibition or performance, thus getting a taste of the college's aesthetic design. The preparations take place in different parts of the campus, giving them hands-on exposure to the spatially distributed training program. The applicants are temporarily housed in the student dormitories and they take their meals in the college canteen, thus deepening their sensory immersion into student life at TaSUBa. Students have access to most parts of the campus, but the Internet room is closed. As a cost-saving device, the management does not pay for Internet access during school breaks, so there is no connectivity during June and July.

At the end of the audition week, students showcase their art projects.[7] The exhibition of fine arts and stage technology projects takes place in one of the classrooms, on three rows of tables covered with cloth, some with the TaSUBa logo. The applicants place their samples in neat arrangements: a sketch of a mug and a glass, an aquarelle of a soda can and bottle, and another one of toothpaste, along with a sculpted ashtray. The stage technology projects include a wooden model of an auditorium, a light arrangement with colored bulbs and a sound mixing board. The head of the academic department walks around the tables with a crew of teachers, asking each student about their displayed items. The process is conscientiously photographed and filmed by TaSUBa teachers and assistants, thus underlining the formality of this ritual event.

The performances of drama, dance, and music projects are staged in the Mwembe theater,[8] to an audience composed of applicants and teachers, with a mixing board managed by stage technology and music tutors. As in the practical exams, the auditors perform the role of an interactive audience, seated on chairs near the stage, which is extraordinarily well equipped, with three large speakers on each side, a drum set, *marimba*, *ngoma*, keyboard, electric guitar, base guitar, and microphones on stands. The music majors start out with a traditional song and dance accompanied by the sound of *ngoma* and *marimba*, using *khanga* as costumes. They then switch to a popular, modern song *Malaika*, using the drum set and electronic instruments. Music minors sing a song, accompanied by some dance movements. The drama majors and minors perform one short play each, followed by traditional dance and song by dance majors. All groups pay homage to culture, arts, and Tanzania, as well as TaSUBa and its Chief Executive. Scholars have associated this praise-singing with socialism (Askew 2004, 310, Lange 2002, xiii), but my material suggests that it is more emblematic of rituals of power than any particular political ideology.

The auditions form part of the initial phases of the ritual performance of schooling (McLaren 1986). The academic calendar is divided into two semesters, from August to December and January to June. During the first semester, the training program is interrupted for one week for the annual arts festival, organized in late September or early October, followed by a week of rest. Classes then resume until the end of November when students get a week to prepare for their exams, carried out over two weeks, followed by vacation. During the second semester, students get a one-week break in March, and in early May they start preparing for their exams, which are completed by the end of the month. In June students go on vacation, or in the case of second-year students undertake fieldwork for their research projects, which they present before the exams in the final semester of their third year.

An elaborate graduation ceremony[9] 🎦 is organized in October, in conjunction with the annual festival. It is a highly ritualized event performed on the main stage of the TaSUBa Theater, with students dressed in colorful gowns designed by a local fashion designer. The college management delivers eloquent speeches while elaborately awarding certificates to each student. After the ceremony, attending friends and family shower the graduates with gifts. Many students post photos of their graduation in Facebook, in memory of this lifetime event and *rite de passage*.

The structure of the auditions reflects the new curriculum that came into effect as of academic year 2006/2007, in conjunction with BCA's transformation into TaSUBa. With the revised curriculum the college acquired formal accreditation according to the standards set by the National Council for Technical Education (NACTE). Major changes compared with the previous curriculum included a higher degree of specialization, with students choosing major and minor subjects from the first year instead of the second year, the introduction of ICT as a compulsory subject, and the removal of many other compulsory subjects, including acrobatics, which is now only taught to students taking dance and drama. Out of the 120 credits students take each year, major and minor subjects constitute 61.2 (51 percent) and 20.4 (17 percent) respectively, while compulsory subjects make up 38.4 credits (32 percent). The training program has also been restructured into modules, with measurable, performance-oriented outcomes and assessment criteria. The structure of the new curriculum represents an exemplary form of audit culture, containing all the core elements of audit technology (Shore and Wright 2000, Uimonen 2011).

The new curriculum is instructive of changes in the aesthetic design, reflecting the worldwide marketization of education (Bartlett et al. 2002). As stated in the curriculum, globalization, urbanization, and technical development necessitate the need for training performing artists for the growing needs of television, radio, the stage, film and upcoming theater groups (TaSUBa 2006, iii). Targeted at the marketability of artists, the curriculum reconfigures art students as "depersonalized unit[s] of economic resource whose productivity and performance must constantly be measured and enhanced" (Shore and Wright 2000, 62). Marketization of education is also evident in the changing constitution of the student body.

These days most applicants have no particular interest in the arts, but join TaSUBa to earn a diploma. Since the entrance requirements at TaSUBa are relatively low, O levels (ordinary certificate) with three credit passes in arts subjects including English and Kiswahili, many students take a three-year diploma instead of the two years it would take to complete A levels (advanced certificate) in secondary education to qualify for university studies. Even so, most applicants are mainly interested in reaching a higher rank in their professional position, especially those employed by the Government. Others plan to integrate arts in their jobs, for instance in their teaching duties. But only a minority has an interest in pursuing a career as artists. During group discussions, I found that among third-year students, 7 out of 15 (47 percent) intended to pursue a career in arts, while among first-year students only 6 out of 17 (35 percent) had such prospects.

The shift in student motivation from arts to educational accreditation reflects global trends in which ICT plays a pivotal role. In his analysis of the social implications of the Internet age, Castells (2001, 260) singles out education and lifelong learning as essential resources for societal development. Having recast itself as the Knowledge Bank, the World Bank is now encouraging the expansion of higher education throughout sub-Saharan Africa, thus reversing its earlier policies of discouraging, even penalizing countries for investing in universities (Wright and Rabo 2010). This renewed interest in higher education is informed by the perceived emergence of a global knowledge economy (ibid.), reflecting the informational development paradigm that has accompanied the expansion of the Internet throughout the developing world (Uimonen 2001, 94–99). Thus it is not surprising that the

World Bank and other major development actors are paying more attention to the role of ICT in higher education.

Increasingly entangled in the dictates of neoliberal capitalism, Tanzania has sought to emulate these new development paradigms. Similarly to countries like Egypt, where education has become a core value in state culture articulated through various channels, including popular television drama (Abu-Lughod 2005, 60), the value of modern education is also a dominant ideal in mediated political discourse in Tanzania and a central feature in young, urban women's aspirations for modernity (Ekström 2010, 212–224). If anything, the distinction of scholarly achievement, one of the postcolonial codes of prestige (Mbembe 2001, 130), is taking on a new significance in the age of digital media. In its efforts to develop tertiary education, the Government has made ICT facilities a requirement for institutes of higher learning, which is why BCA had to have Internet access to get NACTE accreditation for its new curriculum.

It is not only the motivation but also the number of applicants that has changed with TaSUBa's commercial orientation. Shortly after he took over BCA, Bakari increased the annual intake of students from 15 to 30. At the time, the college had as many as 500 applicants (Askew 2004, Uimonen 2009a). Although BCA didn't really have sufficient facilities to house so many students, the issue was resolved by adding more beds to the dormitory rooms, three to four beds per room instead of two. In 2009, the number of applicants had dropped to 200, of which only half were deemed to be qualified. Out of the 105 qualified applicants, 50 were expected for auditions, 48 of whom showed up. The number was lower than the previous year, when 60 applicants had come for auditions. In terms of gender balance, there was a slight decrease in female students compared with the college's 20–25 percent average. Out of the 105 qualified applicants, 23 were female, 10 of whom participated in the auditions. Commenting on the drop in applications, one staff member suggested it may have been due to the price for the interview (TSH 80,000, or USD 50) or the high tuition fees, while another one thought it had to do with lack of information. Within days of completion, the audition results were posted on the TaSUBa notice board: 45 accepted, of which 8 were female (18 percent).

Rather than attracting talent, TaSUBa is now drawing students who can afford to pay for the diploma program. In an effort to become financially self-reliant, one of the first measures taken by TaSUBa management was to increase the annual tuition fee from TSH 150,000 to TSH 985,000 (from approximately USD 100 to USD 650), with immediate effect as of academic year 2008/2009.[10] For students enrolled in the diploma program, the dramatic increase was quite problematic, and some had to drop out. Even at TSH 150,000 students were struggling to pay the tuition fee, relying on financial assistance from friends and relatives, while trying to raise money from their art work.[11]

Artists like Vitali Maembe, who struggled to finance his diploma program, could not possibly afford to study at TaSUBa. When Maembe's father passed away in the second year of his diploma program in 1999, the family was in financial difficulty. Maembe's friends came to his rescue, paying his school fees, while he managed to make some pocket money by selling his paintings. At one point, a friend gave money to the college to pay for Maembe's school fees and pocket money, but he never received this contribution, even though the college had signed for it. Since it took Maembe seven years to complete the diploma program, he lived in poverty for many years, struggling to complete his training as an artist.

### Art Training in Theory and Practice[12] 🎨

Julia Salmi[13] 🎨 enters the stage in response to her tutor's "*tuliho!*" (welcome in Kisukuma), her blond dreads swinging to her rhythmic moves, while students join in her accompanying chant backstage. Dressed up for the occasion, Julia is wearing a simple costume, a waistband of feathers and a *khanga* wrapped around her shoulders, to accessorize her green batik trousers and black t-shirt. At a whistle blow from her tutor, who is one of her three supporting drummers, Julia stops and introduces herself and her dance, *bugobogobo*, a *ngoma ya kazi* (labor dance) from the Sukuma tribe in Mwanza region. She then carries on with her performance, expertly swinging a hoe between her legs and behind her back, her face in deep concentration.

The examiners lean back in their chairs, while students tilt forward, attentively following her flawless moves. Upon completion, Julia gets a big round of applause and she is congratulated by teachers and students alike, not just for her immaculate performance, but for her fluency in Kiswahili. Meanwhile, Julia's nascent expertise in traditional dance is reaffirmed when she is made to lead the group dance that follows the individual performances, quite an accomplishment for a young woman from Finland, only 20 years old at the time.

Julia is Nina's age mate at TaSUBa, a first-year student, majoring in dance and with drama as minor. She has prepared herself well for her first practical exams, relying on tutors outside TaSUBa to teach her the *bugobogobo*. Just like Nina, Julia is one of the few students to have joined TaSUBa to become an artist. She intends to pursue a career in traditional African dance, which to her means she has to dance even better than Africans, if she is to manage the competition, be it in Tanzania or in her home country.

Julia's interest in African dance was awakened back in Finland, where she stumbled across a workshop in West African dance and discovered that the "rhythm and spirit of African dance" felt like her thing. In 2008, she travelled to Tanzania to do some volunteer work for a few months and after the trip her interest in dance grew into a "passion," something she wanted to do for the rest of her life. Someone she knew in Finland told her about an arts college in Tanzania and Julia went on the Internet to find out more. The TaSUBa website did not contain much information, but she managed to track down the Chief Executive via email. When she enrolled in August 2009, Julia was the only international student at TaSUBa. Historically she was the second European to undertake a diploma program at the college, the first one being a young Swedish woman, Mathilda Sundbom, who graduated from BCA in 2007.[14] Over the last few years, a few regional students from Uganda have also studied at the college.

For non-Tanzanian students, the diploma program means intensive language training, since classes are carried out in Kiswahili. During her first semester, Julia often walked around with an English–Kiswahili dictionary in her bag. To speed up her language acquisition she also made a point of hanging out with Tanzanian friends who barely spoke

English. Within a few months of arrival, Julia was quite fluent in Kiswahili.

By the time of their first end-of-semester exams, Julia and other first-year students have become accustomed to the daily routines of student life at TaSUBa. Students wake early and take their breakfast in the canteen across the road from the dormitories. The schedule of classes starts at 8 am and continues until 6:30 pm, with a short tea break between 11 and 11:30 am, and a one-hour lunch break from 1:30 to 2:30 pm. The number of daily classes varies depending on students' major and minor subjects, but in total they have 16–20 hours of class in a week. During breaks students rest or study in the dormitories, practice on campus, or use the Internet room. Evening meals are taken in the canteen and many students also go to nearby churches or mosques for worship. After some rest, students often continue to study or practice, or socialize on or off campus. Weekends are often spent doing chores like washing clothes and cleaning dormitory rooms, as well as resting and relaxing. The beach is popular, and many go there for swimming, others hang out at Bagapoint or similar places in Bagamoyo town. Some students also travel to Dar es Salaam, to visit friends or relatives.

In the liminal condition of student life, some of the ordinary status markers are temporarily suspended, especially in relation to age. As a young female student reflected, having expected she would meet "young girls like me" at the college, she found instead "grown-ups like my mother and father." The mixing of different age groups is socially significant. While the rituals of schooling represent "rituals of status elevation" for all students, who go from novices to trained artists, or at least diploma holders, for older students they can also entail "rituals of status reversal" (Turner 1969, 167). As one older student pointed out to me, "back home I am a district officer, but at TaSUBa I am nothing." This status reversal is evident in terms of address. It is customary to greet people older than oneself with *shikamoo*, but this is often discarded among students who use more socially equal forms of greeting, irrespective of age. Meanwhile, the social hierarchy between students and teachers is maintained. Even young teachers like Hussein Masimbi are greeted with *shikamoo mwalimu* by their students. While age groups

### Digital Mediations of Aesthetic Transformations

The graphic design group[19] of fine art students, five male and two female, wait patiently at the computers for their tutor, who arrives a bit late. His car broke down so he had to take a *dala dala* (local minibus) from Dar es Salaam, he explains upon arrival. Today's class focuses on individual assignments. The students gather around one of the computers in the Internet room to go through their work. Each student has designed a t-shirt and a baseball cap and the group comments on the images one at a time, focusing on balance and harmony in content and form. One student has designed a t-shirt with the words "Jesus never fail" [sic]. Students question his choice of a black background, which he explains by emphasizing that the text, which is written on a cross, is light and surrounded by light spots, to symbolize that even in darkness Jesus spreads light and dispels darkness. Another student uses the words "world designs," text that can function as a logo he explains, adding that we all come from this world and we design for everyone. The students store their work on USB memory sticks.[20] At times they have trouble locating files, but they seem quite used to maneuvering their flash disks. Towards the end of the class, the teacher shows an example of next week's assignment, an article in a magazine, with accompanying graphic images to illustrate the text. He then spends some time with each student, individually tutoring them, before leaving the classroom.

Graphic design is taught to third-year students in fine art, with classes organized once a week. During fieldwork, the tutor was Kiagho Kilonzo, a former graduate from BCA, who acquired an MA in art and technology at the University of Texas in Dallas. After his return to Tanzania, he started working as a part-time instructor at TaSUBa and UDSM. Despite its low-capacity machines, TaSUBa is better equipped than UDSM, and Kilonzo finds that the students are better too; they are "committed" and "grasp very fast." In between his weekly classes, Kilonzo communicates with his students via email and phone. Before Kilonzo started tutoring in February 2009, graphic design was taught by European multimedia volunteers and teachers, starting with Dan Lambert from 2004 to 2005, followed by Kirsten Suhr-Knudsen, who worked as a Fredskorpset exchange teacher through the NOTA project from 2005 to 2007. The fine arts department was the first to integrate ICT into teaching and learning, followed by the music department.

The idea of teaching graphic design is geared at "preparing students to get employment." In a "world moving towards technology," graphic design is becoming a "big market," Kilonzo explains. Most graphic designers in Tanzania have a "shallow background in arts," so TaSUBa students have a competitive edge.

Graphic design forms part of a module on design, with the stated objective: "To enable the student [to] manage design requirements for different needs." (TaSUBa 2006) The module lists several design methods: industrial design, textile design, graphic design, and computer design. Perhaps more than any subject in the curriculum, the design module is geared at reconfiguring students as members of the creative class, preparing them for employment in the creative industries where production is understood in terms of creation (Boellstorff 2008, 206). But the design syllabus is not just a technology of production, it is also a "political technology of the self," offering "a means through which individuals actively and freely regulate their own conduct and thereby contribute to the government's model of social order" (Shore and Wright 2000, 62). This social order is increasingly tied in with the neoliberal culture complex, the morality of which is oriented towards individualism and capitalism in the global market place.

Mussa Sango is a good example of the market value of artists with graphic design skills (Uimonen 2009b). When BCA got ICT facilities in 2004, Mussa was in his third year in the diploma program. He used every opportunity he got to hang out in the computer room and he became very good friends with Dan Lambert, who taught him the basics of graphic design software. After graduation, BCA sponsored Mussa to get training at a desktop publishing institute in Dar es Salaam. His background in fine arts proved most useful and upon completing his training, the institute hired Mussa as an instructor. These days Mussa works for an international branding, packaging, and advertisement company in Dar es Salaam, while pursuing a BA in mass communication/mass media at the Open University of

Tanzania (OUT). He is as inquisitive as ever, while his charming behavior and boyish good looks make him a popular guy, with over 400 friends in Facebook. Mussa's talent has already earned him some material rewards, a small car and a nice little apartment in Dar es Salaam, with a flatscreen TV and a home theater music installation system. Mussa enjoys his upwardly mobile lifestyle, visualized in his Facebook profile photo where he sits at a table full of laptops, wearing a smart, dark suit. But sometimes he misses *sanaa*, not just to create things but to do something for the community.

At TaSUBa, the ICT building offers a visible materialization of modernity, of "keeping up with the times," to use a local idiom, or being "up to date," as Kiswigu put it. This physical exterior is an important aspect of executive management, which is why the ICT building often gets depicted in TaSUBa's promotional material. Digital media form part of aesthetic transformations in more indirect ways as well. The formalization of education would be difficult to achieve without the mediation of ICT, from word-processing software to produce detailed curricula to the online posting of examination results (cf. Strathern 1995).

These days the ICT building embodies not only the reintegration but also the schism of the digital drama of executive transformation. The transformation was supposed to be accompanied by investments in facilities, including 30 new computers for the Internet room, but these resources have not materialized. Similarly, while the executive transformation has provided more freedom for TaSUBa management to adjust staff salaries, this has not been carried through and struggles over job definition continue to be one of the most contested boundaries of this field of cultural production (Bourdieu 1993, 62). During fieldwork, an attempt was made to introduce a new salary scale, but it was vehemently rejected by many staff members. Reflecting the institute's engagements with audit culture, the new salary scale was based on teachers' formal accreditation. Since many senior teachers have very little formal education, the proposed salary structure actually meant a substantial reduction in some teachers' salaries. Tutors and management blamed the newly recruited human resources person, indicating that the administrative structure of new managerialism, in which human resources had been introduced as a new function, was not performing as expected. Meanwhile, the temporary contracts of younger staff members were not adjusted. TaSUBa's only ICT technician left his position at the end of academic year 2008/2009, after three years of service. With the humor that Tanzanians often employ in situations of conflict, students referred to his abrupt departure in terms having "escaped" or "run away." Within a few months, another young teacher left the college, and a few months later, a third.

Since it is the symbolic and material heart of TaSUBa's social body, the new theater complex embodies aesthetic transformations in extraordinary ways. In its efforts to generate more income for the institute, the management prioritizes commercial, money-generating activities over academic ones. The theater complex, which was supposed to contain classrooms and studios for artistic training and production, is primarily used for commercial activities: conferences, commercial performances, or social functions (see Chapter 7). Once constructed to provide a professional setting for artistic performances, then rebuilt to accommodate the training needs of art students, the TaSUBa Theater has now been reconfigured into a place for entertainment and business. Even in a state of creolization, this cultural hybridity is proving challenging, but so are the contradictory demands of an aesthetic design that seeks to master liminality.

TaSUBa's aesthetic transformation is a field of great ambivalence. Many students challenge the implementation of TaSUBa's business orientation, rather than its rationale, indicating how deeply ingrained the "banking system of education," as one tutor put it, has become in the Tanzanian social fabric.[21] For students, commercialization is not just a question of making money, but also getting value for money. Some compare TaSUBa with other executive educational institutes like ADEM or SLADS in Bagamoyo, which boast more modern facilities.[22] Students with an artistic inclination tend to be more critical of TaSUBa's business orientation, which they feel impedes their professional formation as artists. Like many European dance and ballet artists, especially those working for national companies, TaSUBa tutors tend to feel a certain unease and distrust toward the market (Wulff 2005). Although they accept, and even strive to create new markets for their products and performances, they like to perform for a "full, full, full house," as Kiswigu expressed so excitedly; something that only happens during the annual art festival, or the occasional free performance. Meanwhile, teachers are frustrated with management's neglect of academic activities and many feel demoralized.

Given TaSUBa's role and position in a state of creolization, it is no wonder that the executive transformation process is replete with contradictory, even counterproductive, elements, highlighting the ambiguities of liminality. The college is straddling the practical foundation of its past and the commercial orientation of its future. And it is this hybrid condition of social ambivalence that is inscribed in students through TaSUBa's traditional–modern aesthetic design, internalized and objectified in a social body that straddles cultural divides, suspended in a permanent state of liminality.

"Art is life. It is not business," Maembe underlines. Like many other college graduates, he is still struggling to make a living as an artist. His music is becoming more well known in Tanzania, some of his songs are even played on radio, but he has yet to make a stable income from his art work. Occasionally he gets paid for a performance, sometimes he sells a painting, but most of the time he scrapes by, borrowing money from friends when he is in need, paying back when he is able to do so. Social relations of reciprocity are more than an artistic ideal for Maembe, they are also a survival strategy, for him and the majority of Tanzanians who live in material poverty. Even so, Maembe is not too concerned about his financial status. "Music comes from heaven, from God. I will never be poor, because God is rich; he is the nucleus of the universe. He will never let me die poor, because I am doing something that is coming from him."

Maembe spends a lot of his time teaching children, volunteering his time and effort. Like Nina, many college students have the ambition to teach arts, thus making a career out of their own embodied practice of arts training. And many of them end up teaching children, at least for a while. In Maembe's case, teaching arts is not just about passing on skills, but also about social formation and sharing. In his artist's statement, he explains why: "I believe that music and dance can help children to be confident in themselves, helpful and tolerant to others and most of all cooperative. This way as they grow, they set an example and in the long run they will be patriots who will work hard for their nation's development."

# 5
# TRADITIONAL–MODERN HYBRID MUSIC

## Mastering *Marimba*[1]

Seated on tree trunks under a large mango tree, students are playing *marimba*, *ngoma*, and trumpets, the sound of traditional–modern music[2] reverberating well beyond campus. The surface of the trunks is soft from years of wear, while the leafy branches provide some shady relief in this open-air classroom[3] for traditional music. Dressed in a long-sleeved shirt casually worn outside his baggy trousers, *mwalimu* Matitu walks around amidst the students, beating the rhythm with a long wooden stick. From his tall, lean figure and agile movements you would be hard pressed to guess his age, but this Master Musician is soon to retire. Meanwhile, he is passing on his skills to younger generations, as he has done for decades. He does not use written notes, but hums the melody to the students, who pick it up on their instruments. From time to time, he demonstrates on the students' *marimba*[4] how the tune is to be played, thus performing the role of a master craftsman tutoring his apprentices, just like he learned to play traditional music when he was young. The students practice over and over again, until they master the melody. A few weeks later, the whole class performs the song for their practical exams on the main stage of the TaSUBa Theater, with their teacher as one of the attentive examiners, while another examiner captures the student production on a sound recorder.

His honorific title Master Musician notwithstanding, *mwalimu* Khalfan Matitu is a humble, softly spoken man, with a friendly smile and a twinkle in his eyes. He was born in 1951 in Kibaha, Coastal region. Although his formal education is limited to primary education (Standard 7), Matitu's music skills have earned him respectable positions in the production and performance of national culture, facilitated by the social relations he has forged as an artist. As a teenager, Matitu performed with a private group in Dar es Salaam where he was spotted by Mzee Godwin Kaduma who invited him to teach traditional music at the University of Dar es Salaam. At the time Kaduma was lecturing at the university and Rashid Masimbi was one of Matitu's students in traditional music. Matitu was employed as a musician with the National Dance Troupe in the early 1970s. Since it was founded in 1981, *mwalimu* Matitu has been teaching *ngoma* and *marimba* at BCA/TaSUBa. His role in cultural production has been mediated by his instrument, the *marimba*,[5] which is associated with his tribe *wazaramo* in the Coastal region.[6]

Matitu has introduced a new music program in TaSUBa's new curriculum, which he calls *muziki mchanganyiko* (mixed music). It is a hybrid of traditional and modern music, combining Tanzanian instruments and melodies with Western instruments. The program is taught to third-year students majoring in music. Students find it difficult at first, but with enough practice they get used to the new style and by the time they perform for practical exams they master it quite well, Matitu reflects. Matitu uses different tribal songs as a basis. One of them is *Na'embele*, a song originating from the *wanyamwezi* tribe in Tabora. It is a song used to cool people down if they are angry, for example children who are crying. Having heard the song many times, Matitu picked the melody from listening to it, and he now uses it in his *muziki mchanganyiko* classes, the soothing sound of which caught my ear as I was slowly walking to the college one day, reminded of the fact that you actually hear the college before you see it.

It was in 1995 that Matitu started exploring African–Western musical hybrids, when a group of German musicians visited Chuo Cha

Sanaa to collaborate with local musicians. At first Matitu thought it would be difficult but he was encouraged by the German visitors, who were strong musicians, as he puts it. Since Matitu does not read notes, the collaboration was done by ear. The Tanzanian musicians played traditional instruments, which the Germans keenly listened to and then accompanied with their modern instruments, and vice versa. This was Matitu's first experience of this kind of mixed music, and he liked the sound of it.

To Matitu, mixing traditional and modern music is something "good," with a "different intonation," one of hybrid purity. To explain, he uses the allegory of a child of mixed descent. If an African and a European have a baby together, it is "pure," because it is "mixed color." He also sees the commercial value of musical hybrids. In today's world music market, it is better for the new generation to mix traditional and modern to fetch the market, because people will like it, he explains to me. He recalls a popular group Tatunane whose members were trained in traditional instruments at Chuo Cha Sanaa. Their unique style of music, which incorporated traditional instruments, was very popular and they toured in Tanzania, Africa, and Europe. And of course it was his mastery of traditional music that brought Dr Zawose world fame. Indeed, since its establishment in the late 1980s, the world music industry has incorporated a variety of musical styles, promoted through the somewhat contradictory ideals of authenticity, roots, hybridity, and the local (Stokes 2004, 59). In Paris, which preceded London as a center in world music, it was above all African musicians, especially francophone ones like Manu Dibango, who established this genre (Winders 2006). African bands trying to break out of the world music category into popular markets have sometimes met considerable challenges, criticized for selling out their authenticity when trying to reach a larger audience (Brusila 2001).

This musical mix is one of the hybrid genres to have emerged from TaSUBa's traditional–modern aesthetic design. As exemplified by Matitu's experience, the genre is primarily a product of exchange and interaction between artists from different countries. Whether conceptualized as transnational crossroads (Stoller 2006, 100) or global contact zones (Fillitz 2009, 127), these interactions constitute the points at which networks of intercultural production intersect. Intercultural production nodes can involve European and Tanzanian musicians, but they can also revolve around Tanzanian musicians, with European music professionals playing a cultural brokering role, as exemplified by the material presented here. The traditional–modern hybrid is not only a matter of mixing African and Western musical styles but also modernizing traditional African music through the incorporation of Western instruments, thus building on cultural experimentation that predates the world music genre (cf. Winders 2006). In Tanzania, the production of intertribal music has a long history, and the National Performing Arts Company that preceded BCA had an orchestra with a wide range of music instruments of tribal as well as Western origin.

While the traditional–modern hybrid has evolved into a popular genre at TaSUBa, it is rather marginal in the local music market.[7] The Tanzanian music industry tends to favor styles that are widely popular because of the cultural influences of youth, religion, and Swahili, the most recorded genres being *bongo flava* (local hip hop), gospel, or *taarab* (e.g. Askew 2002, Edmondson 2007, Perullo 2005, Thompson 2008, Weiss 2002). There is also a niche market for traditional music, although it is mainly performed live during various ceremonies. A few bands and musicians are known for mixing traditional–modern music or Bongo fusion as some call it, including Kilimanjaro Band, Zemkala, Sisi Tambala, Andrew Ashimba, Tweturobo, and Chiivane. As exemplified by the promotion of the Maasai hip hop band Xplastaz, collaboration with European music professionals, not to mention overseas performances, plays a critical role in boosting the careers of local musicians (Thompson 2008). In the case of the traditional–modern hybrid, such collaboration has played a decisive role for the genre's development at TaSUBa.

To appreciate the social dynamics of intercultural production, it is worth exploring this process in terms of the creole continuum (Hannerz 1996). Hannerz identifies "diversity, interconnectedness, and innovation" to be at the core of creole culture, but emphasizes that it is situated "in the context of global centre-periphery relationships" (ibid., 67). Thus, while recognizing the creative richness and vitality of cultural mixture (cf. Hylland Eriksen 2003), Hannerz underlines that the creole continuum has a built-in political economy of cultural production. This structural inequality is particularly marked in the cultural peripheries of the world, where social actors face numerous constraints in their creative engagements with global cultural flows.

Let me use Matitu's experiences to illustrate this point. In terms of his institutional positioning, Matitu could be seen as a model artist in a state that acts as a transnational cultural mediator (ibid., 72). His years of travel and cultural exchange could even qualify him as a "beento," as West Africans call people who have "been to" Britain, in recognition of their experience of metropolitan cultural centers (ibid.). If anything, Matitu's appreciation of cultural hybridity as something *pure* should earn him considerable symbolic, cultural, and economic capital in the state of creolization that employs him. But this is not the case. Instead we find a professional trajectory replete with conflicting trends, reflecting some of the liminal ambiguities of the creole continuum.

The TRAMO CD is a concrete example of intercultural production, the creation of which Matitu was involved in a few years ago. TRAMO,[8] which stands for "Tanzanian traditional and modern," was part of the NOTA project of cultural collaboration between Norway and Tanzania. When it was released, the CD was described in terms of "creating new combinations," "old and new catching the rhythm and the melodies from each other," and "meetings at the crossroads of cultures old and new," as stated in the laminated cover accompanying NOTA's distribution of the CD to TaSUBa's transnational network of collaborators such as me. The project was initiated in July 2000 in a creative workshop organized by NOTA at Bagamoyo College of Arts, facilitated by Norwegian music professionals. The workshop was concluded with a live performance, followed by another performance during the annual art festival. During a follow-up workshop, the artists expressed their interest in a recording. The TRAMO CD was recorded at Marimba studio in Dar es Salaam in 2001 and 2002. It was distributed in 2006 under the Norwegian Kultur & Spetakkel record label, which holds the copyrights for the production. In online music stores, the CD is categorized as world music/African and as its English language cover suggests, it is primarily targeted at an international audience.

To deepen our understanding of the production of cultural hybrids, let me contextualize TRAMO in terms of a traditional–modern assemblage, thus building on Born's (2005, 13) concept of "musical assemblage" to underline music's multiple mediations and simultaneous forms of existence.[9] In this case, the traditional–modern is embodied in the social constellation of artists involved in its production, the Bagamoyo Players personifying tradition, the Mradi group modernity. In the brochure accompanying the CD, the Bagamoyo Players are presented as traditional musicians, their music and dances coming from different tribes in different regions, thus being representative of the country's rich cultural diversity, while the Mradi group is described as young professional musicians from the city. The composition of artists is indicative of several dimensions of mediation, social (tribal/national), spatial (regional/local), and temporal (old/young), while the social relations of production express complementary social mediations, north/south, center/periphery. The traditional–modern genre itself is expressive of multiple, overlapping mediations, temporal (past/present) and spatial (rural/urban), embedded in a production process containing additional mediations, technological (acoustic/digital), artefactual (instruments/compact disc), and sonic (vocal/instrumental).

What we can discern in these mediations is a high degree of cumulative movement, facilitated by cultural brokering (ibid., 27). Through collaboration with Norwegian music professionals, Tanzanian artists are able to move their production from a creative workshop, to the stage and then a music studio, thus going through different phases of creative practice, from planning, to performance, to recording. The recording process takes this cumulative movement even further, since the music is objectified into a digital cultural artefact for global distribution. This digitization allows the hybrid musical assemblage produced in the cultural periphery to move to the cultural center, for redistribution in the assemblage of world music.

The production of music is of course tied up with broader institutional frameworks, the aesthetic systems of which may or may not be conducive to cultural innovation (ibid., 24). By categorizing Bagamoyo

Players as traditional musicians, TRAMO reinforces BCA's institutional identity as a bastion of traditional culture, thus building on its traditional aesthetic. Since TRAMO is part of the NOTA project, it also ties in with BCA's modern aesthetic design, solidifying the institute's cultural exchange programs with modern institutes. TRAMO even offers an opportunity to explore the emerging commercial orientation of the executive agency in formation, strategically using its position to enter the global market of world music, facilitated by the institute's transnational network of cultural collaborators.

Let us now return to Matitu, who was involved in the TRAMO production, to take a closer look at some of the more conflicting aspects of this musical assemblage. As one of the Bagamoyo Players, Matitu was an actor in the institutionalized performance of hybrid cultural production. He was also the client of powerful patrons. While the artists provided its content, it was the institutes that dictated the terms of cultural production, and as far as Matitu was concerned, the contract was "not understandable." The project itself was good, he thought, in terms of mixing traditional and modern music, but he felt that the artists lost out. As far as he can recall, Matitu received TSH 70,000 (USD 50) for rehearsals and studio recording, and some copies that he could sell, but since there was no special market for the production, he sold them cheaply among his friends. So the project was "good for combination," but it brought "no [financial] benefit," which left him feeling "sad."

Although one could expect a traditional musician like Matitu to be fully endorsed by an art institute seeking to establish itself in the global art market, this is not the case. When Matitu retires, he predicts his instrument, *marimba*, will disappear with him. No traditional musicians have been replaced in the past, so when they have left, there has been no one left to teach their instruments. Out of the original nine musicians for traditional instruments only two remain and he is one of them. He compares the situation to that of traditional dance, which is also neglected by the college. Out of the original ten dancers, only three remain, and they are reaching a high age. Matitu feels that he is not respected and that the college will be happy to see him go. These days they only respect people with "high education."

Matitu's predicament is indicative of the contradictory nature of the commercialization that has come to dominate artistic production at TaSUBa. Although TaSUBa's aim is "to develop, preserve and promote Tanzanian arts and culture and impart knowledge of the same to existing and future generations from anywhere in the world" (TaSUBa 2008, 19), thus building on the initial objectives of national culture production—to revive, preserve, promote and develop Tanzanian culture—this rationale is de facto marginalized in the drive to operate in a more business-like manner. The executive agency prioritizes economic capital over cultural and symbolic capital, while audit culture emphasizes formal structures over cultural creativity. In this brave new moral order, Matitu resembles a victim of progress (Bodley 1990). Management "don't give value to traditional teachers," he laments, because the teachers are "uneducated." Even their instruments are considered to be of little value. The college's mandate was to maintain "traditional culture," but this has disappeared. "Now it's just to find money and eat," he concludes.

### Recording *Masamva*[10]

Dan and I hear the songs over and over again as we prepare the launch of BCA's website, the sound seeping into the ICT building where we are hectically putting together some content for www.sanaabagamoyo.com. At one point I stroll over to the sales stand and purchase half a dozen CDs, thinking they will make nice gifts to friends and family in Sweden, while feeling good about supporting the college's entrepreneurship. By the time the 2004 arts festival comes to a conclusion Dan and I have almost gotten tired of the music. But on the last evening we are captivated by the audience's enthusiastic response. Scheduled as the very last event in the program, when BCA students perform their recorded songs live the auditorium is packed. As Vitali Maembe performs his *Afrika* and *Sumu ya Teja*,[11] the audience reacts with a fervor I have never seen before; screaming, dancing, jumping up on stage and stuffing money in the pockets of the musician. The *Masamva* CD is a hit!

The *Masamva* CD was the "first ever student production at BCA," Idar Hauge tells me with a note of satisfaction. We are sitting in his living room in the exclusive residential compound that NOTA uses for its teacher exchange program. This is the second time that Idar has worked as an exchange teacher at TaSUBa and while he enjoys the comfort, he also feels a little embarrassed about the luxurious housing, far more upmarket than the Kaduma residence where he stayed with his colleague Egil Ovesen back in 2003/2004. At the time, Idar and Egil spent one-and-a-half years at BCA teaching music and stage technology, through NOTA's collaborative partner Fredskorpset. Idar was 25 years old and had recently graduated from the University of Stavanger, with a Bachelor's degree in music. His first visit to BCA was in a two-week student exchange in 2000, and in 2003 he got the opportunity to come back and work at the college. He really enjoyed it, working with teachers who were very engaged and students who really appreciated his efforts. Idar made sure to learn Kiswahili, which he came to master quite well, and forged lasting friendships and collegial ties. After completing his contract, Idar returned to Bagamoyo almost every year on holiday, a place that "feels like second home" to him, and since he missed his friends there, he was happy to return in 2009, this time as a married man.

The idea of recording the *Masamva* CD originated in Idar's and Egil's work with music students at BCA. In addition to teaching, they started some student bands and organized regular student performances. The quality of the music was good and they wanted to encourage the students' artistic development. Towards the end of their contracts, Idar and Egil had some money left in their budget, earmarked for medical emergencies, which they got permission to use for a recording. During a hectic week, they travelled with students to the Marimba Studio in Dar es Salaam, renting a local *dala dala* for transportation. As is "typical in Tanzania," Idar notes, lots of things went wrong: the studio was not ready as scheduled, equipment got lost, and one of the recorded tracks was displaced on the studio's computer. In order to get the sound right, Idar took charge of the postrecording mixing, which he completed at night.

*Masamva* is another product of the traditional—modern assemblage and its title derives from the CD's first track, which means ancestral spirits in Kisukuma, the tribal language of the song's composer,

John Sombi. Most of the songs on the CD are original compositions, by John Sombi, Vitali Maembe, and Francis "Franco" Malindi respectively. The songs combine traditional (drums, bells) and modern (guitar, base guitar, drum kit, keyboard, trumpet) instruments, modern arrangements, local melodies, and lyrics in national or tribal languages. The songs vary in content, from spiritual beliefs and social relations (John Sombi's *Masamva*[12] ♪ and *Mayu*) to political issues and social concerns (Vitali Maembe's *Afrika*[13] ♪ and *Sumu Ya Teja*). In addition, the CD contains some songs by famous Tanzanian musicians recorded by students.

For the students, the CD production offered a unique opportunity to record in a studio, and John affirms that he was "happy to have the progress of recording." When Idar and Egil brought up the idea, he talked it over with some other students and they agreed it was good idea to record their own compositions, to keep as memory. They thought the CD could also help them in the future. Everyone with a song on it would get a copy of the CD, a demo they could use for promotion for the music industry. Since the recording coincided with the week students were supposed to prepare for their final exams, the timing was a bit tricky, with many conflicting obligations. But John appreciated Egil's and Idar's efforts, not least their contributions to the recordings (both performed on John's tracks), and nighttime mixing work. It was "hard work," but "good CV [curriculum vitae, as in experience]," John concludes, noting that immediately after the recording the students got a copy of the CD.

By the time of the annual arts festival in 2004, the students had resumed their studies at BCA and Idar and Egil had returned to Norway, while the copy of the *Masamwa* CD they left with the college's administration had taken on a life of its own. Rather than just keeping it for memory or using it for promotion, BCA's management decided to sell the CD. A recently graduated fine art student was enlisted to redesign the cover and to make copies. The CDs were sold at TSH 10,000 (USD 7)[14] 🔊 by a senior staff member on a makeshift sales stand, a small wooden desk covered with a bright green cloth, with a large ghetto blaster powered with batteries and stacks of CDs, neatly arranged in their original boxes. The sales stand[15] 🔊 was located near the theater entrance, not far from the ICT building where Dan and I were toiling away.

The *Masamva* CD offers an interesting variation of the traditional–modern assemblage. Like the TRAMO project, the production was a result of artistic collaboration between cultural center and periphery, in this case between young Norwegian teachers and young Tanzanian students. In terms of artistic production, *Masamva* was an improvisation produced by artists in formation, while TRAMO was a more carefully orchestrated production, performed by professional artists. In both cases, the Norwegian collaborators covered the financial costs of the project. They also mediated the technical execution of the projects, quite literally in the case of *Masamva*, with Idar laboring in the studio at night to get the sound right.

Although the social relations between Norwegian teachers and Tanzanian students were asymmetrical, the *Masamva* CD was created in a collaborative mode, exemplifying cultural and political solidarities of intercultural music production (Stokes 2004, 67). The labor and means of production were more or less equally shared between teachers and students, each participant contributing according to his/her capacity. If anything, their inputs were extraordinary all around, Idar and Egil diverting leftover funds from their emergency budget to pay for the recording studio and putting in an inordinate amount of unpaid overtime, while students sacrificed their time and energy for an extra-curricular activity that even jeopardized their formal training process. The results were shared according to needs. To underline their artistic ownership, on the original CD cover all songs were carefully attributed to the students and bands that composed and/or performed them, clearly indicating the copyrights of individual artists. And even though they had played such a critical role in its production, Egil and Idar did not mention their own names or that of Fredskorpset, but attributed the CD as a whole to Bagamoyo College of Arts.

While its production was highly egalitarian, institutional hierarchies intervened in the distribution of *Masamva*. When students saw their demo CD being sold at the festival they were quite surprised. Not only had BCA management bypassed the moral and legal obligation to ask them for permission to sell their demo, but they did not share a single shilling from the sales with the students. As far as management was concerned, the CD had been produced by students, who had used college facilities (equipment and electricity) during their time there, so the proceeds from the CD should be considered payment for such expenses. Some of the students complained loudly about the management's exploitative behavior; others kept silent, for fear of reprisals. Rumours circulated that the CD was sold in both Norway and Tanzania in thousands of copies, which is quite unlikely, and in Norway, Idar asserted, it certainly was not the case. Even so, when it came to the distribution of the CD, students felt they had lost out. In the words of Maembe (by email):

> Honestly I was not positive of BCA selling the CD, not because I didn't want them to sell but they had to follow the process of doing that business. First of all appearance of the cd was very poor it seems that they just only need money, they didn't think about how to protect it, nice cover but it was just a photocopy in a very cheep [sic] paper, cd was just plain with its word 'sony' on the top. Also they didn't talk to us about the selling, that is not a good example to people and other small institution when this big instate [institute] of arts do not think about the quality and the rights to artist.

Let us briefly return to the discussion on how institutionalized aesthetic systems intersect with the production of the traditional–modern assemblage, this time in terms of protentions and retentions (Gell 1998). Art works are always spatially and temporally distributed, forming "nodal points in a network of temporal relationships of protention and retention" (ibid., 235).[16] To phrase it in different terms, when viewed as a system or a network, one can discern that the individual parts or nodes are related to one another over time, earlier work being something of a prototype of later work, while later work is inspired by earlier work. Using Gell's terminology, we can analyze TRAMO as a protention of *Masamva*, which is also a retention of TRAMO in the sense of building on similar ideas. If we want to go further back in time, we can see that Matitu's jamming sessions with his German colleagues were a protention of TRAMO. In terms of creativity, we are dealing with a cumulative process (ibid., 237), a subject we will return to later on. In terms of social analysis, we can see the production of TRAMO and *Masamva* in relation to institutional developments, both processes being protentions of TaSUBa. Since both CDs were completed before BCA became TaSUBa, they cannot be accounted for as products of the institute's new business orientation, but they anticipate this shift. In both cases, we also find retention of the traditional aesthetic, the music assemblage being a celebration of traditional cultural forms.

In terms of production, we thus have a rather close fit between creative work and aesthetic design, but when it comes to distribution, there is a performative disruption. Even though the artists themselves welcomed the commercial opportunities that TRAMO and *Masamva* offered, TaSUBa's embryonic business mode did not operate in their favor. In the case of TRAMO, the economic conditions were probably stipulated in the contract, but the terms were incomprehensible to artists like Matitu. In any case, TSH 70,000 is rather meager compensation for professional musicians for two weeks of rehearsals and two days of studio recording, even by Tanzanian standards. For *Masamva*, there was no contract, nor was there any agreement not to sell the CD. But it was understood by those involved in its production that the music was the property of the composers, as clearly indicated on the original CD cover and as stipulated by Tanzanian copyright law.[17] These copyrights were ignored by BCA's management and instructively enough they did not appear on the redesigned CD cover. The institutional usurpation of the product was expressed on the CD cover in other ways as well. While the original CD cover[18] 🎥 depicted a band playing, the new CD cover[19] 🎥 showed the main stage of the old theater building, with the reconstruction of the burned-down theater on the back cover. Contact details for the CD, an email address and web page that Egil had put up under his personal website to facilitate communication for the students, were also removed. When the college tried to sell the *Masamva* CD again at the 2005 annual arts festival, Maembe smashed the copies on display. The college did not try to replace them.

### Animating *Nakupenda Afrika*[20] 

Standing at a roughly constructed wooden table, with a video camera fastened above on a structure of wooden poles, the student is modeling letters in clay.[21]  He gently thumbs it into long strings, which he then uses to form the letters he needs, carefully arranged on a large piece of light blue paper. He checks constantly against a laptop screen on a nearby desk to make sure that the words appear correctly. Once he has completed the writing, another student suggests that the color does not come out quite right. After a short discussion, they change to another color and repeat the tedious process. When the letters have been completed, they start the arduous task of preparing the animation. A few letters at a time are placed on the paper, and photographed. They are slightly shifted, then photographed again. More letters added, captured with the video camera, and so on. The whole process takes about an hour, with three students working together with the teacher. When completed, the words NAKUPENDA AFRIKA appear rhythmically, a few letters at a time. Once spelled out, the words morph into an image of the African continent. The title of the song *Nakupenda Afrika* (I love you Africa) is completed.

*Nakupenda Afrika* offers yet another variation of the traditional–modern music assemblage, this time in multimedia format, combining digitally composed music with computer animation. The song and its accompanying animation were created by TaSUBa students participating in extracurricular short courses organized by university students from Holland. The courses form part of a collaborative project between TaSUBa and HKU, geared at developing a training program targeting the creative industries in Tanzania. While the overall aim is to assist TaSUBa develop a Bachelor program in arts and media, it also includes an interim training program, the products of which are meant to contribute to the development of an artistic portfolio, for students and TaSUBa.[22] Since 2008, small groups of HKU students have spent ten to twelve weeks at TaSUBa each semester, training a small number of students in film and video, music and animation.[23] During the second semester of academic year 2008/2009, three young Dutch students, Alexander Mooij,[24]  Marlyn Spaaij,[25]  and Laura Roncken organized courses in documentary filmmaking, computer animation, and music composition, carried out through concrete productions. *Nakupenda Afrika* was one of them.

*Nakupenda Afrika* exemplifies the collaborative ethos of intercultural production and the improvised style of artistic production at TaSUBa. Music students pooled together their ideas for a song, each of them writing what they felt, while discussing among themselves what they wanted it to be about. They composed the song on the computer, with the help of their Dutch teacher, trying out different sounds as they went along. They also recorded some traditional instruments, which they mixed with sounds available through the computer software (Logic Pro), thus creating a hybrid production of real and machine-made sounds, traditional and modern. After completing the song, the animation team proceeded in a similar manner, listening to the song while coming up with ideas for suitable images. They drew and painted the images on paper,[26] while their Dutch teacher helped them use the software and equipment for the animation. Again, it was a hybrid production, combining traditional visual art with modern technology: hand-painted images animated with the help of split pins,[27] a video camera, and a laptop.[28] In both cases, the Dutch teachers mediated the use of new technology, while their presence also served to inspire the art work.

The music students wanted the song to be about the "beauty of Africa," they explained to me. Knowing all too well the "reality of Africa," where "still we have bad things," they wanted to talk about its "beauty," to "welcome" people to Africa, as exemplified by their teacher just arriving from Holland, for which they included some ambient "bus stop atmosphere" in the song. What would be new for someone arriving from the outside? They wanted to emphasize that people are happy and hospitable, "welcome to my home," that they are "not that busy" but take the time to greet each other properly. And similarly to the customary greetings of how are you (*habari*), students wanted to convey the standard answer fine (*nzuri*), for when you welcome somebody new, you want to show everything that is good. They also wanted to emphasize that as Africans "we are living in peace, as one," "one continent, one country," enjoying our "freedom" and "helping each other," as

if we live in the "same village." Indeed, from the students' perspective
it was "simple to speak of Africa, instead of Tanzania, Nigeria or other
countries," since we are all "proud of it [Africa]." They compared their
song to the national anthem, *Mungu Ibariki Afrika*, which sings about
Africa first, then Tanzania.

*Nakupenda Afrika*[29]

| | |
|---|---|
| Intro: | Intro: |
| Yeye ye oh yee! | Yeye ye oh yee! |
| Nchi yangu Afrika | My country Africa |
| Yeye ye oh yee! | Yeye ye oh yee! |
| Karibu Afrika | Welcome to Africa |
| Yeye ye oh yee! | Yeye ye oh yee! |
| Bara langu Afrika | My continent Africa |
| | |
| 1. Verse: | 1. Verse: |
| Watu wanafurahi | People are happy |
| Mandhari safi tena ya kuvutia | Good and attractive atmosphere |
| Tazama milima, mabonde na mito | See mountains, valleys and rivers |
| Mbuga za wanyana wanyama tena wa kupendeza Afrika | National parks and beautiful African animals |
| | |
| Chorus: Ninakupenda Afrika. Bara langu Afrika | Chorus: I love Africa. My continent Africa |
| Japo mi sina pesa, nakupenda Afrika x 2 | Although I don't have money, I love you Africa x 2 |
| | |
| 2. Verse: | 2. Verse: |
| Uhaligani Afrika | Hi Africa |
| Dunia nzima wanakujua | The whole world knows you |
| Karibu nyumbani Afrika | Welcome home to Africa |
| Karibu twende shambani | Welcome, let us go to the farm |

| | |
|---|---|
| Karibu kwa bibi na babu | Welcome to grandmother and grandfather |
| Ujionee maajabu | Come to see for yourself the amazing things |
| Oh maajabu ujionee maajabu | Oh, amazing, come to see amazing |
| Karibu kwetu Afrika | Welcome to our Africa |
| | |
| Conversation: | Conversation: |
| Karibu muka tata! | Welcome home! |
| What? | What? |
| Karibu nyumbani! | Welcome home! |
| You are welcome Africa, especially Tanzania | You are welcome Africa, especially Tanzania |
| Tusherehekee! | Let us celebrate! |
| | |
| Chorus | Chorus |

In the computer animation, these cultural identities and sentiments are visually displayed through hand-painted images. To convey their sentiments about Africa students use images of landscapes and people, of different cultures and nature, which they select so that "anyone will understand it is Africa." Although they use images typical of Tanzania, they are representative of other parts of the continent. Kilimanjaro symbolizes mountains in general as well as Africa's highest mountain, while the rivers and savannahs could have been anywhere on the continent. Wild animals (elephant, giraffe, and lion) serve as illustrations of national parks, while grazing cattle are used to show that African societies are still largely agricultural. Similarly, the image of jumping Maasai men is representative of the "traditionalism of Africa," expressing cultures different from Europe, while underscoring tradition. People praying in a church and a mosque are used to display the "two big religions in Africa" and people dancing and drumming to show traditional culture and entertainment.

I am elaborating on the students' own reflections on their production in order to anchor my social analysis of cosmopolitan world
making in their culturally shaped views of the world. Since *Nakupenda
Afrika* is about cultural encounters between Africans and non-Africans,
it offers analytical insights into the (re)creation of social worlds
through the medium of digital art. It might seem odd that I would like
to discuss this process in terms of cosmopolitan world making, seeing
that *Nakupenda Afrika* is so replete with visual and oral expressions of
more localized attachments and sentiments. My reason for doing so is
threefold. First, *Nakupenda Afrika* demonstrates that students construct their African identity in a postcolonial context, shaped by the
gaze of the European other (Eriksson Baaz 2001). Second, two of
the most salient aspects of Tanzanian cultural identity are inherently
cosmopolitan, offering an exemplary illustration of rooted cosmopolitanism or cosmopolitan patriotism (Appiah 1998, 91). And third, these
cosmopolitan expressions diverge from the Dutch students' cosmopolitanism in interesting ways, pointing to a creole continuum
(Hannerz 1996). Let me elaborate.

In *Nakupenda Afrika*, students perform several layers of cultural
identity, which coalesce into a cosmopolitan construction of the world.
It is by being able to step outside their own world that students can
look at their world from a broader perspective, their definition of
Africa being inseparable from their understanding of a world outside
that is not Africa. To them, Africa exists, because the world exists, and
Africa is part of that world. In *Nakupenda Afrika*, these cultural boundaries are drawn through imagined and real encounters between us
(TaSUBa students/Africans) and them (Dutch teachers/Europeans).
This might not seem particularly controversial if it wasn't for scholarly
debates on globalization, especially in relation to Africa. It was not
least in response to anthropologists' problematic relation with the concept of Africa as a whole and Africa's absence in much literature about
globalization that Ferguson (2006) came up with the concept of Africa
as a place-in-the-world. My ethnographic material clearly supports his
argument that "a wide range of social actors on the continent understand their own situations, and construct their strategies for improving
them, in terms of an imagined 'Africa' and its place in a wider world"

(ibid., 6). Ferguson underlines that place-in-the-world is not just a matter of spatial location, but also social ranking, with Africa being on the lower rungs of the world's social hierarchy. Even so, *Nakupenda Afrika* reminds us that Africa is not just a place of material scarcity and social inequality, but a place celebrated for its beauty by artists seeking to mirror their place-in-the-world to the world at large. In constructing their world through sounds and images, TaSUBa students express their "pride" and "love" of Africa as one, "Africa unite."

This cosmopolitan appreciation of the world at large is rooted in Tanzanian nationalism and Pan-Africanism. In her analysis of the rising popularity of Congolese music in Tanzania and the mounting international reputation of Tanzanian musicians, especially in East Africa, Edmondson suggests a shift toward cosmopolitan nationalism (2007, 135–137). While I agree with her postulation, I would argue that Tanzanian nationalism has been cosmopolitan all along. First of all, Tanzanian nationalism is inseparable from Pan-Africanism, as exemplified by the words of the Father of the Nation: "African nationalism is meaningless, is anachronistic, and is dangerous, if it is not at the same time Pan-Africanism" (Nyerere cited in Shivji 2006, 303). Tanzania's active contribution to the freedom struggles around Africa is still visible in the vicinity of Bagamoyo, where a sign for a school in Kaole[30] proudly states "The school used to be a vocational training centre for FRELIMO freedom fighters." Through socialism, this brotherhood was extended even further to encompass ideological counterparts around the world, from China to Cuba, although Nyerere maintained that he was "African first and socialist second" since he "would rather see a free and united Africa before a fragmented socialist Africa" (cited in Mwakikagile 2006, 34–35). Unity and freedom were not just an African or socialist concern, but covered the so-called Third World, Nyerere playing an active role in constellations that sought "unity for a new order" to cite the title of his address to the Group of 77, a "unity of nationalisms" and a "unity in our diversity" transcending national, cultural, economic, and ideological boundaries (Nyerere 1979, 63–64). I could go on, but the point I wish to underline here is that nationalism in Tanzania was never a matter of chauvinism or xenophobia (Gingrich and Banks 2006), but a sense of shared history and destiny with a much larger imagined community, thus constituting what can be defined as anti-imperial cosmopolitanism (Malcomson 1998, 238).

Interestingly enough, the students' cosmopolitan use of cultural symbols contrasts in certain ways with the Dutch teachers' cosmopolitan understanding of Africa. Marlyn, the softly spoken animation teacher, and Alexander, the extroverted music teacher, are surprised that students use such stereotypical images of Africa, resembling the tourist art for sale on the streets of Bagamoyo. Before coming to Tanzania, they had learned that Africa is not one but diverse, just like Europe is composed of different cultures. Yet the students pick all the "cliché images" of Africa, animals in parks, Maasai, and so on. They note the Tanzanian tendency to "copy," whether in popular music styles like *taarab*, which to Alexander sounds all the same, full of musical "clichés," or the art work sold in shops.

We thus find some variations in cosmopolitanism that can be appreciated in terms of the creole continuum. When defined as a perspective, a state of mind or a mode of managing meaning (Hannerz 1996, 102), cosmopolitanism has a built-in political economy of its own. While the Dutch students' perspectives would seem rather typical of the travelling metropolitan elite (ibid., 107), the Tanzanian art students' perspectives are shaped by their everyday life in the cultural periphery, illustrating that cosmopolitanisms are plural and particular (Robbins 1998), in other words situated (Werbner 2008). Indeed, the "cosmopolitanism of the rich" can be distinguished from the "cosmopolitanism of the poor," even when their techniques and imaginaries have common elements (Stokes 2004, 62). TaSUBa students' digitally mediated world making is constrained by material scarcity, which they transform into a virtue by portraying a romanticized image of traditional rural society. Implicit in the production of *Nakupenda Afrika* are the asymmetric power relations between the technology-rich Europe and technology-poor Africa, as exemplified by the sheer absence of images of modernity. Even so, we should take careful note of the fact that in performing their imagined selves and their imagined world, these students emphasize beauty and unity, thus engaging in the cosmopolitics of world making (Robbins 1998). And as far as they are concerned, Africa is a place to love.

### Intercultural Creativity and Digitization

The reason why I have chosen music as the analytical focus of this chapter is to capture its importance in daily life in Tanzania. Not only is music one of the most popular subjects at TaSUBa, but it is also an important feature of everyday social life in Tanzania. In Bagamoyo, the soundscapes of public and private spaces are punctuated by music, mediated through TVs in beauty salons, CD players in bars and restaurants, and radios and cassette players in people's homes. Wherever you go, you hear music. Music is also on the move, blasting from loudspeakers in *dala dala*, from tape recorders in taxis, and from mobile phones carried by people walking. Music is performed in various daily contexts, school children starting their school day by singing national songs, adults gathering for religious worship through hymns and prayers at the end of the work day. Social, cultural, economic, and political events are mediated by music, from religious rituals and social functions to electoral campaigns and sales promotions, whether stationary or mobile. The types of music vary tremendously, *taarab*, *bongo flava*, reggae, traditional music, band music, and *kaswida* being the most popular ones in Bagamoyo, most of them hybrids of some kind. While tastes in music vary, loudness is a widely shared ideal, which is another reason why music dominates the sensory landscape. Music is also illustrative of institutional transformations at TaSUBa. The sound of traditional instruments is common during the day, but at nighttime the soundscape is dominated by more commercial tunes.

Sound in general and music in particular are important parts of the sensory repertoire of TaSUBa's *mzungu* collaborators, key actors in intercultural production. Both Alexander and Idar were trying to teach music students about distortion, to fine tune their auditory skills, and Idar noted with some regret that the preference for loud music had ruined some of the concert-quality sound equipment that NOTA had contributed to the college. Alexander was fond of saying "the importance of sound is often overlooked" and his own cultural immersion into Tanzania was mediated by sound, as he listened his way through this new cultural environment. Tanzania was the loudest country Alexander had ever visited and towards the end of his stay he was looking forward to the silence of Holland. Loud *taarab* music had made one of his bus rides a rather painful experience, but his favorite sound was that of neighborhood dogs howling in unison at night. I got to enjoy the sound of wailing dogs myself on a few occasions and a Tanzanian friend explained that the dogs were reacting to something that their senses, unlike those of humans, could pick up. I am sharing this as an example of how both sound and silence are bound up with socially inhabited worlds as well as invisible spiritual ones, beckoning us to be more attentive to the acoustics of African worlds (Peek 1994), not least the in-between worlds of musical experience (Friedson 2009).

Having thus briefly contextualized sound and music, let me explore the concept of intercultural creativity to deepen our understanding of intercultural production in the peripheries of the creole continuum. From an anthropological perspective, creativity is above all a social phenomenon, rather than an expression of individual genius (Hallam and Ingold 2007, Liep 2001). This is not to say that individual artists are irrelevant, after all they constitute nodes in the networks of intercultural production that I have explored here. But individual artists, no matter how talented they may be, never work in social isolation. Gell (1998) reminds us that the production and circulation of art objects mediate social relations, to the extent that art objects themselves constitute social actors (or indexes), a point of view more commonly associated with Latour's (2005) notion that things have social agency. It is perhaps no coincidence that Gell and Latour arrived at the same conclusion from slightly different perspectives, since art and science can be conceptualized as two ends of the cultural continuum of creativity. Lévi-Strauss (1966, 17–22) positioned art between scientific knowledge and the bricolage of mythical/magical thought, arguing that the artist combines structured thinking out of the box with making things out of the odds and ends at hand.

We can appreciate this social position of creativity in terms of liminality, that ambiguous space of the between so full of stimulating complexity (Stoller 2009, 114–115). When appraised in terms of intercultural artistic production, it becomes quite clear that the power of the between is very much a question of being here and there, then and now. And at the crossroads of being-there and being-away, we find that things begin to separate and coalesce at the same time (Friedson 2009, 35). To understand this simultaneous division and fusion, let us explore additional dimensions of the state of creolization, in this case not in terms of a form of statehood, but in the sense of a condition, a state of being, expressed through intercultural artistic production. I am by no means negating the relation between the state of creolization, as in a body politic, and a state of creolization, as in a condition of cultural hybridity. Since art is a mirror of society, artistic production at TaSUBa is all about a state of creolization in both senses of the word. But let me use this opportunity to explore the cultural underpinnings of creolization in somewhat more abstract terms. For artists in a state of creolization, cultural creativity is always a process of mixing different cultural traditions, to create "pure" forms, as Matitu so succinctly put it.

I would like to expand the concept of creolization to capture not only the spatial dimensions of intercultural creativity, but also temporal ones. The liminality of the state of creolization is not just a question of the creative interplay of cultural currents from different places, but also from different time periods. The traditional—modern music assemblage exemplifies creative processes through which older cultural forms are mixed with new ones, thus creating novel forms of artistic expression, while remolding existing ones. Although the modern part is associated with the West, it is also associated with the present, while the traditional is associated with rural Africa as well as the past. By blending past cultural traditions with contemporary ones, Tanzanian artists thus engage in what could be described as temporal creolization. It would be rather misleading to read this process in terms of conventional creativity/improvisation as opposed to true creativity/innovation, thus insisting on creativity as a form of modernity (Liep 2001). If anything, intercultural production in a state of creolization is all about the improvisational creativity that goes into the making of a world that is always being made rather than ready-made, demonstrating the creativity in copying and imitation as well as the maintenance of tradition (Hallam and Ingold 2007).[31]

Cosmopolitanism is another characteristic feature of intercultural creativity. I have used *Nakupenda Afrika* as an example of cosmopolitan world making, but a similar argument could be made for TRAMO and *Masamva*. In the traditional–modern assemblage, the modern is associated with the outside world, the source of modern instruments and potential destination of locally produced music. This cosmopolitan orientation is a prominent feature throughout the cumulative movement of artistic production, from the performance of modern sounds (guitars, drum kits, trumpets, keyboards) to the production of cultural artifacts for global distribution (music CDs, computer-animated songs). If anything, the digitization of music promotes an aesthetic remediation, an intensified circulation of music through spatial, geographic, and cultural mediations (Born 2009). Not only do these remediations affect music production, but they also mediate how artists view themselves in an increasingly interconnected world. Digitally mediated intercultural production enables Tanzanian artists to explore and express their views of the world at large, which in turn are shaped by their place in it, cosmopolitanism having its own political economy of cultural production. This cosmopolitan sense of belonging to a world at large can be attributed to a greater degree of digitally mediated global interconnectedness (Uimonen 2001, 78–79), a sense of being part of world society constructed as an interactive social network mediated by the Internet (Hart 2000). But cosmopolitanism in Tanzania is also rooted in cultural identities characterized by nationalism and Pan-Africanism.[32]

While creolization and cosmopolitanism point to its more positive aspects, intercultural creativity also beckons us to take a hard look at the asymmetric structure of the global art world, which continues to be demarcated by center–periphery relationships. Indeed, the "Eurocentric gaze and strategies of the global art market system" demonstrate that for African artists "interconnectedness does not enhance an egalitarian space of reciprocal flows" (Fillitz 2009, 116–121). This is exemplified by the categorization of the traditional–modern assemblage as world music, thus reinforcing the distinction between the West and the rest

(Brusila 2001, Stokes 2004). As much as the possibility of recording a music CD in the traditional–modern genre may stimulate fantasies of global success (Stokes 2004), thus feeding on the mediated fantasies of global inclusion so common among Tanzanian youth (Ekström 2010, Weiss 2002), such efforts tend to be thwarted by social and material constraints. Artists at TaSUBa are dependent on European collaborators for the cumulative movement of digitization, from production and recording to distribution.

Global asymmetries are expressed temporally as well, Tanzanian artists having a hard time keeping up with the times. It was only in 2004 that TaSUBa students got a chance to record a CD. For the artists this process represented significant progress, although as I have discussed here, it also revealed a new set of problems. Meanwhile, the music industry, along with the creative industries in general, is undergoing fundamental structural transformations, the outcome of which remains uncertain. The Internet has created a new mode of cultural production, an important aspect of which is the value of open and modifiable technology, or recursive publics (Kelty 2008). Far from being just a moral code shared by computer geeks, the ideals of freely available and modifiable cultural products have spilled onto other domains, like copyrights, as exemplified by the Creative Commons license (ibid.).[33] Since music and other cultural products are increasingly shared freely over the Internet, thus bypassing the commercial channels of the music industry, the boundary between production and consumption of music is increasingly blurred, promoting new forms of creative agency, not least relayed creativity (Born 2005, 2009). Existing copyright regimes are now being questioned and even the supremacy of individual creators is challenged by legal theoreticians who call for a decentered model of creativity (Cohen 2007). Meanwhile, it remains to be seen to what extent music's remediation in the digital age will promote musical invention (Born 2009). So far, existing copyright regimes have tended to exploit rather than protect local musicians whose spheres of influence are so distant from the metropolitan centers of cultural production (Stokes 2004).

Although one should not overlook these challenges, neither should one underestimate the *ingenuity* of intercultural creativity in the cultural peripheries. If necessity is the mother of invention, then there should be little doubt that Africa is one of the most creative places in the world. While it is true that dominant readings of creativity focus on innovation (e.g. Castells 2004), thus underestimating the generative, relational, and temporal aspects of improvisation (Hallam and Ingold 2007), we should also recognize the creative powers of ingenuity. I know that by insisting on ingenuity, I am making a virtue out of necessity, but so do Tanzanian artists. Art students at TaSUBa may not have the state-of-the-art digital technologies that artists in the cultural centers of the global network society enjoy. But they are exceedingly creative when it comes to making something out of what little they have. Not only do they treat the digital technologies available to them with the reverence of sacred objects, but they also exploit them to the utmost. It takes an incredible amount of scientific thinking and magical bricolage to produce a computer-animated song like *Nakupenda Afrika* at an under-resourced arts college in one of the world's poorest countries. If this kind of ingenuity is not true creativity, then I don't know what is.

I would like to conclude this chapter with the emotional dimensions of intercultural creativity. Anthropological theories of art and creativity, from Lévi-Strauss to Gell, tend to privilege cognitive processes. Yet there is something to be said for that magical quality of art that strikes a chord in us, which has more to do with sentiments than reason. In recognition of the cumulative movement of scientific creativity, let me thus explore another layer of music's multiple mediations: music's affective mediations. The social interrelation between music and sentiment has been elegantly explored in the analysis of sound as aesthetically coded sentiment among the Kaluli (Feld 1990). While writing this chapter I came across a citation online that captures this linkage ever so succinctly: *music is what feelings sound like*. The words strike a chord with me because my Tanzanian interlocutors often talk about the sentiment of music: even if people do not understand the words they use, they will still get the feeling of their songs. And this is an interesting aspect of intercultural creativity. Feelings vary across cultures (Wulff 2007), yet there is something to be said for Tanzanian artists' notion of music's universal emotional qualities that seemingly transcend cultural boundaries. Our friend Matitu is a good example of this. He has traveled around the world and performed with artists from different countries, yet he does not speak any English. Music offers him a means of communication with cultural others, a universal language so to speak, which is how TaSUBa music students often talk about their music. It has been noted that African sounds travel with remarkable ease around the world (Stokes 2004, 66), so perhaps there is something to be said for the global appeal of African music. Africa's latest contribution to the global soundscape, the *vuvuzela*, certainly conveyed the emotional attachments of Pan-Africanism and cosmopolitanism when South Africa hosted the World Cup in football in 2010.[34] Either way, I can safely conclude that the very notion of music's emotional universality is instructive of the cosmopolitan dimensions of intercultural creativity among TaSUBa artists.

# PART III
## CULTURAL DEPENDENCIES

# 6

# CULTURAL EXCHANGE AND
# FRIENDSHIP

Travelling Troupes and Gift Exchange

The first acrobats learned their skills in China. This was when
our relationships with China began. Mwalimu [Nyerere] had
some very close relations with Chou Enlai, then Prime Minister
of China, who said when he visited the country he was going
to give a present to Tanzania, he called it a flower, in the shape
of trained young people in acrobatics. A group from China had
performed here and it was much appreciated. A number of young
people were selected to be trained in China. This was in 1964,
they stayed for 4 or 5 years, and came back in 1969.

(Rashid Masimbi, July 2009)

It was through this exchange of artists between Tanzania and the
People's Republic of China that acrobatics[1] was brought into the
repertoire of national culture, and as Masimbi recounts, it was initiated
as a present. As Mauss (1967) reminds us, a gift is not simply a volun-
tary act of generosity, but a transaction that involves complex social
obligations between the giver and the receiver. Like debt, the gift has
the power of founding either dependence or solidarity (Bourdieu 1977,
192). The gift of acrobatics served to solidify social relations between
the giver, Chou Enlai/China, and the receiver, Julius Nyerere/Tanzania,

145

in the domains of culture, economy, and politics. In postsocialist Tanzania, these social relations have been reinvigorated in the age of digitally mediated globalization. A Chinese company has been contracted to construct the national Internet backbone in Tanzania, and Chinese suppliers are entering the lucrative mobile phone market, not least through cheap models of smart phones. These business investments are greatly facilitated by historical ties, with China presenting itself as a "neutral, non-imperialist, value-free outsider that wants simple relationships of trade and friendship with African governments" (Dowden 2009, 495), following the principles of *guanxi* capitalism (Smart 1999).

Mathias Kihima was one of the musicians selected by the Government to go to the People's Republic of China in 1968. At the time, some 24 Tanzanian trainees had already been in China for three years studying acrobatics and for their final year ten musicians were added, to study music for acrobatics. Mathias was one of them. Born in Ngeza district in the Tabora region in 1952, Mathias had played the flute and side drums in school. When he was selected to go to China, the Government prepared everything for him: air travel, passport, luggage, costumes, and even Western suits with necktie and shoes; a modern look. Mathias returned to Tanzania on 6 November 1969, and the following day on 7 November he was employed by the Ministry of Education and Culture as a musician in the National Acrobatics Troupe. When Chuo Cha Sanaa was established in 1981, Mathias was recruited for the college and has taught there ever since. He has also travelled to other parts of the world, but the trip to China stands out in his memory. He often talks about differences in food cultures and he is clearly proud of the Chinese words and phrases he still remembers, four decades after his travels to the People's Republic of China as he calls it.

As with Mathias, Master Musician Mzee Matitu's first overseas travel was to Asia, but in his case the destination was Japan. This was in 1972, during his work at the University of Dar es Salaam. Matitu spent three weeks in Japan, playing *ngoma* and *marimba* in a group of Tanzanian performers. For Matitu, the experience was quite frightening, starting with the travel itself, since he was scared of the airplane. While his fellow artists walked around after their performances,

Matitu stayed at the hotel, watching TV. He was scared of the city and the country, which was so highly "developed," making him feel like a "bush man," and he was afraid of getting lost. Nonetheless, the trip to Japan was but the first of his many journeys abroad. As far as Matitu can remember, he has performed in Japan, Nigeria, Angola, Mozambique, Norway, Denmark, Sweden, Canada, the United Kingdom, India, Bulgaria, then Czechoslovakia, Russia, Korea, Tunisia, Ethiopia, and some other countries.

For most of the teachers at BCA who were drawn from the National Troupes, the first overseas journey was to Lagos, Nigeria in 1977, to perform at the Second World Black and African Festival of Arts and Culture, or African Festival, as they tend to refer to it. For the host country, this festival, popularly known as FESTAC 77, offered a lavish display of oil wealth, a cultural spectacle serving as a form of cultural commodification (Apter 2005). Matitu performed at the festival, along with Kiswigu and Mary, to name two of the characters you have already met in this book, in a drama group led by Mzee Rashid Masimbi. In his CV, the Chief Executive, Juma Bakari, notes "1977: Performed as Kinjeketile in Ebrahim Hussein's Kinjeketile in Lagos Nigeria during the 2nd World Black Festival of Arts and Culture" as the first in a long list of "INTERNATIONAL PERFORMANCES, CONFERENCES, SEMINARS AND WORKSHOPS."

Even now, TaSUBa teachers who performed in Lagos mention the festival in casual conversations. Once during fieldwork I was wearing a t-shirt with an image of Stevie Wonder, purchased after his concert in Stockholm in September 2008, when Kiswigu noted that the image looked familiar. She recognized the "blind American singer" who had performed at the African Festival. Similarly, when I first started working at BCA in 2004, I was told with great pride how staff had performed in the same event as world stars like the Jackson Five. The festival has clearly made an imprint in the social memories of TaSUBa artists, stimulating their imagined selves as globetrotting artists and members of a global art world, in this case a Pan-African art world constituted by black artists from around the world.

In return for their services to the national government, Tanzanian artists have been awarded cultural and economic capital. This capital has taken the form of artistic skills and cultural prestige, as exemplified by Bakari's listing of the Second World Black Festival of Arts and Culture as the start of his career of international performances and collaborations. It has also taken the form of material benefits. In recalling her first journey abroad, to the African Festival in Nigeria in 1977, Mary noted with pleasure that she got "a little money" to buy "gifts" for her family back home. As mentioned above, Mathias listed Western suits as part of the preparatory package that the Government bestowed upon him when he was sent off to China.

I prefer to discuss these forms of capital in terms of gift exchange rather than contractual arrangements between employer and employee to capture the cultural underpinnings of Tanzanian artists' engagements in nationalist pilgrimages. Being a member of a National Troupe was never just a matter of work, in the sense of contracted labor, but involved a complex set of social obligations between the Government and state-employed artists. It was through the social alchemy of gifts that the state was able to transmute economic into symbolic capital, thus asserting its legitimate authority (Bourdieu 1977, 192). The meager salary played a minor role in this process, since it was the gift of travelling abroad and its associated capital benefits that assured the loyalty and piety of artists.

"Thanks to God that I can travel around like that, with my ignorant knowledge and ignorant instrument. I was happy. Without that I would never visit Europe or somewhere else," Matitu reflects on his travels. Once when he came back from Europe and his friends were asking him about his trip, an educated man who overheard the conversation was surprised Matitu had been to Europe and asked him about his profession. The man found it difficult to comprehend that someone specialized in *marimba* could have travelled so far. Equally, he could not understand that someone who looked so "normal" had been to Europe, since he expected Matitu to wear nice clothes and have a car and a huge house. But even without the material goods associated with journeys abroad, Matitu is "happy" about his travels: "I can even jump on a plane to perform, my people count me and appreciate my profession."

While the National Troupes' journeys abroad centered on African and other so-called Third World countries, with BCA the focus shifted towards Europe. As mentioned in Chapter 3, one of the main reasons why BCA was set up was that the Tanzanian government could no longer afford the journeys of the National Troupes. Instead of engaging in cultural exchange with other postcolonial countries, state-employed artists came to rely on exchanges supported by European donor countries.

For Nkwabi Ng'hengasamala, the World Festival of Culture and Arts for Black People, as he calls the event, was his first trip abroad, but his second one took him to Sweden. Born in Sengerema district in Mwanza region, also known as Sukumaland from the tribe *wasukuma*, Nkwabi started dancing and singing at an early age. By the age of twelve he was quite well known locally, having performed with his father, who was a singer, dancer, and song composer. After completing primary education, Nkwabi was keen to go to secondary school, not so much to get an education that would lead to a job, but because he wanted to be able to sing in Kiswahili and English, rather than just his tribal language Kisukuma. In 1975, Nkwabi saw an announcement in the paper that the Government was looking for artists for the National Theatre Group. He sent in his application and after being selected he was enrolled in a two-year drama course at the Dar es Salaam College of Theatre Arts. On 1 July 1977, Nkwabi was employed as an actor in the National Performing Arts Company, where he also did some dance choreography. In 1980, the Swedish Theater Director Martha Vestin came to Dar es Salaam as a guest lecturer at UDSM and later for acting and training at the National Company, which led to a play that she directed. The following year, she invited the Company to perform in Sweden. Some Company members remained for a while, working with Friteatern in Sundbyberg, Stockholm, and they also performed together at a theater festival in Copenhagen and in Mannheim, Germany. When the artists returned to Tanzania, they were accompanied by their Swedish colleagues and performed together in Dar es Salaam, Arusha, and Morogoro as well as Zimbabwe.

Just as specific events stand out in the social memories of artists at TaSUBa, so do specific people involved in cultural exchange. Although I have never met Martha Vestin in person, I have heard about her throughout my years of engagement at BCA/TaSUBa, always spoken of in warm, even loving, terms. By brokering cultural exchanges between Swedish and Tanzanian artists, Martha has occupied a central position in the social networks of intercultural production. She has also played a key role in advancing the professional careers of individual artists at BCA. While in Stockholm, Nkwabi visited the Mime School at Danshögskolan (University College of Dance). In January 1983, he was invited back to Sweden for interviews and auditions and in August he was admitted to a three-year BA program in mime through the prestigious Dramatiska Institutet (Dramatic Institute). Nkwabi was the first East African artist trained in mime and he helped spread this art form in the region.

This emphasis on social relations is a distinctive feature of everyday life in Tanzania, as elsewhere in Africa. The old idiom "it is not what you know but who you know" takes on a powerful meaning in this cultural context where social networks are of overriding importance in all spheres of social activity, including the executive operation of the state apparatus. It is not for nothing that social anthropologists have developed some of their most intricate theories on social organization in African contexts, including early social network theory (Kapferer 1973, Mitchell 1969). When it comes to modern statehood, Tanzania offers an exemplary case of Wolf's (2001 [1966], 167) early observation that "we must not confuse the theory of state sovereignty with the facts of political life." Instead of a tightly knit and well organized social unit, the state itself is divided into and traversed by different concentrations of power and "the formal framework of economic and political power exists alongside or intermingle[d] with various other kinds of informal structures that are interstitial, supplementary, or parallel to it" (ibid.).

As can be expected, in the state of creolization, various constellations of social relations coexist and overlap with formal structures, especially the informal structures of friendship, kinship, and patron–clientism (ibid.). In addition to being good friends, Westerners collaborating with Tanzanians are often addressed through familial kinship terms, as *dada* (sister), *kaka* (brother), or *mama* (mother/elderly woman, also wife). The honorific *mzee* used to address older men (as well as husband and boss) tends to be less common, but some men are addressed as *baba* (father). Far from being just an expression of Tanzanian hospitality, the use of these kinship terms serves to solidify social relations of reciprocity and obligation. Since most relations between Tanzanians and Westerners are asymmetrical, even kinship and friendship tend to be tied up with patron–clientism. The *mzungu* friend/brother/sister/patron is expected to help his/her Tanzanian friend/brother/sister/client in times of need.

### Norwegian Centers, Tanzanian Peripheries

"So they have the same kind of behavior in Norway like we have here in Tanzania," Sixmund Begashe remarks when I tell him Idar is coming back to work at TaSUBa. "It is easy for Idar to get the job since his friends are on the selection committee," he explains when I ask him what he means. When I tell him that they actually had problems recruiting people in Norway, Sixmund looks astonished. He assumed that the opportunity to work as a teacher in Tanzania would be as sought after as positions to work in Norway. But whereas 20 Tanzanian students and graduates compete for three positions in Norway, NOTA had to advertise the position for a Norwegian music teacher twice to find a qualified candidate willing to spend a year in Tanzania. The center–periphery relations of what is referred to as a mutual, intercultural collaboration network between Norway and Tanzania could not have been more explicit. Nor could the politics of cultural exchange have been any more implicit.

Before Sixmund started working as a temporary teacher at BCA in 2004, he spent almost one year in Stavanger in Norway through the NOTA project, studying sound engineering. Over the many years I have known him, Sixmund often talks about his experiences in Norway, from technical details that his teachers taught him to reflections on differences in lifestyles. Sixmund still remembers some words and phrases in Norwegian, which he uses whenever he gets a chance. His recurring story telling about Norway is part of his cosmopolitan identity and he often plays the role of a cultural broker, his skills as an intercultural mediator enhanced by his understanding of cultural differences between Europeans and Tanzanians. If anything, Sixmund's remarks about possible similarities between Norwegian and Tanzanian recruitment processes rested on an assumption that they should in fact be different.

Our conversation takes place in the small office in the ICT building that Sixmund shares with Hussein, a place where we often laugh a lot. Sixmund's desk is often cluttered with CDs, CD covers, video cameras, notebooks, and pens. Ever since the late Mzee Kaduma remarked that the ICT office looked like a "ghetto," I poke fun of the mess on Sixmund's desk. Sixmund has a great sense of humor, and he loves playing with words, in Kiswahili as well as in English. Verbal wit is much appreciated in Tanzania where people prefer suggestive subtexts and subtle insinuations over direct talk. Since he himself is such a joker, people often play around with Sixmund's name, usually referring to him as Six, sometimes as Seven, and his colleague Solomon calls him Zeromund on occasion. Six is quite handsome, with sparkling eyes and a charming smile, so people also refer to him as Sexy. Now in his early thirties, Sixmund grew up in Manyara region with his grandmother, brother, and sister. He graduated from BCA in 2002, with a major in drama and minor in music. In 2009, he left his teaching job at TaSUBa for a position at the newly constructed House of Culture in Dar es Salaam. He combines his work with undergraduate studies at the Open University of Tanzania, where Mussa is his classmate.

In the coming days, eager applicants go through various exercises aimed at determining the most suitable candidates to work in Stavanger, Norway. Between the exercises they hang around on campus, nervously chatting with each other under the shade of trees. The auditions last for three days and the stakes are high. The jobs focus on teaching and performing Tanzanian music, dance, and culture in kindergarten, primary, and secondary schools, and at the Stavanger School of Culture. The job announcement is posted on the TaSUBa notice board on 4 April 2009, stating 30 April as the deadline for written applications, to be submitted with CVs and certificates to the Chief Executive of TaSUBa. Prior to the auditions, a list of applicants is posted on the notice board, categorized into women/girls (six in total) and men/boys (14 in total), along with a tentative timetable for the auditions on 20 to 22 May and some information about the jury team, composed of two jurors from Stavanger and two from TaSUBa.

The auditions start with an interview and a short dance performance, after which the number of candidates is reduced from 20 to nine. The individual dance is followed by a teaching exercise, for which a class of primary school students is brought in from a nearby school and taught in one of the TaSUBa classrooms, then another round of selections. The remaining group of six applicants is interviewed again, this time with more personal questions about moral character and expectations of living in Norway. They are also asked to perform group dances, a traditional dance and an improvised one. Out of the six, the jury team identifies four suitable candidates, one of whom is discarded since he has not completed his diploma, leaving one female and two male candidates to fill the positions.

For the applicants, the process is somewhat unclear until the results are announced on the notice board on 25 May, following which rumours and gossip start circulating. Some of the applicants communicate with one another via text messages and phone conversations, confirming what they have suspected all along, that the outcome is a result of candidates' affiliations with college staff. It is only one of the winning candidates they consider to be fully qualified, despite him being a relative of college staff; the other two are contested. As one student tells me: "It is not fair, it is always those who are related to staff who get to go. Last year, it was one, two years ago two of them. It means outsiders don't really stand a chance."

Since the mandate of the NOTA project is targeted at institutional development, it is an important actor in the digital drama of executive transformation. As stated in the NOTA project document, during its second phase 2006 to 2011 the project's goals are "to promote cultural collaboration between Tanzania and Norway" and "to contribute to transforming BCA into an effective and efficient Executive Agency" (NOTA 2006, 5). The mode of collaboration follows the dictates of audit culture, with clearly specified objectives and measurable outputs, structured according to the logical framework approach (LFA) that has come to dominate development cooperation. Following the LFA management tool, the project document lists detailed outputs, strategic objectives, and activities, along with an activity plan, management structure, and risk analysis. These audit technologies replicate the neoliberal rationale of public sector reform, not least by concealing competing paradigms of governance through the illusionary structures of a "culture of legality" (Comaroff and Comaroff 2006). Culturally patterned power structures are subsumed under a seemingly neutral governance model that glosses over the contradictory pulls of existing power relations.

As exemplified by the audition process, the NOTA project tries to introduce audit technologies that are detached from the cultural context of TaSUBa, emphasizing professional requirements over social obligations. The audition process is highly formalized, with a carefully worded job advertisement, a publicized list of candidates, and a carefully scripted and publicly displayed selection process. The impression of an objective, legalistic process is further ascertained through the physical presence of an equal number of Tanzanian and Norwegian jurors. But this staged performance of legitimacy conceals as much as it reveals. Although the Tanzanian jurors are quite willing to play along with the *langue* of legality, they can also play around with its *parole* (ibid., 24). It is a well known fact that the state in Africa functions as a "rhizome of personal networks" that assures the "centralization of power through the agencies of family, alliance and friendship" (Bayart 2009, 261). And this is why students interpret the outcome of the auditions in terms of social relations. They expect nothing less, since "what is classified as nepotism and cronyism in Scandinavia, may well be regarded as a moral duty to help one's friends and family in parts of Asia and Africa" (Haller and Shore 2005, 9).

"We are looking for a job, anywhere, that's the most important for us," an applicant explains to me while waiting for his turn to audition. A second motivation is the chance to travel to another country, "to see how they live, their geography and their culture." Related to this is the opportunity to exchange culture, "we can show them our culture through the arts." The opportunity to work in Norway is thus associated with economic and cultural capital, yet the former is quite substantial, far surpassing the salaries Tanzanian artists could possibly make at home. And this is why the positions are so contested; their allotment has everything to do with the redistribution of wealth. This is also why the applicants interpret the results in terms of power relations, for this is the logical conclusion of the moral culture of belly politics (Bayart 2009). Meanwhile, similarly to how witchcraft is used to denounce the concentration of undeserved enrichment (ibid., 243), the applicants resort to gossip to express their disappointment and moral outrage. Contrary to the ideals of the culture of legality, they have no legal recourse to challenge the informal structures at work, no evidence to prove that the results are rigged. Nor can they officially challenge the outcome for fear of reprisal, since they themselves are entangled in networks of power: "We don't want to say something; the college can do something to us, even fail us," I am told.

The capital gains of cultural exchange are reversed for Norwegian teachers working in Tanzania, which to some extent explains why NOTA has such a hard time recruiting Norwegian professionals. This capital reversal exemplifies some of the "general patterns of frustration in a gift relationship" observed in the aid relationship between Norway and Tanzania (Simensen 2010, 62).

It was her interest in different dance traditions that prompted Ingrid Remmen[2] 📷 to apply for the job as dance teacher in Tanzania. At the time she was between jobs and although she had no previous experience of African dance or culture, her "interest in different dance forms" made her "open for it." After a three-week preparatory course in Norway, during which 70 professionals from the North and the South were instructed on various aspects of working in different cultures, Ingrid arrived in Tanzania in mid-March 2009, contracted to stay until August 2010. She was struck by the heat, which captured much of her early focus, as well as the "laidbackness" of the school and Bagamoyo at large. Professionally her first few months revolved around waiting, for information and instructions. Language was also an obstacle, since she didn't speak much Kiswahili. Her early "frustrations" were "balanced out" by learning African dance, taught to her by some students. With time, she got to teach her own classes in choreography.[3] 🎥 She also came to appreciate the way dance is taught in Tanzania, not as "technical" or "intellectual" as in Europe, but "full body and mind engagement," so you "feel the rhythm" and "feel it is part of nature." Overall, it is the social and cultural aspects of her experience that Ingrid enjoys the most, making her feel "more relaxed" and "confident" than she sometimes feels at home, while enjoying the "powerful" cultural expressions of daily rituals.

The imbalance in capital gains is far from visible to Tanzanians, who tend to assume the opposite when they see how Norwegians live in Tanzania. Fredskorpset participants from Norway are housed in an executive residential area, a walled compound with exclusively fur- nished apartments and houses, equipped with A/C, satellite TV, and a stand-by generator. The housing complex is one of the most luxurious in Bagamoyo and it is only the newly constructed residence of the Chief Executive that comes close to this standard of housing among TaSUBa staff. Some exchange teachers purchase a car, not least to enjoy some tourism in Tanzania. Although they pay for them with their own money, with the intention of selling them for almost the same amount once they leave, the cars tend to be upmarket four-wheel drives, costing USD 10–20,000 (second hand). None of the teachers at TaSUBa can afford such expensive vehicles and most of them do not even own a car.

This is why the political economy of cultural exchange has such deep social ramifications, reflecting global inequalities framing varia- tions in capital accumulation. While Norwegian teachers may be attracted by the cultural authenticity and exoticism of Africa, their Tanzanian collaborators can ill afford to overlook the material gains of cultural exchange. In a digitally mediated neoliberal world order, Africans know that social mobility is a question of "individual spatial mobility," that it is primarily "by leaving, going elsewhere," if even temporarily, that one can "escape the low global status of being a 'poor African'" (Ferguson 2006, 191). In Togo, the desire for spatial mobility has even produced a Lotto visa culture that has given rise to all kinds of inventions of kinship (Piot 2010). Tanzanians are not quite so des- perate, but kinship ties do play an important role in attempts to achieve social and spatial mobility. If the destination of the Promised Land of wealth and modernity is a rich country like Norway, the opportunity to travel will not be left to the whims of some abstract culture of legality but firmly entrenched in social networks of power.

### Dutch Brokerage and Digital Cargo[4]

It takes some time before I realize that the young *wazungu* outside the ICT building[5]  are Dutch students from HKU. I had simply assumed that they were volunteers in Bagamoyo, young Westerners, often American, spending a few months helping out at one of the local orphanages or schools. I did not think they were young backpackers, since they lugged around their laptops, and having seen them on several occasions, they were clearly not day trippers from Dar es Salaam. When John Sagatti, one of the younger music teachers, informs me that the group is from HKU, I ask him to introduce me to them. Over the next few weeks I hang out with Alexander, Marlyn, and Laura as often as I can, observing their classes during the day and enjoying a cold beer and friendly conversation at night. Ned is always with us, Laura's inanimate soft, furry friend who has travelled around the world with her and has a page of his own in Facebook.

TaSUBa's collaboration with Holland is directly focused on digital media, which makes the HKU project an interesting cultural broker in the digital drama of executive transformation. As mentioned in Chapter 5, the HKU project is geared at developing a training program in multimedia, targeting the creative industries in Tanzania. So it builds on and contributes to the process of executive transformation, assisting TaSUBa to realize its mission of producing arts products, services, and multimedia productions, while offering training in skills that are increasingly sought after by the media industry in particular.

The HKU project is also contributing to the digitization of culture in a material way, by literally bringing the cargo of millennial capitalism, the tools of techne (Boellstorff 2008, Comaroff and Comaroff 2000). By lugging around all kinds of digital media, the Dutch students embody the status markers of a "privileged 'first class' world" (Ferguson 2006, 166). This cultural assumption is so deeply embedded that Tanzanians have a hard time categorizing *mzungu* who lack such material attributes, a telling example of which is Julia, the Finnish student you encountered in Chapter 1. When Julia arrived at TaSUBa, she had very little money. Not so surprising since she was only 20 years old, recently graduated from high school, thus falling into the European social category of poor, young student. In Tanzania, this social status is inconceivable for *mzungu*, which is why Julia's Tanzanian friends had a hard time classifying her. "What kind of *mzungu* are you?" they were asking her. "You are supposed to have a laptop, flash disk, camera, iPod and a nice phone. But you have nothing!"

It was above all their interest in working in a different cultural environment that inspired Alexander, Marlyn, and Laura to come to Tanzania for their third-year project work at HKU. Alexander and Marlyn were only 21 years old at the time, Laura was 27, and unlike her fellow students who had not been outside Europe, she had travelled extensively in Asia, Latin America, and Australia. This was, however, the first time in Africa for all of them, and as they came to learn, the place was quite different from the negative media portrayals they had been exposed to.

In my recurring interactions with the Dutch students, I notice how keen they are to understand the social and cultural life around them, discussing their observations and experiences amongst themselves or with their Tanzanian friends. Laura, who is taking a pre-Master in anthropology, combined with practical studies of documentary making, is paying close attention to everything going on around her, but so are her fellow travelers. The group is closely knit and spends most of their time together. They live together in a simple house owned by one of the TaSUBa teachers. They have their lunches together with some of the younger staff in the TaSUBa resthouse, a daily treat sponsored by HKU. Towards the end of their ten-week stay in Tanzania they travel together to one of the national parks, before returning to Holland.

John Sagatti, the cultural broker who introduced me to the Dutch students, makes a lasting impression on *mzungu* visitors. A giant of a man, he is at least a head taller than everyone else, with broad shoulders and a deep voice that can be heard at quite some distance. Sagatti took the diploma program at BCA in 1990 to 1993, majoring in music, with dance as a minor. He then worked with a children's program on the newly established TV station ITV for a year, before taking his BA degree at UDSM, with a double major in theater and music. From 2000 to 2004 he worked as a producer and artistic director at Marimba Studio, after that the Zanzibar International Film Festival (ZIFF), and are mixed, dormitory life is socially structured according to gender, with male students housed in different buildings from female students. Students regulate the social norms of dormitory life in a rather egalitarian and artistic manner, while reproducing gendered patterns of social behavior. If someone breaks social codes, for example by hanging their washed lingerie to dry in public, they can expect a cartoon on the dormitory notice board.

A printed schedule of classes is displayed on the TaSUBa notice board, the formal structure of which conceals the flexibility and mobility of teaching. Many classes have temporary or improvised "classrooms."[15] Traditional music classes are usually held under the mango trees near the entrance gate, with students sitting on logs, or in the aisle of the main theater hall, while music theory tends to be organized in the classrooms. Dance is taught at the Mwembe theater, or in some other open space, occasionally upstairs in the theater hall. Drama classes are usually held in the classrooms, sporadically on the main theater stage. Fine art classes are often organized in the canteen, or under the trees nearby, while stage technology is taught wherever space allows for it. ICT classes are always held in the Internet room, although frequently cancelled due to power failure.

Students often roam around looking for their teachers, who may or may not be present, and many students skip class altogether. Despite the high teacher–student ratio (around 1:3), students don't enjoy much tutoring due to the high absenteeism of teachers. In order to complement their meager salaries, many teachers engage in side activities, ranging from consultancies and cultural exchanges to running businesses of their own. Participation in workshops, meetings, and other collective government events is a common source of income and used as a means to reward the loyalty of select members of staff. Some teachers are absent due to their own studies, pursuing undergraduate or postgraduate degrees. Teacher and student absenteeism is supposed to be carefully recorded and reported, but this bureaucratic formality is largely ignored.

The training program also suffers from deteriorating facilities. The three to five working computers in the computer room are shared by a student population of 120. Some students have laptops of their own, but most students cannot afford to buy their own computer. ICT is by no means an exception: all subjects suffer from a lack of facilities. For instance, keyboard is compulsory for all music students, yet there is only one keyboard for 45 learners, while instruments like guitars and trumpets are in short supply, as are materials for painting, sculpting, and design in fine arts.

During ICT class,[16] most students sit together two to three on each computer, some sit on the floor between the desks, and a few at the back of the room with their own laptops. The teacher stands at the front of the room, using a projector to display materials from a computer onto a screen. The screen is worn out, patched to its frame with some string. As with other subjects, the written teaching material is in English, but when speaking the teacher mixes English and Kiswahili to explain the different functions of computers and computer applications. To deal with infrastructure limitations, ICT classes are conducted in groups of 12 to 16 students, each year divided into three groups. Between classes, students have little opportunity to practice, since the room is busy during breaks and closed after school hours.

Although TaSUBa continues to promote itself through its practical training program, the rituals of schooling illustrate the liminality of the traditional–modern aesthetic design. These days standardization according to the dictates of audit culture is combined with a drive to make more money out of the institute. Neither aspect of the modern aesthetic is particularly conducive to the traditional aesthetic, which builds on training through the slow development of embodied artistic mastery. This ambivalence is, however, rooted in the college's aesthetic design. Traditional culture is increasingly disconnected from modern culture, the former associated with the rural past, the latter with the urban future. In its attempts to straddle this cultural divide, the college finds itself in a liminal position, unable to provide the temporal and spatial requirements for embodied practical mastery, but equally incapable of supplying students with the modern facilities they expect in their quest for formal accreditation.

The conflicting trends in aesthetic design are evident in the perspectives of teachers and students, who lament that the training is "too theoretical" and "not practical enough." Teachers are frustrated by the lack of facilities, while the growing number of students impedes their efforts to develop artistic talent, the transmission of embodied practical mastery being compounded by the lack of artistic talent and interest among students. For the students, the lack of modern teaching and learning facilities is a common source of complaint, illustrating that the college is not living up to the ideal of providing them with "educational resources for upward mobility" (Bartlett et al. 2002, 7). Many students also complain about the lack of formally qualified teachers, exemplifying the extent to which they have come to adapt the rather "impoverished view of education as a matter of acquisition and inculcation" achieved and measured through standardized accreditation (Varenne 2007, 22). Rather than appreciating that the mastery of artistic skills takes time, students complain about the slow pace of learning. Those who are more serious about becoming artists are frustrated by the lack of personal tutoring, the lack of facilities to practice, and the fact that most students in their classes have no talent or inclination for the arts, thus slowing down their learning.

This is why Julia relied on external tutors, in her case friends and alumni, to prepare for her practical exams. As often as she had a chance, she practiced with friends who mastered the *bugobogobo* and John Sombi, a college graduate who originated from Mwanza, gave her private classes free of charge. Between classes, Julia practiced on her own, spending hours and hours refining her movements, until she mastered them well enough. Julia had the ambition to dance the *bugobogobo* with fire, but after burning herself on the blazing torch when she first tried to hold it, she settled for a heavy wooden stick. It is not only Julia's learning that takes place outside the college, but her living as well. Like other international and regional students, Julia has opted to stay off campus, renting a small room in town, instead of sharing a room in the student dormitory.

External tutoring is but one of the strategies students use to overcome limitations in the training program. Upon completing the diploma program, one student estimated that he had learned 60 percent from other students and on his own and only 40 percent from the teachers. Collaboration between students is very common and teachers encourage students to help each other by practicing together after school hours. Collaborative learning is an expression of the cultural ethos of *pamoja*, but it is also indicative of material scarcity. To circumvent material limitations, students try to acquire learning materials on their own. Those who can afford it buy their own instruments and equipment; others borrow from friends or relatives.

Given the lack of learning materials, students rely heavily on the Internet to look up relevant information, often typing in questions for assignments in Google or generic sites like www.answers.com or www.definitions.net, and to a lesser extent Wikipedia (Uimonen 2011). Students often sit at the computers with a notebook and pen, copying the answers from their online searches onto paper, for future reference. In this cultural context, the Internet resembles a global library, giving students access to information they would otherwise not find, especially in the under-resourced college library. But students also find that online information on topics like African art tend to be limited and sometimes inaccurate, often originating from Western rather than African sources. This lack of locally relevant content indicates that the digital stratification of online content is possibly even greater than gaps in access and use.

The social context of teaching and learning can be contrasted with the highly ritualized performance of examinations, which are divided into practical and theoretical exams, each allotted one week. As exemplified by Julia's dance routine, the practical exams[17] are elevated to the status of artistic performances, while fine arts and stage technology exams are performed as artistic productions. The theoretical exams[18] are no less ritualized. Often carried out in the modern flexible hall, they are performed in silence, supervised by examination guards who carefully manage the administrative process, from the distribution of exam questions to the collection of students' answers on handwritten sheets of paper. Like the auditions, the exams serve important social functions in the rituals of schooling, framing practical art training in the bureaucratic procedures of a modern educational institute. They also structure the liminality of schooling; arranging the marginalized position of students into successive phases of ritual transition, the passing of exams serving to qualify practical mastery.

then at Kingdom Production Studio in Dar es Salaam, which specialized in gospel. In February 2007 he returned to BCA, where he was
given a temporary contract as a music and stage technology teacher.
Sagatti often manages the sound set-up for performances, towering
over the mixing board in the main theater or its back stage. Fluent in
English, Sagatti is a skilled cultural broker, helping visiting *mzungu*
understand what is going on and facilitating their interaction with
teachers and students at the college. No wonder Sagatti was good
friends with the HKU team.

The Dutch students carry out most of their work in the new theater
building, in spaces allocated for digital media production. When
the HKU project started, Dutch students constructed a makeshift
recording studio in a small room located at the end of the ICT building. This annex was built in 2004, when the ICT building was inaugurated, to house a small cafeteria operated by an external entrepreneur.
The business activity did not last for very long and the space was left
empty, until Dutch students installed a computer and basic recording
equipment. In 2009, the music studio was shifted to the main theater,
to a spacious room cooled with A/C.[6] 🎥 The acoustics in the new
theater studio are far from ideal, yet a great improvement compared to
the stuffy small room at the back of the ICT building. Documentary
film production and computer animation are allocated a small, win-
dowless room upstairs. The room is furnished with simple wooden
tables and chairs, and a makeshift stand for computer animation placed
in a small alcove, a cramped space where only two people can work at
the same time. The multimedia room is stifling, with no inlets for fresh
air or air conditioning. The students use a rusty old fan to cool down
the iMac[7] 🎥 used for video editing, but there is no respite from the
musky, hot air. Even so, this is where multimedia classes are conducted
through practical training, with students editing images and sound
tracks for video documentaries, or painting landscapes and figures,
carefully captured with a video camera for computer animation. While
the music studio is cool and loud, the multimedia room is usually hot
and silent.

The Dutch students worry that their project is "exclusive" and "out
of balance," showing students "things they can never have." All the

equipment is sponsored by HKU and literally brought to the college by the Dutch students, each group bringing as much equipment as they can carry. The project emulates the technical standards of HKU, which means Macintosh rather than PC equipment. Maintenance of equipment is rather problematic, since Macintosh is quite rare in Tanzania, and students often bring faulty equipment back to Holland, for repair or replacement by the next batch of students. The equipment is exclusive and unequally distributed. There is only one iMac for video editing, only one Mac mini for music production, and only one Macbook for computer animation. Furthermore, use of the equipment depends on the presence of Dutch students. When they are absent, only management can utilize this precious cargo. During fieldwork, the iMac was used to showcase TaSUBa at the annual Public Service Week exhibition, transported in the TaSUBa pickup used for domestic travels. Some of the younger staff members used the iMac to edit a film production for senior staff members. The HKU cargo is thus tied in with internal social hierarchies and power relations.

The Dutch students could not fail to notice how enthusiastic students were about "walking around with fancy equipment," when shooting video documentaries, or how careful they were in handling the equipment, treating the iMac with the reverence of a "holy grail." They also noted that students assumed they needed the same kind of equipment, clearly not fully realizing how expensive it was.

Inadvertently, the HKU project started a Macintosh trend at TaSUBa. Students were not just dreaming of computers of their own, but they wanted Macintosh, which they assumed to be superior for artistic production. One of the students, Mcwilliam Langole, who adopted the Mc in his name after watching a lot of American movies, even got his name associated with Macintosh, since he was the first student on campus with an iBook. These fantasies of acquisition should be understood in terms of deeply felt desires for global inclusion, cultural mimickry being synonymous with aspirations for membership in modern world society (Ferguson 2006, 158–161).

Digital media serve as important status markers for younger teachers like Sixmund and Sagatti who thereby achieve some degree of social mobility. Both possess technical skills that TaSUBa is in short supply of, their digital literacy enhancing their temporary positions at the college. Sixmund started playing around with the college's video camera early on, and over time he has become quite proficient in recording and editing video. Not only have Sixmund's technical skills earned him continued contracts at the college, and a role in the NOTA documentation project that uses him for field trips, but they have also enabled him to earn some extra income, by tutoring students or making videos for staff. Sagatti has been closely involved with the HKU project from the outset, especially the music production part, where his professional experiences are valued. He dreams of a music recording studio at TaSUBa, something he hopes HKU might help with.

Reflecting the cultural hybridity of art production in a state of creolization, the HKU project is an example of hybrid media engagement (Uimonen 2011). Due to their state of partial inclusion, TaSUBa students are unable to emulate the more elaborate forms of media engagements typical of Western youth (Ito 2010). Marlyn noted that while Dutch students tend to produce all their computer animations digitally, at TaSUBa students rely on non-digital methods, drawing on paper rather than on digital drawing tablets, of which there is only one. Even paper is expensive and in short supply, so students shift their drawn objects by hand when photographing them. For the students, hybrid media engagement comes rather naturally, building on the traditional–modern aesthetic described earlier. Thus, when David Estomihi commented on how he combines hand-drawn and computer-drawn images, he referred to this style in terms of mixing traditional and modern (Uimonen 2011).

The Dutch students adapt the social practices of hybrid media engagement while working at TaSUBa. In many cases, they have to rely on the ingenuity so characteristic of intercultural creativity discussed in Chapter 5. For instance, to facilitate animation of drawn objects, Marlyn used split pins, while another Dutch teacher used duct tape to strap together two video cameras. Alexander, who was relying on various ingenious methods to manage TaSUBa's sound equipment, called such efforts "low-tech solutions to high-tech problems."

### Facebook Friends, Selfhood, and *Pamoja*[8]

In Facebook, David Estomihi is friends with Marlyn Spaaij, Laura Roncken, and Alexander Mooij, along with some 320 other people. Marlyn was David's tutor in computer animation, and he became friends with Laura and Alexander when they were working at TaSUBa. David is also friends with other Dutch students he has met through HKU and some of the Norwegian teachers who have worked at TaSUBa, as well as the international students at BCA/TaSUBa, Mathilda Sandbom and Julia Salmi. He has some additional "friends from abroad" that he has met outside TaSUBa, while they were visiting Bagamoyo, and a few he has met online. The great majority of David's friends are Tanzanian. Many of them are "students" or alumni from BCA/TaSUBa, a few are younger teachers/former teachers at TaSUBa. Some are "relatives," others are "friends" he studied with before. These were the social categories David used when describing what kind of friends he has in Facebook. At the time (December 2009) he had 151 friends in total, so his network has clearly grown quite a lot up to now (May 2011). David has also started his own blog entitled *sanaa*,[9] where he posts some of his art work.[10]

David's Facebook profile exemplifies digitally mediated identity construction, combining visual and textual elements. Trained as a visual artist, David creates rather elaborate profile photos, which he often changes. He used to have 95 images in his profile photo album, most of them graphically designed, from digitally reworked photos to computer-drawn images. David's professional identity as an artist is evident in form and content, many times showing him as an artist at work, often in contexts featuring digital media, thus displaying his imagined self as a modern artist.[11]

David also expresses his tribal and national identities in his profile photos. For a while he used Dauu in his images, a tribal version of his Christian name, thus underlining his *wachagga* identity[12] and for a while his Facebook surname was Ndosi, his clan name. David's visual expressions of national identity are equally creative, as exemplified by an image of his face in the colors of the Tanzanian flag. Or a photographic portrait of himself within an outline of the map of Tanzania, with the letters MTIIZII,[13] thus playing on the Kiswahili prefix m- used to denote people and the .tz denoting the domain name for Tanzania, pronounced tii zii in Kiswahili (tee zee in English). David expresses his Pan-African identity as well, through images of his portrait with a map of Africa, accompanied by the words Strictly African or Strictly Afrikan[14] (following the Kiswahili *Afrika*), or in another version, a map of Africa that he has remodeled into an eyeball inside a drawn image of an eye with the words LOVE AFRIKA.

David's creative expressions of cultural identity in Facebook can tell us something about the creation of selfhood in virtual social environments. Although Boellstorff (2008, 247) makes a distinction between virtual worlds like Second Life and social networking sites like Facebook, referring to the former as a place, the latter as networks, I am not sure if this distinction is necessary. Like Second Life, Facebook is a place because it is a site for social interaction. While it is true that "one connects relationships 'through networks', but lives relationships 'in' places" (ibid., 247), in an increasingly interconnected world, relationships tend to be distributed over different places, so there is not much point in privileging local social relationships over more translocal ones (Hannerz 1992a, 51). Thus, I would suggest that Facebook is a place, even a networked place, rather than a networked public (Ito 2010):[15] a virtual node in which networks of social relations coalesce, offering social spaces for cultural expression and experimentation.

Visual expressions of selfhood are an important aspect of David's Facebook identity, exemplifying the significance of techne in digitally mediated social interaction. Like Second Life, virtual places like Facebook "provide contexts for self-fashioning—techne in its most basic sense" (Boellstorff 2008, 122). Of course in Facebook, it is not a question of fashioning elaborate avatars, but even so, there is something to be said for virtual embodiment and the supremacy of the visual (ibid., 134). Far from merely replicating his offline physical body, David reconfigures his corporeal appearance in creative ways, thus communicating his sense of selfhood to his friends in Facebook. Digital technologies play a critical role in mediating this process, allowing him to capture his image (digital camera), modify it (computer software), publish it (Facebook platform) and distribute it (Facebook network). Facebook is thus an important place for digitally mediated performance of selfhood.

David performs his identity through text as well. In some cases, he uses text to modify his images, as exemplified by the profile photos described above; in other instances he relies on text alone. For instance, in the box below his profile photo David has written GOD IS GOOD, a statement he is "not ashamed for people to see because I believe." For David, religion forms an important part of his identity, and he sometimes posts citations from the Bible in his status update, or more general moral messages, thus communicating yet another dimension of his selfhood: "The words of his mouth were smoother than butter, but war was in his heart: his words were softer than oil, yet were they drawn swords. ~Psalms 55:21; confidence makes it all the way to the end." These postings exemplify how Facebook can function as a "moral encompassment," displaying "a sense not only of who we are but of who we ought to be" (Miller 2010, 15). In performing his cultural identities, David also makes his political views known, by simply stating "none" in this box in his profile, while he locates himself physically in "Bagamoyo, Tanzania" in the box for current city.

Facebook clearly offers a place where David can visually meet his friends, regardless of where they are physically located. This is also what David likes about Facebook: "how much we can share information, really easy and lots of people see it." Most of the time, his communication and interaction in Facebook are asynchronous, as he uses the status update, wall or message function rather than chat. David rarely has the time or ability to hang out in Facebook for any length of time. Instead, he logs in sporadically and stays online for a short period of time. This is quite different from youth in the United States, who often use Facebook to continue hanging out with their friends after school, thus incorporating social media into their "friendship practices in the context of their everyday peer groups" (boyd 2010, 80).

Since the only category for social relations in Facebook is *friend*, it offers analytical clues into cultural variations in friendship. Recent research on social media (boyd and Ellison 2007, Ito 2010) and virtual worlds (e.g. Boellstorff 2008) highlight the cultural significance of friendship, but the complexity of this social category has yet to be fully explored anthropologically.[16] For instance, Boellstorff (2008, 157) underlines that "friendships are the foundation of cybersociality," a social category he defines in terms of choice and egalitarianism. Similarly, in their extensive ethnography of digital media engagements among American youth, the researchers distinguish two main genres of participation, friendship driven and interest driven (Ito 2010, 15). The former refers to "shared practices that grow out of friendships in given local social worlds," the term "friend" denoting "a subset of the peer group that individual youths have close affiliations with" (ibid., 16), which is also how boyd (2010) approaches friendship in Facebook and other social media. My research can hopefully nuance our understanding of digitally mediated friendship.

One of the most salient features of my ethnographic material is the extent to which Facebook mediates translocal social relations, as exemplified by the social composition of David's network of friends. Friendship can be constituted through local, face-to-face interaction, but it can also take the form of long-distance social relations, mediated by virtual meeting places like Facebook. What I have noted among my research collaborators at TaSUBa is that their Facebook friends often correspond to their offline social relations, in the sense that the great majority of their friends are people they have met in real life. Nonetheless, they do not interact with most of these friends on a daily basis, since they are located elsewhere. This spatial distribution of Facebook friends demonstrates the anthropological view of culture as socially organized meaning, distributed as a network of perspectives (Hannerz 1992a). If anything, Facebook makes the social distribution of culture quite visible:

> When culture as a collective phenomenon is understood to belong primarily to social relationships and their networks and only derivatively and without logical necessity to particular territories, then we can see how it is nowadays organized in the varied connections between the local and the long-distance.
>
> (Ibid., 40)

The translocal distribution of social relations makes for interesting variations in language use. David usually updates his status in English, thus catering to all his friends, regardless of their location. Similarly, Nina who has over 370 friends in Facebook, mostly non-Tanzanians, tends to communicate in English. Julia on the other hand tends to write her status updates in Finnish, thus using Facebook to stay in touch with friends and family back home. Over time, Julia has acquired more Tanzanian friends, who communicate with her in Kiswahili, and recently she wrote a status update, starting in Finnish, but then switching to English, wondering if she should perhaps start using English instead so everyone could understand what she was writing. Sagatti, a very extroverted person with more than 800 friends in Facebook, tends to write his updates in English, but since he went to South Africa for a year to take a MA degree in theater, he has used more Kiswahili.

This code switching illustrates that it is not just the translocal distribution of social relations that determines language use, but also where people are geographically located in relation to their homes. When people are at home, Facebook can offer a means to stay in touch with friends located elsewhere, while it mediates relations with friends back home for people who are away. The translocality of social relations is thus related to both actual and imagined mobility.

Another salient feature of Facebook is the extent to which it mediates transtemporal social relations. Through Facebook David reconnects with friends from school, people he may no longer interact with, but who nonetheless form part of his life history, just like he can stay in touch with *mzungu* friends he met at TaSUBa, people he might never see again in person. The ways in which Facebook transcends time and space demonstrate the temporal and spatial fluidity of social relations in a world characterized by a greater degree of interconnectedness and mobility, even for those social actors who may be quite stationary, like David, but whose social relations span across the world and across different time periods.

Having thus teased out some of the spatial and temporal dimensions of social relations, let me now return to friendship. As exemplified by the composition of David's network, his Facebook friends span relatives, students at TaSUBa, friends he studied with before, and friends from abroad, to use his own social categories. From an anthropological perspective, one could recategorize these as kin, colleagues, and peers, but in Facebook there is only one category, that of friends. For David and my other research collaborators at TaSUBa, this is by no means a problem, because in a Tanzanian social context, friendship is a broad social type, one that can easily accommodate other social groupings. While some anthropologists approach friendship as a modern social construction, quintessential to Western ideas of autonomous, equal individuals (e.g. Boellstorff 2008, Carrier 1999, Kaplan 2007, Paine 1999), I prefer to look at other social contexts to arrive at a better understanding of friendship, since it illuminates fundamental aspects of identity and selfhood (Bell and Coleman 1999).

The Tanzanian self is constituted, activated, and realized through social relations. In Tanzania, you are who you are in relation to others.[17] This statement may come across as a universal truism, but it holds particular validity in an African context where the social whole is superior to its individual parts. Friendship has become more common in East Africa through the development of modern institutions and lifestyles, schools being a primary example, but it would be a mistake to reduce friendship to a distinction between localized kin and globalized friends (Aguilar 1999).

Since Tanzanian selfhood is relational, it is no surprise that young people at TaSUBa enjoy Facebook, showing the same kind of natural affinity observed among users in Trinidad (Miller 2011). The idea of being able to "connect and share with people in your life," to cite one of the Facebook slogans, makes complete sense for Tanzanians, as exemplified by David's internalization of this concept. A gentle-mannered young man, David tends to be rather quiet in social situations, but in Facebook he is not shy to express himself, a platform where he can explore and perform his cultural identities. Using Facebook to connect with social relations corresponds to his notions of modernity and global inclusion, both when it comes to the materiality of digital media and the sociality they mediate. It also connects with Tanzanian culture.

The fact that Facebook friends cut across social hierarchies and social groupings matters little in this social context where friendship is a matter of *pamoja* (togetherness). As in Brazil, where people increasingly refer to one another, even strangers in the street, as friends, the

Tanzanian notion of friendship is above all "an idiom of affinity and togetherness" (Barcellos Rezende 1999, 93). In Tanzania, the sense of social empathy and unity is present in all social interactions in everyday life, as exemplified by the frequency of the words *tukopamoja* (we are together) or *pole* (sorry), to express social bonds forged through cognitive as well as emotional understandings of social life, expressed through sentiments of sympathy.[18] This is also why total strangers can be referred to as *dada* (sister) or *kaka* (brother) as well as *rafiki* (friend). The term "*ndugu*" (comrade) that was popularized during *ujamaa* is also sometimes used.

The Tanzanian notion of friendship is evident in cultural exchange, Facebook being but the latest constellation of meeting places with cultural others. Throughout TaSUBa's history of cultural exchange, social relations of friendship have been forged between cultural selves and others, demonstrating that friendship exists at the individual as well as the collective level (Kaplan 2007). Thus it makes sense to reconceptualize the nation "not as an imagined community of strangers, but as a political community of friends" (ibid., 241). Friendship can also incorporate sentiments of solidarity with distant cultural others, Tanzanian cosmopolitanism adding but another layer of social relations to the moral order of *pamoja*.

Facebook-mediated friendships also incorporate the asymmetrical social relations of cultural exchange. While young people like David can use his position at TaSUBa to leverage cultural capital through Facebook, not least by having a Facebook profile that he can access almost daily, he is quite privileged. Most students do not have such frequent access, nor do they have Facebook pages. But even David is restricted in his use. Since he does not have a computer or camera of his own, he has to rely on digital media equipment at TaSUBa, while the development of his digital skills depends on the presence of *mzungu* collaborators. The Dutch students are well aware of these discrepancies, and try their best to accommodate them. Nonetheless, as much as David, Marlyn, Alexander and Laura are friends in Facebook, the real-life contexts in which they access this virtual meeting place vary tremendously.

When it comes to the digital drama of executive transformation, Facebook allows David to master the liminality of TaSUBa's online presence. David is the web master of the official TaSUBa website, but the site contains little information and is rarely updated. The main reason for this lack of content has to do with formal channels of approval, which have proven cumbersome ever since the college launched its first website in 2004. By contrast, Facebook straddles both professional and personal online spaces. So David uses his Facebook page to share personal information as well as more public announcements and photos of events taking place at TaSUBa. Since Facebook-mediated communication is targeted at networks rather than the general public, it is often a more efficient channel for online interaction than a website. This is why Facebook figured so prominently in the promotion of the *Tuwaenzi Wakongwe* commemorative event. Interestingly enough, since Facebook is not subject to TaSUBa's information management procedures (or the lack thereof), it gives individuals like David greater opportunity to communicate more freely with a vast network of interested groups and individuals. In this way, Facebook is also contributing to the individualization of social interaction, while reinforcing a sense of community. This cultural hybridity of individualism and collectivism is yet another example of the complex mix of cultural strands that people manage on an everyday basis in the state of creolization, a condition of permanent betweenness.

# 7
# ARTS FESTIVAL AND EXECUTIVE VISION

## Tamasha la Sanaa na Utamaduni

The auditorium is packed with people, visiting artists dressed in traditional costumes interspersed with Bagamoyo residents of all ages, women with babies wrapped in *khanga*, men wearing traditional Muslim caps, boys in t-shirts, girls in pretty dresses. The TaSUBa community is spread throughout the auditorium, students, alumni, tutors, and administrators, many dressed up for the festive occasion. A few *mzungu* sitting here and there, their white faces sticking out in the crowd of black people: volunteers, tourists, and artists. It is hot and stuffy, a pungent smell of perspiration emanating from hundreds of warm bodies, tightly squeezed together on the hard concrete steps of the auditorium. It is noisy, the murmur of people chatting and laughing blending with announcements by the Master of Ceremony, his voice carried by a sophisticated sound system. In the middle of the auditorium, some tables covered with bright cloth and a few rows of upholstered chairs, reserved for top management and high level guests. Above the VIP area,[1] the elaborate sound mixing board securely walled off with concrete and behind it the main entrance, where streams of people enter after buying their tickets, scuffling to find a spot to sit on. It is 13 October 2008 and the audience has

171

gathered for the opening of the 27th Tamasha la Sanaa na Utamaduni (Festival of Arts and Culture), and the inauguration of the new TaSUBa Theater.[2]

A torch is lit on stage, the flame flicking as artists and audiences pass on the torch[3] to the VIP section, where it is triumphantly raised by representatives from the Swedish Embassy, the Ministry of Information, Culture and Sports, and the Chief Executive of TaSUBa. Touched by the historical grandeur of the moment, I take some snapshots and video clips to document this ritual inauguration of the new TaSUBa Theater. I cannot help but smile at the audacity of the organizers, lighting a fire inside the theater to celebrate its reconstruction, an emblematic reminder of the fire that destroyed the old theater building. The symbolic value of the torch[4] is unmistakable, but I am unsure how to interpret it. A challenge of power, a daring act of lighting a fire in a building that donors insisted should be fireproof, thus a roof of aluminum rather than *makuti*? A nationalist stance, replicating the torch that is annually toured around the nation, a ritual initiated by Nyerere, as depicted in his statue outside the administration building? Or a submission to power, demonstrating to development partners and political figure heads that the fire that once ravaged the theater building has been tamed, controlled, and contained? That the crisis of governance has been resolved and the redressive action of executive transformation has brought harmonious reintegration, a ship of enterprise now securely anchored in the harbor of new managerialism, along the shores of millenial capitalism? If so, is this yet another carefully scripted frontstage performance concealing backstage schisms?

The Head of Swedish Development Cooperation delivers a congratulatory speech, his stage act illuminated by a bright spotlight. The speech is distributed through the website of the Embassy of Sweden in Dar es Salaam, in the spirit of transparency and accountability.[5] After diplomatically greeting everyone and recognizing the partnership with the government of Tanzania through its two ministries, Education and Vocational Training and Information, Culture and Sports, he recounts the history of Swedish support to the college. Starting in the 1980s with enhancement of the training program, construction of the theater building in the early 1990s, together with Norad, coupled with assistance to improve the college's operations in the mid-1990s. He remarks on the "2002 tragic event: the burning into ash of the prestigious theatre building" and how, without hesitation and upon request from BCA, Sida commissioned consultancy work that culminated in a Master Plan approved in a workshop in 2005, "which justified this project whose output, as we witness today, are the THEATRE and FLEXIBLE HALL!" He proceeds with explaining the value of the agreement, signed on 17 July 2006 between the government of Tanzania and the Swedish government, to SEK 14,600,000 or TSH 2.336 billion (approximately USD 1.8 million), out of which the government of Tanzania contributed TSH 800 million, the Norwegian Embassy TSH 160 million, and the Swedish Embassy TSH 1.376 billion. The audience applauds at the staggering numbers, incomprehensible amounts of Tanzanian shilling.

The speeches by dignitaries and the stunning torch parade are followed by an equally spectacular theater performance. The tall wooden doors of the reconstructed stage are opened, revealing a more elaborate setting than ever shown on this stage. A two-story house facade, complete with a functioning staircase and door, offers the backdrop of a living room furnished with a plush sofa set, a carpet, tables decorated with flowers, and a small, brightly lit aquarium. In this urban, middle-class setting, TaSUBa artists perform *KWENYE UKINGO WA THIM* (At the edge of Thim)[6] 🔊 written by Ebrahim Hussein. It is about the conflict between traditional and modern ways of life, represented by the Umma clan and the family of Dr Herbert Palla respectively.[7] In the interactive space between actors and audience, the magic of acting is performed, conjuring a possible world through the power of persuasion (Hastrup 1998, 42–43). Following Ebrahim Hussein's classic script, known to secondary school students throughout the country, traditional rituals win over modern cultural practices, collective rural values conquer urban individualism. At the end of the performance, credits written on a computer are projected against the wall, a sophisticated use of digital media that reminds me of the college's spectacular multimedia theater *Once Upon a Dotcom*, performed at the World Summit on the Information Society (WSIS) in Tunis in November

2005 (Uimonen 2009a). The cast line up on stage to receive the audience's approval, an impressive number of staff, many of them close to the Director, the Chief Executive of TaSUBa. The cultural performance reveals itself as a dramatization of status, traditional cultural forms conquered by modern executive power, thus reversing the very message of the play!

The festival carries on until Saturday 18 October, with a daily program of performances. Dance groups dressed in elaborate tribal costumes, bands playing traditional–modern fusion music, and acrobats performing reckless stunts take turn on the stage, along with drama performances, ranging from oral recitations to theater plays. The daytime audience rarely reaches more than a few hundred people, but at night the auditorium reaches its full capacity of 1,500 people. International performers are scheduled at night: NOTA productions with Norwegian and Tanzanian students[8] and a group from Okinawa[9] performing Japanese traditional dance and music. Local performers are also popular, especially the *taarab* prima donnas, who tend to be showered with tips of cash. Tickets are cheap, only TSH 500 for children and TSH 1,000 for adults, a whole day of performances for the price of a soda or two. Outside the theater, an exhibition area[10] with vendors selling their goods in small makeshift shops, mostly art work and handicrafts, a few serving food and refreshments. Some visiting artists pitch their tents on campus; others stay in local guesthouses. TaSUBa is alive with the spirit of *sanaa*.

The annual art festival is an important ritual at TaSUBa, a cultural spectacle through which the college performs its cosmopolitan identity. Membership in the global art world is embodied in the international cast that performs the opening ceremony, in stage acts by local and visiting artists, and the reputation the festival has built over the years as one of the most important cultural events in the region. Organizers, actors, and audience all take part in the artistic enactment of an imagined world of global interconnectedness and cultural diversity. The theater itself plays an important role in the performance of cosmopolitanism, a landmark in the regional art world, constructed and reconstructed with the help of international patrons of art. A modern place where artists from around the world can get together and perform their culturally diverse selves.

Reflecting its cosmopolitan ethos, the TaSUBa arts festival is a celebration of traditional culture,[11] reified and performed by groups of artists from different parts of the country. While this reification of traditional culture reflects TaSUBa's role and position in the management of national culture, it also resonates with the general public, who view these performances as the real thing. Like the Zanzibar International Film Festival (ZIFF),[12] also known as the Festival of the Dhow Countries, it is a staged performance of culture for local and domestic purposes as well as foreign guests (Kirkegaard 2001). And similar to the Second World Black and African Festival of Arts and Culture (FESTAC 77), TaSUBa's annual art festival is "a kind of commodity fetish writ large—whereby an exhibited 'people' became more real and authentic than the lands and peoples themselves" (Apter 2005, 88). The more exotic and "authentic" the performance and appearance of the artists at the TaSUBa festival, the more positively the audience responds. I have often been struck by the almost burlesque reification of tradition performed on stage, but the audience, primarily composed of Bagamoyo residents, seems to appreciate this exoticism. The most popular combination tends to be women in traditional costumes performing traditional dances with exaggerated erotic movements, to the excited cheers and lavish cash contributions of the male audience (cf. Edmondson 2007).[13] Thus, organizers, performers, and spectators all take part in the process of cultural commodification (Apter 2005). In so doing, they also engage in the "touristic ways of seeing" and the "culture industries of otherness" (Favero 2007).

This cultural spectacle is of course tied to power structures, which in the state of creolization are as multifaceted and complex as are the cultural identities of its citizens. We are not dealing with an oil-rich state like Nigeria seeking to transform the public sphere through the production of a national culture dictated from above and detached from its popular base (Apter 2005, 89), but a liminal state that tries to mix and balance contradictory ideological paradigms of *maendeleo*. Postcolonial sentiments still linger on in the public imaginary, inspiring the production and consumption of staged performances of traditionalism.[14] 🔟 Even TaSUBa's *mzungu* friends appreciate the idea of cultural authenticity, to the extent of giving the generous gift of millions of Tanzanian shillings for the reconstruction of a theater where cultural spectacles can be performed. It is of course no coincidence that it is Sweden and Norway that offer this gift, Tanzania's political history resembling the ideological underpinnings of the Nordic welfare states. So it is cultural exchange of solidarity, helping Tanzanian artists build a modern theater, complete with international-standard light and sound equipment, to perform traditional culture. But this act of solidarity cannot be separated from the dependencies of gift exchange, which is why we need to return to the words of advice that the Swedish representative expressed, for herein lie some of the contradictions of the digital drama of executive transformation.

> We, at Sida, are immensely pleased with the greatest achievement. However, we believe that these two physical facilities will not be seen as an end in themselves but as a means to an end. We already anticipate an enhanced learning environment, which is critical for quality learning. Of cause [sic], the situation of moving from learning in an open air theatre and a mango three [sic] down there is but one important step but requires leadership to ensue [sic] requisite facilities and programmes are in place for realization of intended objectives. This is particularly important considering that the BCA has been accredited to an Institute of Arts and Culture as a centre of cultural excellence in Eastern and Southern Africa.
>
> In addition, we expect management of Bagamoyo Institute of Arts and Culture will ensure that these facilities are run and managed in as sustainable manner as possible. To mention a few, management of the Institute ought to have [a] meticulous maintenance programme coupled with strategic and operational plans to ensure maximum utilization of these invaluable facilities. In this case the College will be able to contribute to [the] country's goal of enhancing economic growth and reducing income poverty.[15]

Quality learning, excellence, sustainability, economic growth, and poverty reduction, these are the ideals and values constituting the gift wrapping of the new theater, a generous package of audit culture, helping Tanzania nudge a little bit closer to the centers of the world. The gift is gracefully received, the cargo of millennial capitalism corresponding to local aspirations for membership in modern world society, the bright lights of the stage illuminating TaSUBa's imagined self, a step away from the global shadows, a step closer to the metropolitan centers of the global art world. So there is some progression, things are moving forward, but perhaps not the way it was expected. As discussed in Chapter 4, learning has not moved from the open-air theater or the mango trees to the modern stages and studios in the theater. Nor have the requisite facilities been put in place for an enhanced learning environment. Management has introduced a meticulous maintenance program, outsourced to a local security company. Strategic and operational plans to ensure maximum utilization of the facilities have also been implemented, with the help of NOTA, focusing on income generation and economic growth, as exemplified by the program of performances discussed below. So there is some change, but is this progress? And might something have been lost in the process?

"The building itself, it's just a building," Hussein concludes when filming the theater to complete our walk around campus. After telling me his life history, through recollections of people and activities embodied in different parts of the campus where he grew up and where he now works, we return to the ICT building where his office is. The tone of his voice changes as he talks about the here and now instead of the then and there, shifting from joyful memories of the past to a perturbing concern for the present.

Hussein knows that it takes much more than bricks and concrete to convert a building into a social space, as he has been struggling to build his own house over the last few years. Many of his relatives, friends, and colleagues were quite surprised when Hussein bought a plot in Kaole. Why would anyone want to live in this small Swahili community, so far from urban comforts? But Hussein is an artist, with a mind of his own. Over the last few years, he has struggled to build his house the way many Tanzanians do, adding bricks when he can afford it. He had to make an extra effort when his young wife Saphia and newborn baby girl Nyamizi moved in with him in 2009, a conjugal liaison that was celebrated with a lavish wedding reception at TaSUBa.

Introductions of the respective families thus joined together took several hours, while Hussein's lifelong engagement with the college was expanded to his marital life with the beautiful daughter of Mary Chibwana. Hussein looked quite out of place in his two-piece suit, but at one point he got up from his upholstered chair at the front of the well decorated flexible hall, spontaneously joining Maembe, Shabani, and others in their improvised dance.

Hussein directs the video camera[16]  to the new theater in front of us and recalls the old one, it really reflected the image of art, African art and culture. But this one, he notes, "it's difficult to think it's [an] arts place, it doesn't really reflect art. So the architectural thing, maybe it doesn't really matter, but maybe we have now to transform it from a building into a creative place and that would make a lot more sense. Because the building itself can be there, no matter how decorative it is, but if there is no art in there, then it won't make sense. Maybe now we are critical with the structure because we are not putting so much art in there and maybe especially students they don't have access to it as much as they want and maybe the facilities in there. So maybe that's why it looks like a building." Hussein keeps his focus on the theater and adds with emphasis, "So, what I think we need is facilities that can be used to make creations and then we feel this building is having big value because it has a lot of stuffs that we can use to create. But the building itself, it's just a building."

### Bagamoyo Kamambe Nights[17]

Vitali Maembe is on stage,[18] performing some of his songs in the traditional–modern genre that he has explored ever since he was a student at BCA. He is accompanied by his friend John Sagatti on bass guitar, along with some local musicians from Bagamoyo and Dar es Salaam. The band arrives in a rented *dala dala*, with some *ngoma* and guitars of their own, but most of the equipment is provided by TaSUBa, a drum kit, electric guitars, and microphones. The Master of Ceremony introduces the band in Kiswahili and English, to the mixed audience of *mzungu* and Tanzanian spectators, tourists, volunteers, and local residents, seated on plastic chairs in front of the outdoor stage at the back of the TaSUBa Theater. Traditional African food is served by the Bagamoyo Women's Group, a scrumptious buffet of local dishes sold at the reasonable price of TSH 5,000 (USD 3.50), along with refreshments of water, soft drinks, and beer. The senior tutors are dressed in beautifully tailored batik dresses, proudly accentuating their full figures.

Demonstrating his skills as a multi-talented artist, Maembe puts on an artistic show, sometimes taking off his acoustic guitar to move his tall, lean body more smoothly, as he combines singing with rhythmic dancing. Some members of the audience know his music quite well, having performed with him on previous occasions, and they dance in front of the stage, with synchronized movements. His songs *Afrika* and *Sumu ya Teja* are particularly popular; known from the *Masamva* CD discussed in Chapter 5, but over the years, Maembe has written more songs, some with a distinctly Swahili/Zanzibari flavor. TaSUBa can count this talented musician as one of its alumni, yet Maembe's career has been anything but straightforward. It took him seven years to complete the three-year diploma program, as the college failed him twice, even in subjects he felt he mastered quite well. In 2008, Maembe auditioned to go to Norway through TaSUBa's NOTA exchange program, but he failed to get a position. The following year he applied through an institute in Zanzibar instead, for a similar job, with similar requirements. He was selected and in February 2009 he went to Norway for a ten-month assignment through Fredskorpset, returning to Tanzania in December. During this period he got a holiday back home, which is why Maembe was able to perform at TaSUBa on this cool Saturday evening of 11 July 2009.

Maembe is one of the first artists to perform in the *Bagamoyo Summer Nights* program, later renamed Bagamoyo Kamambe Nights. This regular program of performances was initiated in 2009, with the help of Norwegian collaborators. The TaSUBa Theater management team consists of Mary Chibwana (Conference Manager) and Nkwabi Ng'hangasamala (Event Manager), housed in a shared office in the main theater building, and assisted by technical staff at the college. Initially the team was led by a Norwegian adviser who served as general manager.

The Bagamoyo Kamambe Nights program is aimed at presenting a variety of art performances, while generating income for TaSUBa, thus complementing earnings from the rental of theater facilities for conferences and social functions. In addition to performances by music bands and dance groups, Bagamoyo Kamambe Nights contains more commercial spectacles, like the Vodacom Miss Tanzania beauty pageant and the Star Light disco on Fridays, as well as cultural events like a free weekly African Film Program organized with ZIFF.

The ticket price reflects a socially stratified audience, TSH 5,000 (USD 3.50) for non-residents, TSH 2,000 for *wakubwa* (adults) and TSH 500 for *watoto* (children). This demarcation of resident and non-resident spectators is new at TaSUBa, which previously only charged different prices for adults and children. It reflects a more explicit focus on cultural tourism, reproducing the differentiated pricing structure employed by some actors in the tourist sector. For some people it also comes across as discrimination. At one point John Sagatti wrote "stop racism" on one of the promotional posters.

Mary suddenly jumps onto the stage,[19] swinging the promotional *Bagamoyo Summer Nights* t-shirt, while rhythmically dancing to Maembe's music. After a while she grabs a microphone, and the band switches to soft jamming after she instructs them "*pole, pole*" (softly/slowly). Mary starts pitching the *Bagamoyo Summer Nights* program and the t-shirt that is for sale, in Kiswahili. She then switches to English: "In your country you are always speaking German, sometimes you are speaking Norwegian, you are speaking Swedish. So, here we speak Kiswahili." She continues by encouraging the *wazungu* standing in front of the stage to "please learn Kiswahili" so they can meet and speak with people "who can't speak good English," "so that you can understand." Mary stays on for a few minutes, promoting TaSUBa and the program, while rhythmically dancing, before returning the microphone to Maembe, who effortlessly resumes his performance.

The Bagamoyo Kamambe Nights program is emblematic of TaSUBa's aesthetic transformation, recasting the theater facilities as a stage for touristic spectacles. No other activity has had such a profound effect on the social aesthetic design of the college, reconfiguring its material and social environment according to the dictates of TaSUBa's new business orientation. And no other program has so manifestly championed the logic of new managerialism and its code words of excellence and performance, geared at the commercial market. Artistic performances are elevated to the level of cultural excellence, through marketing lingo that repackages Vitali Maembe as a musician "famous all the way to Scandinavia!" We find an intensified commodification of culture, brokered by external social actors, a process whereby cultural performances are repackaged as objects for the tourist gaze.

Digital media play an important role in this transformation, the use of which also clarifies some of the contradictions involved. The program has a website of its own, set up through the free host weebly.com, thus the address http://tasubatheatre.weebly.com. Not only is this a completely different address from the official TaSUBa website http://www.tasuba.ac.tz, but the Bagamoyo Kamambe Nights site does not even have a link to the institute's own site. Rather than pointing to its institutional home, the site usurps TaSUBa's institutional identity, as visually expressed in an image on the home page that reproduces the official TaSUBa logo, with the added word Theatre, thus forming a logo for TaSUBa Theater. The design of the Bagamoyo Kamambe Nights website is reproduced in all kinds of digitally designed promotional material,[20] ▶ a large poster mounted at the campus entrance (see Chapter 1), another large poster at the town entrance, flyers distributed around Bagamoyo, and even a postcard, distributed for free.

It is noteworthy that this program is carried out *beside* rather than *within* TaSUBa, as shown by its website, at the same time that it is so firmly anchored in the very *center* of TaSUBa, illustrating yet another variation of the multifaceted condition of liminality.[21] ▶ In fundamental ways, the Bagamoyo Kamambe Nights program is in a state of betwixt and between, neither here nor there. It is not a state-run campaign, targeted at the local population, nor is it an artistic production, geared towards a local audience of art consumers. Rather it is a state-operated initiative targeting the commercial market of touristic cultural spectacle. Similarly to the coexistence of TaSUBa's two online identities (Chapter 3), the Bagamoyo Kamambe Nights program straddles the state apparatus and the world of commerce.

The cultural hybridity of liminality makes for interesting language shifts. Mary's encouragement to spectators to learn Kiswahili exemplifies the pride Tanzanians have in their national language, a welcoming gesture to *mzungu* to interact with local people through their own cultural medium. As exemplified by the Master of Ceremony, announcements of the program are performed bilingually, thus catering to two worlds at the same time, that of cultural others and that of cultural locals. But the website departs from this bilingualism in telling ways. Unlike the official TaSUBa website, all the text on the theater site is in English. While detaching the TaSUBa Theater from its cultural roots, the site reconfigures traditional culture in the form of visual images of exotic artists, thus intensifying the touristification of culture.

Since the promotion of Bagamoyo Kamambe Nights is the only promotional campaign for TaSUBa, it has come to dominate the institute's public image, thus redefining the very identity of TaSUBa. The touristic image may or may not correspond to how different social actors imagine TaSUBa, nor does it necessarily give an accurate portrayal of the institute, but since the program has access to such sophisticated marketing tools sponsored by the NOTA project, it plays an influential role in frontstage impression management. Through "the act of seeing" and driven by "the logic of spectacle, enjoyment and entertainment," the program positions TaSUBa in the culture industries of otherness (Favero 2007, 52). The back stage is, however, less glossy, revealing some of the "cultural politics of (in)visibility" (ibid., 70).

By repackaging art as touristic spectacle, the program of performances renders the institute's core activities invisible. It does not seek to promote TaSUBa's own artistic talent, but relies heavily on external performers. Some of these artists, like Vitali Maembe, are alumni from the college, but many of them have no particular relations to TaSUBa. Meanwhile, no effort is made to organize performances by students, like the Friday Show the college used to run free of charge, thus giving students an opportunity to perform for an audience, while offering the local community a chance to consume arts, regardless of their financial ability to pay entrance fees. And since the main focus is on running a professional program of performances, with an eye to generating income, efforts to use art for educational purposes are left by the way-side, replaced with money-generating entertainment.

The hosting of the beauty pageant Vodacom Miss Tanzania,[22] run by one of Tanzania's largest mobile phone operators, offers a telling illustration of cultural digitization and commercialization. During the 2004 arts festival, the college set up a critical drama to address prob-lems of sexual exploitation of young women entering beauty pageants. By contrast, since 2009, TaSUBa has hosted Vodacom Miss Tanzania, thus renting out its art facilities to a cultural spectacle that is modeled after global trends, repackaging women as objects for modern con-sumption. As you may recall from Chapter 2, in explaining the mean-ing of *ujumi* (aesthetics), the beauty of a woman was used as an example, valued according to character and behavior as well as physical appearance. Beauty pageants, which are increasingly popular in Tanzania, espouse a different value system. Here a woman is above all judged by her physical appearance, which unlike the traditional ideal of a full figure is modeled according to the standards of the Western cul-tural other: slim, tall, and light skinned. It is a cultural model promoted by a transnational mobile phone company that uses the objectification of women to increase sales: commodification of culture for the sake of cultural commodification.[23]

By trying to attract audiences that can pay entrance fees, the pro-gram ignores the great majority of the local population who do not have the financial means to pay for cultural performances, rendering them invisible. In so doing, TaSUBa facilitates, even encourages, the touristification of culture. Performers and spectators who seek to emu-late Western cultural models, even to the point of celebrating Western aesthetic ideals that contradict the ideals of *ujumi*, are offered a space in the place for *sanaa*. So the "divides between places and cultures and between 'us' and 'them'" is actually "reproduced and incorporated," demonstrating how the industries of otherness actually "reproduce the power gaps of a globalizing world" (Favero 2007, 77).

In usurping power over the theater complex, the Bagamoyo Kamambe Nights program is redirecting the institute's capital invest-ments. The new theater and flexible hall are gradually transformed into modern venues for business and entertainment, rather than enhanced learning environments for art training and production. Since the theater is the heart of the social body of TaSUBa, the social and cultural ramifications of this transformation are exceedingly profound.

The program is able to play this role because of the contradictory aims of the executive transformation, which creates a space of ambivalence, a liminal space in which multiple paradigms are supposed to coexist.

Ironically, the economic gains of this capital reversal have yet to materialize, despite efforts to capitalize on urban popular culture. Six months into operation, the Bagamoyo Kamambe Nights program was running at a financial loss. Even the evening of *bongo flava*,[24] with well known artists like Ray C, Fid Q, and Joh Makini failed to generate a profit. Again, it was an attempt to encourage the consumption of Western cultural models, digitization of culture emulating the cultural switchboards of metropolitan centers. Local hip hop stars mimicking urban American rappers, a DJ with a computer instead of musicians on stage, and a young male audience[25] capturing the performance on their flashy mobile phones. Out of respect for the arts college, Ray C, who is well known for her revealing stage clothes and erotic dance moves, toned down her stage act. A senior female tutor commented that she should have been swinging her hips more, as that is what the audience expected, seemingly impervious to the *bongo* star's attempt to be culturally sensitive, in deference to the traditional cultural norms she associated with the college.

One can of course see this program as a long-term investment, the economic benefits of which will take some time to realize, but one should not lose sight of the cultural and symbolic losses incurred by the prioritization of commercial touristic spectacle over art training and production. Can the recasting of TaSUBa for the tourist gaze accommodate the institute's aim "to develop, preserve and promote Tanzanian arts and culture and impart knowledge of the same to existing and future generations from anywhere in the world" (TaSUBa 2007, 7)?

### Executive Vision and Digital Seduction

"Right, now this is the ICT building, a very, very important building here at TaSUBa," the Chief Executive comments as we are standing in front of the building. "This is a project that started in 2004, which in a way we can say it connected what used to be BCA into the world. Because before that we never had Internet facilities, we never had computers, and we never had any internal or local area network. Many, many thanks to Sida for their generosity in funding this particular project, which is now going on very well, but of course there are a number of challenges because after we had developed the new curriculum now it is a requirement for every student coming to TaSUBa to study ICT. So the number of students that we are getting is bigger than the space that we are having but we are in the process of finding ways of having a bigger space than this one." As we enter the Internet room, he adds: "Hopefully we will be able to get funding from some donors. Earlier on we had requested the Germans to assist us in building four classrooms, two of which were going to be ICT. Unfortunately, all their funds were allocated to other commitments. Now what we are thinking is to put forward an application to Tanzania Education Authority for funding."[26] The Chief Executive looks around the room, which is empty save for some Dutch students, "Yeh, so nice, very well put by our fine arts students, very, very interesting. OK."

We are walking around campus with video, and I have asked Bakari to start with the ICT building, after which he is free to choose what to film. He prefers that I hold the camera, while he directs our walk and what to record. After the ICT building, we walk to the "famous mango tree theater," a place where training and performances used to be done. Bakari recounts how a Swedish television team covered the annual festival in 1988, after which the Embassy of Sweden decided to fund the construction of an open-air theater, the small Mwembe theater.

Bakari directs me to film "the new theater building," explaining how "the first theater building that was built in 1990 burned down in 2002." He adds with theatrical emphasis: "It was a very, very big tragedy, not only for Bagamoyo College of Arts, but for the entire Bagamoyo community. Because almost all the community was here, looking very, very helplessly to the big fire. It was destroying our theater." "What caused the fire?" I ask, to which Bakari responds "It was still unknown, because it was thought it was an electric fault, but it was not said, it was not known. So we never know exactly what caused the fire." In the background I hear Matitu instructing students playing the *marimba* and the trees around us are filled with the gentle sound of birds singing. It is late afternoon and the campus is enveloped in tranquility.

After elaborating on the increased capacity of the new theater, which can seat 1,500 people, Bakari adds: "So with this new building, there are so many things that can be done here. All sorts of performances can be put here, but all other events like conferences, workshops, seminars, wedding receptions, training can also be done here. Now for the last couple of months we have been hosting a series of conferences and workshops here.

"We are very proud of this building because it is the only modern theater facility that we have in all of Tanzania, and probably in the whole of East Africa," he concludes with emphasis.

We proceed to the flexible hall, outside of which Bakari points to the remnants of the walls of the old theater, which has been kept as part of the college's history. These low walls often serve as seating areas during the discos, receptions, and performances that Bakari mentions. He directs my gaze to the flexible hall, "a very nice building" used for "conferences, receptions, and training, and students doing their exams." We pass the nearby resthouse, used for hosting visiting guests. He recollects a Swedish consultant who spent some time there, doing a study for Sida. This was in the 1980s and it opened up more support from Sida over time. The house is still kept as a resthouse, so as not to lose its history, he explains to me. We continue to the administration building and Bakari recalls how the offices used to be student dormitories. His narrative is muddled by the sound of a lawn mower, which a laborer starts up to attend to the lawns being sprayed by water sprinklers.

We return to the area between the campus entrance and the theater, where Bakari visualizes future developments. He points to the house of the college's founding principal, which will be demolished to make room for a new administration building. Opposite, near the current entrance, a gallery will be built, a shop where some of the college's products will be sold, thus framing a space he calls public interface. "So the public will be connected by these buildings, especially the theater," Bakari explains, noting that the entrance will be shifted, near to the new signpost, which is behind the mango trees where some students are now practicing on their trumpets. He then directs my camera to the current entrance, explaining that behind the post for the security guards, facing the road going to Kaole, they will construct another building, which they will hire "for someone to come and run a super-market." "So this place will be busy," he concludes, "these are the future plans that we are having."

He asks us "to go closer to that house that used to be the Principal's house," adding "as a comparison we will go and take some pictures of the new building where the Principal is living." We walk up to the simple house that Hussein and his father used to live in, which Hussein remembered in terms of privilege, now in a state of neglect. "So this is where the founding principal was living, let's go to see where the new principal is living." We walk down the slope towards the beachfront, passing an undeveloped area, "spaces for future developments," Bakari explains, referring to the Master Plan[27] and the plans for starting a Bachelor's degree, for which new buildings will be constructed. We pass through a large opening in a corrugated iron fence and approach the Principal's house, with its guest wing. It is a large, two-story construction, with spotless white walls, doors and frames of dark wood, and a solid roof, a design matching the new theater and flexible hall. The private residence is separated from the guest wing by a concrete staircase, with stylish wooden railings. The guest wing contains four rooms, two on each floor, for rental to guests coming for TaSUBa's functions, Bakari explains to me. He adds, with a note of pride, that the Principal's house contains three bedrooms, a master bedroom, a very big living room, a kitchen and an office. He makes sure to underline that "this is a project that was 100 percent financed by the government of the United Republic of Tanzania." It was built in the second phase of the Master Plan along with three hostels, after the first phase, which was the theater and flexible hall, he explains. Bakari's private vehicle, a four-wheel drive Suzuki, is parked at the entrance.

As we stand at the back of his house, Bakari outlines more future plans, this time concerning a space by the sea, where they will build a beach motel. This project "is purely for business," he emphasizes, and the motel will have a capacity of twelve self-contained rooms, along with facilities for preparing meals for guests. "It's a way of having some sources of income for the development of TaSUBa, because in the long run the Government is not going to support us 100 percent. We have to generate our own money." I direct the camera towards the tree tops to capture the rustle of the ocean breeze, before switching it off.

I am sharing this reflexive video narrative in some detail, because it captures the cultural perspective of TaSUBa's Chief Executive, one of the main protagonists in *Digital Drama*. After our walk, I go to Bagapoint to gather my thoughts over a cold soda. I am quite stunned by Bakari's insistence on filming both the old and the new Principal's house, his visions of all kinds of commercial activities, a supermarket, a gallery and even a motel, and his constant neglect of art training and production, as if these activities have been submerged in a pool of activities, "events" he calls them, primarily geared at generating income. Over the next few days, I share my bewilderment with some of my research interlocutors, who explain that Bakari just wants to show me the progress of TaSUBa. Progress? What kind of progress?

## Virtual Liminality in the Neoliberal Culture Complex

It takes an exceptionally creative performer to manage the overlapping paradigms of executive power in a state of creolization. On the one hand, an almost permanent condition of material and financial scarcity, on the other, internal and external pressures to conform to global trends and standards, dictated by the powerful centers of the world, improvised by the peripheries. It would be naive to neglect the structures of power, to think that Tanzanian state actors enjoy such a degree of agency that they can freely reconfigure the development models of their *mzungu* friends and partners. Yet it would be unduly cynical to think that Tanzanian state actors are mere pawns in the invisible hands of global market forces. Instead, they juggle a state of betweenness, being neither here nor there, while trying to maintain a foothold both here and there.

This is what liminality is all about, a state of belonging but yet not belonging, a state of being but yet not being, a state of never quite reaching, but always grasping, a state of constant becoming. It is a condition of pure hybridity.

The Internet mediates this condition of liminality to the point of unraveling its virtual characteristics. Remember Bakari's remark about the very, very important ICT building, embodying a project that "connected" the college "into the world." Of course the college was connected before the arrival of the Internet, as discussed throughout this book. But there is something to be said for the intensity of connectedness mediated by the Internet, a reconfiguration of time and space in terms of translocality and transtemporality. This temporal and spatial conflation is, however, virtual, not just in the sense of being digitally mediated, but above all because it fortifies a condition of being virtual, in the philosophical sense of an "almost" or "as if" state of being (Boellstorff 2008, 19, 249). Connectedness to the world does not necessarily entail being part of the world, it can also entail a partial state of being, a virtual, *as if* state of connectedness, an *almost* form of inclusion. This is yet another dimension of liminality, a state of virtual membership in the modern world, a state of partial inclusion in the global network society.

If in the past the college was meant to play a pivotal role in national culture production, to *revive, preserve, promote* and *develop* Tanzanian culture, as Masimbi summarized so succinctly (see Chapter 3), these days it engages in cultural production dictated by the market forces. While this redirection is aimed at generating income in the absence of government funding, it is not just a result of partial autonomy from the state, but a reflection of a state that is partially privatized as a result of its partial inclusion in the global capitalist economy. The executive transformation that is embodied in the new buildings reflects the animating forces of millennial capitalism, especially "its impulse to displace political sovereignty with the sovereignty of '*the* market'" (Comaroff and Comaroff 2000, 333, emphasis in original).

And this is why the ICT building is so very, very important, because it embodies access to and participation in the global market place, the world of .com.

Since we are dealing with a state of creolization, we should appreciate the virtual liminality of these visions of progress, as so clearly
expressed in Bakari's outline of future developments, the supermarket,
the gallery, and the beach motel. None of these buildings have been
constructed; they are no more than plans. Yet, in Bakari's imagined
world, they virtually exist, in a near future that is about to come. And
since his gaze is directed at the future, he can close his eyes to the
pressing needs of the present. A master of impression management,
well versed in the "paper accountability" of development cooperation
(Finnström 2007), Bakari focuses on the front stage rather than the
back stage (Goffman 1990 [1959]). The front stage is not just the
places visible to the public eye, but the places to be constructed in
the time ahead, in front of the now, places like the public interface and
the new entrance. Similarly, the back stage is not just the places of
under-resourced classrooms, underpaid staff and overcrowded student
dormitories, but places to be demolished, like the old principal's house,
or kept for memory, like the walls of the old theater, depending on how
the past, the time before now, is to be reconfigured according to present
and future needs. Whether we focus on the front stage or the back
stage, one thing that remains constant is the state of virtual liminality,
the present being a state of betwixt and between, neither here
nor there, at the same time being almost here and there, as if then
and now.

While frontstage impression management can gloss over social
conflicts in the state of creolization, it cannot bridge the backstage
schisms of the digital drama of executive transformation. Not only is
Bakari's gaze directed to the future, it is also directed to the outside
world. His connectedness with the centers of power translates into
alienation and disconnectedness from the social worlds of TaSUBa and
the surrounding Bagamoyo community, spaces in which the effects of
executive power are felt on a daily basis. The staff members are segmented, many of them demoralized, others trying hard to share the
spoils of institutional transformation. The students are critical of the
lack of modern facilities, not necessarily because they cannot fulfill
their visions of becoming artists serving their community, but because
they do not get enough value for their capital investment in modern

education. As for the vast majority of the Bagamoyo community, all those people who witnessed the tragic fire of the theater, they are now excluded from the campus, kept outside by corrugated iron fences, thorny bushes, and uniformed security guards. And since they do not possess much economic capital, they are no longer welcome at performances, except the annual arts festival, the occasional free performance, and the public interface of the future.

# 8

# CHAOS, CONFUSION, AND MORAL CRISIS

## Post-Nyerere Dependencies

"If Nyerere could come back from the dead, he would drop dead right away," Sagatti responds, and Nkwabi adds in a regretful tone: "He would be so sad, we haven't followed through with his vision." I have posed the question "What would Nyerere think if he saw what is happening in Tanzania now?" to stimulate some reflections, noting that Sagatti joined a group in Facebook a few weeks earlier: NYERERE UNSUNG HERO OF AFRICA WHO MADE MANDELA. We are seated on beige plastic chairs around three tables, arranged under a large tree that provides some respite from the hot afternoon sun. The flexible hall behind us is not in use, so we are left undisturbed. Having completed our lunch in customary silence, we all proceed with washing our hands, while some female staff members clear the plates away. The meal has been prepared by the TaSUBa Women's Group, a tasty buffet of rice, *ugali*, banana stew, fried chicken, fried fish, thick tomato sauce, and cassava leaves cooked in coconut milk, with a slice of water melon for desert. We drink the accompanying soda straight from the glass bottles, which are collected for recycling. I set up my video camera on a tripod at some distance from the table, as I explain the purpose of our group discussion on art and the role of art in society. This group of teachers is mainly composed of senior staff, with lifelong careers in art, their life trajectories intertwined with institutional developments of TaSUBa. Their collective experience is remarkable, and the discussions are rich and eloquent, animated with vivid gestures and artistic metaphors.

After a while, Kiswigu notes that the problems started even during Nyerere: it has to do with the "economy," which has been a fundamental problem for social development. The economy has never been strong and culture has not really been prioritized; it has been an "appendage" in the Government, as exemplified by the way culture has been shifted between different ministries (cf. Askew 2004). Now it is under the Ministry of Information, Culture and Sports, but the bulk of the budget goes to information, then sports, and lastly culture. Even the new Culture Policy, dating a few years back (the teachers are unsure of what year it was launched), is still minimal, "shallow" one of them calls it, while the role of district culture officers has been reduced to what they describe as "Master of Ceremony" (cf. Askew 2002). The teachers conclude that since the Government has not placed any emphasis on culture in national development, people do not see the value of their culture today. This is particularly evident among the rich, educated urban elite and the youth, who are taken in with modern, Western-inspired lifestyles rather than traditional culture and arts. For the young, who are easy to manipulate, cities like Dar, Mwanza, Arusha, and Mbeya are like Europe, and they dream of going to the USA. They know more about Michael Jackson, whom they try to copy from television, than about Tanzanian musicians (cf. Ekström 2010). Meanwhile the rich elite send their children to international schools and buy their food in supermarkets, wrapped in plastic, Sagatti notes wryly.

The nature and pace of change are quite perplexing to the state actors entrusted with the production and performance of national culture, as evidenced in how these tutors view current modernity as a "polluter," something that is "out of balance" and "out of control," taking place at a "high speed" that is impossible to catch up with. In their view, modernization has been going on since old times, but now it is abrupt, bringing "out of control change." They trace this socially and culturally disruptive force back to colonialism, the arrival of colonialists who started to change them and introduced their culture to Africa, not least religion: "The colonialists came with Christ, and stopped us from doing our dances, which they called satanic." Following independence, it was understood that culture had been "distorted" by the colonialists and there was a "movement back to tradition." This is why the National Troupes, the Faculty of Arts at UDSM and then BCA were set up, the tutors recollect. But then the speed changed to globalization, which they periodize in terms of the commercialization of the 1980s and the development of media in the 1990s, especially television. They see globalization as a "common universal reality" that is bringing in aspects they cannot control. They feel confused: the future is "unclear," the world is "chaotic." This very speedy globalization is perceived to be Janus-faced; they "help us" but they also "try to destroy or control us," just as capital represents their "best friend" as well as their "enemy."

In order to understand this sense of chaos and confusion, it is worth revisiting Tanzania's place in the world, in the global shadows of the neoliberal world order (Ferguson 2006). Fifty years of national independence has not reduced Tanzania's dependence on external forces; quite the opposite. One-third of Tanzania's national budget is still financed by donors, which means that external social actors dictate the terms of national development.[1] While each actor has its own perspective on development, greater coordination also means a greater degree of consensus. In the impression management of development discourse, this ideological homogenization is recast as yet another "moral badge": harmonization (Dahl 2007). By focusing on whether or not nations are pursuing the correct policies, donors perform the depoliticization of development, "masking the relations between rich and poor regions behind the false fronts of sovereignty and independence that have never existed" (Ferguson 2006, 65). Although ideologically concealed, this power imbalance is by all means material. In May 2010, donors cut funding pledges for Tanzania's annual budget "due to concerns about the slow pace of reforms in the country" (Reuters Dar es Salaam, 14 May 2010).[2] While local analysts pointed out that the economy would potentially suffer as a result, donors warned that "rising concern over the government's weak governance, economic policies and failure to stick to agreements could affect future aid disbursements" (ibid.). Meanwhile, conditions for future aid included a bill to parliament to facilitate joint projects between private business and government. So donors are pressuring the Tanzanian government to push forward with neoliberal public sector reforms, the ambivalent results of which I have shared throughout this monograph.

This is why Kiswigu is absolutely right in pointing to the problems of the economy, because it was the weakness of the national economy that put an end to the visions of self-reliance formulated in the Arusha Declaration. When Nyerere realized that his debt-ridden country was losing the battle against the International Monetary Fund (IMF), he stepped down from his presidency in 1985, leaving it to his successor Ali Hassan Mwinyi to come to an agreement with the international financial power house (Edmondson 2007, 33). The austere structural adjustment program that followed affected the very core of Tanzanian national culture production (see Chapter 3). Despite political efforts to implement the moral badges dictated by foreign donors, Tanzania's national economy has yet to succeed and the country continues to be trapped in cultural gift exchange of solidarity and dependence (Chapter 6).

It is this continued dependency on forces beyond their control that shapes the perspectives of TaSUBa tutors as they discuss the plight of art and culture in Tanzania and its disconnectedness from an increasingly stratified population. Positioned in the artistic field, an in-between position in the social structure of the state, they differentiate themselves from the rural population as well as the urban elite. The villages are retaining our culture, they note, but the cities are a different story. Educated people avoid traditional culture, thinking it is backward. Even political leaders are at fault, their gaze being directed elsewhere, looking at Europe instead of our culture, they lament. They tell me how Kikwete was criticized for organizing a traditional initiation ritual for his son; the elite felt it was not appropriate for someone in his position to engage in such backward traditions. Meanwhile, traditional rituals are being commercialized and what is supposed to be secret knowledge is now open, people even using microphones when organizing kitchen parties, rituals performed on open stages.[3]

"Perhaps these are the calamities they were talking about, when they said our secret rituals should remain secret," Kiswigu ponders, since "something is wrong with our country." And it is perhaps no wonder that she refers to the traditional ways of the elders, when trying to make sense of a confusing present, because somewhere along the way, it appears that Tanzania lost its cultural direction and leadership.

Sagatti knows all too well what crisis, chaos, and confusion means in everyday life. Having reached the age of 40, he is still struggling to secure a stable income, to support himself as well as his mother and two younger brothers, not to mention his two children with his ex-fiancée. Sagatti's late father was from Mwanza, his mother is from Musoma, and he has grown up in different parts of Tanzania: Mwanza, Arusha, Lindi, Mtwara, and Dar es Salaam. Sagatti is often dressed in jeans (in conscious defiance of TaSUBa's dress code) and oversized second-hand t-shirts, always with a cap on his big head, usually a baseball cap. Sometimes he wears a Muslim shirt, another expression of social life in a state of creolization—Sagatti is Christian, but in Facebook he describes his religioius view as "kristhizzlam." While his dressing style comes across as urban hip hop, Sagatti's behavior is firmly anchored in cultural traditions: he is respectful of elders and his selfless concern for the well-being of others is evident in his professional trajectory.

Sagatti returned to the college in early 2007, because of his "passion for teaching." He felt indebted to his country, which had educated him, so he wanted to "invest in my country, especially in art and culture." He also "wanted to give something back to the school, which I love, and Bagamoyo, which I love." Like the other young teachers Sixmund and Hussein, Sagatti got a part-time teacher contract, with a monthly salary of only TSH 200,000 (USD 150), minus TSH 19,000 deducted for government tax, leaving him TSH 181,000. This salary was well below what he should earn in government service, what with his BA degree and all, and certainly not enough to live on. But Sagatti struggled on. His technical skills were very much needed by the college, along with his academic merits, yet he found himself "in the middle of battle," caught between people fighting over resources and positions. Sagatti had many creative ideas for how to modernize the college while retaining its cultural essence and he often shared his views and opinions with his colleagues, an approach he realized was too "violent."

"They say they want to be a dynamic center of excellence," but I felt "like I was throwing a seed on a rock; it will never grow," Sagatti notes disappointedly. He is now struggling to complete his MA thesis in South Africa, not to earn greater personal wealth, but to improve his knowledge and understanding so he can serve his country better, especially future generations.

### Moral Crisis in a State of Creolization

Tanzanian statehood is above all a moral order, which is why the digital drama of executive transformation is not just about a crisis of governance but about a *moral crisis*. Turner (1996 [1957], 289) reminds us that the "consciousness of national unity" depends on "a common system of values and a common set of norms regulating behaviour," which is why "unity is a moral, rather than a political, unity." It would thus be inadequate to appraise Tanzanian statehood in terms of an imagined political community (Anderson 1991). The concept *imagined moral community* comes much closer to emic understandings of the nation, as mirrored in *sanaa*. It also comes closer to the "ethical core of Tanzanian and African traditional life" that was expressed in the *ujamaa* of early statehood (Havnevik 2010, 44). The Tanzanian sense of moral unity is in turn interlinked with Pan-Africanism and cosmopolitanism, the sense of belonging to an imagined moral community encompassing the whole continent of Africa as well as the world at large. It is only by making these transnational connections that we can appreciate the depths of Tanzania's moral dilemma.

The Tanzanian state has not always been in a state of moral crisis. Early forms of statehood built on a language of legitimation that drew on key popular moral themes (Ferguson 2006, 75). Central to this moral order was the notion that production, accumulation, exchange, and consumption are inseparable from *social relations*, as illustrated in the very concept of *ujamaa*, which means *familyhood*, thus building on

Tanzanian notions of selfhood, which by definition are relational (see Chapter 6). This sense of familyhood is replicated in the national anthem, which speaks of citizens in terms of children, *Tubariki watoto wa Tanzania* (Bless us, the children of Tanzania), within a moral universe that is ultimately in the hands of spiritual power, *Mungu ibariki Tanzania* (God bless Tanzania). In Nyerere's case, *ujamaa* or familyhood was not just empty political rhetoric, his "refusal to 'eat' his fellow man," his "conspicuous lack of a belly," and his "rejection of material luxury" (ibid., 74) setting him apart from African Big Men and belly politics (Bayart 2009). Succeeding Tanzanian presidents have not come close to the moral stature of the *mwalimu*. Their engagements with the neoliberal culture complex have led to continued dependency, growing inequalities, and a moral crisis that is articulated in terms of the most fundamental features of daily living, *eating*.

"Everyone is hungry and everyone wants to eat," a tutor explains to me, with theatrical gestures of grabbing and chewing. We are discussing possibilities of sponsorship for TaSUBa and I am told that whether staff members turn to mobile phone companies or NGOs, they have to pay a kickback. This is but one of many instances when people talk about how much eating is going on in Tanzania, a recurring topic in informal conversations throughout my fieldwork. It is well recognized that the culture of corruption has become pervasive in Tanzania. In this context of material scarcity, social inequality, and postcolonial struggles for political legitimacy, corruption can be viewed as "the simple manifestation of the 'politics of the belly' ... [a] rush for spoils in which all actors—rich and poor—participate in the world of networks," yet it should be noted that "not everybody 'eats' equally" (Bayart 2009, 235–236). Indeed, the higher up the food chain (pun intended), the bigger the belly. No surprise that interlocutors often explained corrupt behavior in terms of our culture, African leaders, and Tanzanian politics, demonstrating its embeddedness in social, economic, and power relations (cf. Heilman and Ndumbaro 2002).

The cultural meanings of hunger and eating offer powerful idioms for morality and modernity, articulating a cultural critique of contemporary society. Hunger is contextualized in relation to material scarcity: people have been deprived for so long, now they are hungry.

Those who get a chance to do so are eating; people satisfy their hunger for material wealth. The idioms of hunger and eating are thus related to notions of development, *maendeleo*, which is evaluated in material terms.

Even though interlocutors explain corruption as a cultural phenomenon, they are far from complacent about it. Like Nigeria, corruption has become a dominant discourse of complaint (Smith 2007, 11). Most commonly, eating is condemned in terms of selfishness, a lack of sharing that should be appreciated in terms of the relational nature of selfhood. When you sit down to eat, it is customary to invite everyone around you to share your meal: *karibu chakula* (welcome to food). Not offering to share your food is indicative of selfishness, which is antithetical to the normative ideals of *pamoja*, togetherness. In contrast with the ethos of capitalism, notions of hunger and eating thus serve as a moral critique of individualistic greed. As Sagatti puts it "To me a new culture is emerging in our community, a culture of 'greedy' people are becoming kleptomaniacs and they have no fear of GOD at all."

I wish to underline that the idioms of hunger and eating must be appraised in relation to broader social processes, especially the sociocultural forces of global capitalism. As in Ghana, the forms of desire that fuel corruption are shaped by the global trends of capitalism, consumerism, and neoliberal governance (Hasty 2005, 271). If anything, neoliberalism and corruption seem to go hand in hand, not just in postcolonial peripheries, but in the very centers of global capitalism (e.g. Comaroff and Comaroff 2006, Haller and Shore 2005). And far from being immune to corruption in their partner countries, Western donor agencies are very much part of the problem, whether directly or indirectly (e.g. Hancock 1989, Wrong 2009). For instance, in the much publicized scandal involving the purchase of an overpriced air traffic control system in 2001, well beyond the means and needs of Tanzania, the £28 million deal was pushed by none other than Tony Blair (Dowden 2010). So the potential for rent-seeking behaviour and perverse outcomes of Tanzania's first Executive Agency go well beyond the local power structures investigated by Caulfield (2002), reaching well into the political heartland of DFID, one of the central actors in the introduction of neoliberal public sector reform in Tanzania.

The moral critique of selfishness can be contrasted with the impression management of donor agencies. As much as transparency is touted as a moral badge, in many ways synonymous with good governance, it is quite remarkable that neoliberal governance has been accompanied by occult cosmologies, accusations of witchcraft being but one example of the proliferation of conspiracy theories (West and Sanders 2003). These cosmologies capture how "modernity is experienced by many people as a fragmented, contradictory, and disquieting process that produces untenable situations and unfulfilled desires" (ibid., 16). The idioms of hunger and eating should be understood in this wider social–political context, since they "mirror structural cleavages and tensions in society" which are "connected to transnational politics and economic structures" (Haller and Shore 2005, 14). So, it is not just the eating that is problematic, but the hunger from which it stems, a desire for material wealth that is intrinsic to the illusionary promises of millennial salvation.

It is these structural cleavages that underline the moral crisis of *Digital Drama*, a deep-seated crisis that remains unresolved. A crisis is a condition of instability and upheaval, but it is also a turning point. As Turner (1996 [1957], 161) notes, "the social drama is a process which reveals realignments of social relations at critical points of structural maturation or decay" and "a trial of strength between conflicting interests." The digital drama of executive transformation should be appreciated in terms of the restructuring of a moral order, the realignment of social relations constituting an imagined moral community. The crisis of governance that set off this drama constituted nothing less than a turning point in morality, while the trial of strength that was exposed in the phase of redressive action assured that the interests of powerful national and global actors were ascertained.

This moral crisis is not a matter of a failed state, but a state of creolization, cast in a condition of permanent liminality, forever caught between different cultural worlds, while trying to straddle all of them. It is a state that seeks to master the complexities of cultural hybridity, caught in a condition of continuous liminality, embodying a state of betweenness that never ends (Chernoff 1979, Stoller 2009). Although the state of creolization offers an exceptionally flexible form of statehood to deal with conflicting global trends, let there be no mistake of the stresses involved. Not even the masters of cultural ingenuity and improvisation are able to make sense of social life in a permanent state of crisis. In this age of creativity, these artists should enjoy the benefits and privileges of their talent, yet they continue to be strapped down by structural conditions beyond their control. Even when equipped with the tools of techne, TaSUBa artists have to struggle to convert cultural and symbolic capital into economic wealth, while their most immediate market is the cultural industry of otherness, commodification of culture for the sake of cultural commodification.

If art is a mirror of society, we should pay attention to these stories of chaos and confusion told by individuals who have devoted their lives to educating and entertaining a nation that once tried to break the yokes of colonialism by reviving and remodeling its traditional culture. A nation that made great sacrifices to liberate other African countries, from South Africa and Mozambique to Uganda, its values of nationalism always inseparable from the ideals of Pan-Africanism, even at the cost of its national economy. A country where it is well worth asking not just the tired old question "what went wrong" but the more probing "what went right" (Swantz and Tripp 1996). An African nation, free from tribal conflict, war and disaster, that continues to play a key role in peace keeping and peace negotiations throughout the continent. A postcolonial, postsocialist state that has never been heralded as a model, but has served as a laboratory for Development Incorporated, a place where development policy "stops and starts, lurches forward and then doubles back, kangaroo-hops in a particular direction one year and then veers off drunkenly in quite another the next" (Hancock 1989, 74). This experimentation in development is replicated in audit culture, the questionable validity of which I have discussed throughout this book. And when all else fails, strangle the funding and blame it on weak accountability and rising corruption (Reuters 14 May 2010), while avoiding that painful moral question of "transnational responsibility", or more explicitly: "My God, what have we done" (Ferguson 2006, 88).

For people like John Sagatti, who never tires of political discussions, Tanzania's plight is very much tied to the country's dependency on external powers, as posted to his friends in Facebook in June 2010 (emphasis added):

> Try to read how Conspiracy Theory applies and If possible check on CFR—Council on Foreign Relation, you will understand what is going on now in our country ... those are people are just merely political figures who dont have final decision for our destiny ... dependency syndrome ... poor governance ... + obeying orders from Illuminati institutions like WB, IMF, Paris Club ... *we are slaves of NWO—New World Order*!

Given the current lack of control, it is perhaps no wonder that Tanzanian artists, intellectuals, and even some politicians are turning to their past for guidance, as indicated by the recent revival of Nyerere and the Arusha Declaration. In 2009, at the tenth commemoration of Nyerere's death, the Arusha Declaration resurfaced in public and popular debates: "*Azimio la Arusha and miiko ya viongozi* (the leadership code) was on everyone's lips—from the lumpens of Dar es Salaam to the learned of the university," with media playing a pivotal role in these public debates: "On TV talk shows and in newspaper columns, ordinary people repeated tirelessly: Mwalimu gave us dignity; the Arusha Declaration cared for us, the oppressed and the disregarded" (Shivji 2009).[4] In the 2010 electoral campaign, the Arusha Declaration was invoked as a moral commentary on growing social inequalities and rising corruption.

It remains to be seen whether this renewed interest in the visions of the *mwalimu* will translate into a new moral order, guided by the ideals of Pan-Africanism, thus breathing new life into the cultural ethos of *pamoja*.

### Coda of *Digital Drama*

When honoring the legends at the *Tuwaenzi Wakongwe* commemorative event, Maembe pitches his latest album: *Chanjo* (vaccination).[5] Dressed in light blue jeans and a black long-sleeved shirt, his charismatic face framed by a short beard, his eyelids slightly lowered over his large eyes, Maembe stands barefoot on stage. *Chanjo* is now available, he informs the audience, with 14 sound tracks. The CD is displayed at the ticket counter of the TaSUBa Theater. The cover shows a photo of Maembe on stage, with the guitar in his hand, dressed in a light brown cotton shirt decorated with batik, one of the few nice shirts that he owns. Maembe produced *Chanjo* in conjunction with Tanzania's national election in 2010. He had to borrow money to make copies of the CD, which he is now selling by hand, or giving away for free to people who cannot afford to pay the low price of TSH 10,000 (USD 7.50). The purpose of *Chanjo* is vaccination against corruption.[6]

*Chanjo* offers a mirror of a society in crisis, the reasons for which are global in scope, the solutions for which can only be found from within, in the cultural roots of past visions for the future. Most of the songs are in Kiswahili, all of them are about Tanzania. In one of the songs, *Hotuba* (remarks), a speech delivered to the rhythmic accompaniment of his guitar, Maembe includes some words in English:

Good morning house!
I give you comradely salute, "salaam"
I am the one who built you and put you where you are
I hope you know about this
I haven't much time to spend here,
but I would like to tell you something!

Meetings come, meetings go
What shall I remember you for?
What have you done for the betterment of life?
Now and then I give you my good people
I also gave you power and I kept you in my home
What haven't you received from my house?

To whom much is given much is required!
You have given education and professionalism to your youth,
respect to the aged with experience,
but the moment they get into your sitting rooms they
become weak

I expected to see the power of youth on these red chairs,
wisdom of grey haired, magic of Beijing,
but my expectations were not met!

Whom should I blame for this?
Maybe the one who advised me to decorate you with these
luxuries!

"Paula, a few years from now you can write a different book about *sanaa* in Tanzania," Maembe tells me after reading the manuscript for *Digital Drama*, "some of us are working hard to change things here." God willing, you will manage to bring back the spirit of the nation and relight that candle of hope on Mount Kilimanjaro. The world needs *pamoja* more than ever before.

*Mungu ibariki Tanzania. Mungu ibariki Afrika. Mungu ibariki dunia.*

*Asanteni!*

# 9
# POSTSCRIPT

*Behind the Scenes*

### Digital, Visual, and Sensory Research Methods[1]

As I am lugging my heavy backpack to TaSUBa, I reflect on how heavy digital anthropology can be in practice. On my shoulders I am carrying a laptop, a charger, a digital camera, video camera, and voice recorder, a mobile phone, two notebooks and some pens, all stuffed into a backpack, along with a tripod in a separate shoulder bag. While the ergonomic bag protects my spine, halfway through fieldwork an old injury sets in, and I remain housebound for two weeks with an excruciatingly painful slipped disk. When I explain my absence upon my return to TaSUBa, staff do not question the connection I make between my back problems and spending too many hours in front of a computer, some of them having noticed similar problems when working long hours in their offices. In my case, the problem has only gotten worse over the years, but as my PhD supervisor Ulf Hannerz kindly pointed out when I traced the origin of the problem to the last stages of completing my dissertation a decade ago, surely it is worth it. And when it comes to exploring new ways of doing ethnography, it certainly is, for all that digital equipment I have been lugging around has opened new opportunities for anthropological knowledge production.

It is probably no coincidence that anthropologists interested in digital media are paying more attention to materiality, suggesting a sensory turn in studies of the virtual, venturing beyond analyses of technology as material culture. Anthropologists have questioned the analytical distinction between the virtual and the real since the beginning of digital anthropology (Boellstorff 2008, Miller and Slater 2000, Uimonen 2001), but a great deal of scholarly attention has been placed on the virtual dimensions of digital media, while underscoring the cultural nature of virtuality. Some scholars are now turning to more sensory aspects of mediated sociality, with a renewed emphasis on corporeal aspects of cultural digitization.[2] Perhaps this scholarly trend is not altogether surprising, seeing that digital technologies are becoming increasingly mobile, portable and ubiquitous, designed to merge with our everyday lives, rather than set us apart from our material existence. Meanwhile, technological advancements are serving the needs of a discipline that always prided itself in its empirical understanding of human complexity. If anything, the sensory orientation of digital anthropology that I explore in this book builds on a well established subdiscipline in anthropology that has advanced the theoretical and methodological appreciation of the senses more than any other branch within the discipline: visual anthropology.

Throughout my years of ethnographic engagement at TaSUBa, I have used digital recording techniques to capture everyday life on campus, as well as more ritual or spectacular events, such as auditions, classes, examinations, and performances. When I first visited BCA in October 2002, I had a camera in my hand, and throughout my engagements as an ICT consultant from 2004 to 2007, I used photo and video documentation to complement meetings and interviews. These images form an important data resource for this project, capturing social activities during the initial phases of Internet development. When I returned to carry out ethnographic fieldwork in 2009, I was equipped with a variety of digital gadgets. From the very beginning of fieldwork, I used these devices to document what was going on around me and to make people used to being recorded. Many Tanzanians dislike being photographed or filmed and thinking that photos taken by Europeans will be sold, many expect some payment for being captured on camera.

In my case, the camera was an important research tool and having included visual research methods in my introductory note posted at TaSUBa, staff and students accepted it as a form of research practice.

My own use[3] of digital recording techniques is not unlike the cultural practices of my research interlocutors,[4] who tend to record and document all kinds of events at TaSUBa. Over the last few years, the college has acquired some digital cameras and video cameras as well as a digital sound recorder, which are used to document auditions, examinations as well as performances. Most of the time, these recordings are merely stored for a while and eventually they tend to be recorded over. In collaboration with European institutes, most notably the NOTA and HKU projects discussed in this book, TaSUBa is making a more concerted effort in video documentary. Meanwhile, as people acquire smart phones, many also use their mobile phones for photography and video and it is increasingly common to see members of the audience record performances on their phones. Digital recording is thus becoming a more common feature in everyday cultural production at TaSUBa.

The use of digital media to capture audiovisual material points to the domain of visual anthropology. Whether defined as the anthropology of visual systems and visible cultural forms (Banks and Morphy 1997, 5) or visual communication (Ruby 2005, 159), visual anthropology encompasses the study of visible cultural forms as well as the use of visual media to describe and analyze culture (MacDougall 1997, 283). In other words, visual anthropology is concerned with both "the visual in the process of cultural and social reproduction" and "the recording of visual or visible phenomenon" (Banks and Morphy 1997, 14–17). Since the subject of my research is an arts institute, it is quite evident that visual research methods offer many advantages for data gathering on a variety of visual cultural forms, which can be recorded for subsequent analysis. If anything, my field site embodies Ruby's (2005, 165) rather theatrical view of culture as "manifesting itself in scripts with plots involving actors and actresses with lines, costumes, props and settings." The TaSUBa campus itself can be approached as a visual representational system that is part of wider cultural processes (Banks and Morphy 1997, 23).

Over the years, visual anthropology has evolved into a means with which to reunite sensory and cultural landscapes, a way of appraising social environments in experiential terms, as "social aesthetic fields" containing both natural and cultural elements (MacDougall 1999, 3–4). Like MacDougall's experience at the Doon school in India, since my first encounter with BCA, I have experienced the college with my senses, intuitively understanding it in terms of what he describes as a complex composed of a wide range of elements, "whose interrelations as a totality … are as important as their individual effects" (ibid., 5). These sensory elements range from the geographic location of the college and the designs and functions of its buildings to dress codes and information flows. Thus my audiovisual material contains sounds, images, and movements depicting the physical environment, material objects, social activities and events, as well as social interaction, recorded from different perspectives and at different times, to capture the "disposition of time, space, material objects, and social activities" (ibid., 6).

Digital anthropology lends itself quite readily to further exploration of insights gained from visual anthropology, not least to capture more sensory forms of data, thus leaning toward the anthropology of the senses. The idea that "if one can see culture, then researchers should be able to employ audio visual technologies to record it as data amenable to analysis and presentation" (Ruby 2005, 165) takes on even greater relevance when digital media and communication technologies are brought into the research process, allowing the researcher to capture not only what is *seen*, but also what is *heard*. Although it is still quite difficult to actually record the sense of taste and smell, the sense of touch is more or less explicit in the materiality of social life, while audiovisual techniques can be explored to capture the sense of balance or body movement and temperature that also form part of the repertoire of sensory perception.

Sensorial anthropology or anthropology of the senses has been around for several decades. The notion of social aesthetics reflects this scholarly tradition, focusing on the cultural patterning of sensory experience (MacDougall 1999). Similarly to MacDougall, I have not tried to investigate the sensory order of the people I have studied (cf. Geurts

2002, Stoller 1989). Instead, I have tried to incorporate the senses, especially my own, in the data gathering processes, thus using sensuous immersion as a complementary means of investigating everyday life at TaSUBa (Herzfeld 2007, Stoller 1989, 1997). I have mostly focused on visual and auditory senses, rather than for instance smell or taste (cf. Stoller 1989). This preference is largely related to the focus of my investigation on visual and auditory cultural forms, not least sound and music (Chernoff 1979, Feld 1990, Friedson 2009). I fully agree with Stoller's (1997) argument that sensuous and embodied ethnography can help anthropologists unravel the complexities of transnational spaces of various kinds. I also strive to incorporate the senses in my writing, thus aiming for a greater degree of melange in what is hopefully "tasteful ethnographic writing" (Stoller 1989).

In this chapter, I will share some reflections on different methods I have employed in this project, offline as well as online. My aim is to show a variety of ways in which digital media can be studied ethnographically in a specific cultural context, while exploring how digital media can assist in the research process. If the dual aims of visual anthropology are anything to go by, digital anthropology should be able to follow a similar path. To paraphrase MacDougall, *digital anthropology should be concerned with the study of digital cultural forms as well as the use of digital media to describe and analyze culture.*

Let me first note, however, some of the epistemological drawbacks, technological vulnerabilities, and cultural ambiguities of digital research methods. First, while digital video and photography offer great ways of recording ethnography, their usage introduces a layer of mediation in the sensory immersion characteristic of anthropological fieldwork. Watching a cultural performance through a camera lens is not the same thing as observing it directly, the gain of capturing data for later analysis also resulting in the loss of a sense of immediacy and presence. Second, digital equipment is not only heavy, but also susceptible to malfunctioning. During fieldwork, my digital voice recorder stopped working and the files I had uploaded to my computer turned out to be corrupt. Luckily I had taken detailed notes during the interviews I had recorded, while my mobile phone proved more reliable for voice recordings, so there is lasting value in combining high-tech research methods with low-tech ones. Third, in cultural contexts where digital media are in short supply, the use of high-tech research equipment tends to underline rather than bridge social differences. Digital gadgets stimulate fantasies of and desires for material goods that are associated with wealth and privilege, thus feeding into cultural patterns that we try to maintain a critical stance against. I do not think the solution is to avoid using digital equipment, but it begs us to be critically aware of our own role in reproducing relations of social and material inequality.

## Media, *Mzungu*, and Participant Observation

I ask the student sitting behind me to help plug in my power adapter, which he jerks into the wall socket. I switch on my laptop and plug in one of the network cables lying on the floor. While waiting for the computer to start I walk up to the door and turn up the fan, having felt mosquitoes biting me under the table. It is morning and most students are in class, but a few are in the computer room. I spend some time responding to email and searching some websites, while observing what is going on around me, noting how students are checking their Yahoo email accounts, or typing research reports. A few are watching music videos, some log into Facebook, others search in Google. I note that several students sit at each computer, and wonder if this is an expression of the collective forms of learning that the Dutch students have noticed. During a group discussion later on I ask about this habit of sharing the computers and while an older student says it is our culture, some younger ones say they do it because there are not enough computers; otherwise they would prefer to sit alone, especially when checking email or chatting.

After some hours, I shift to my desk in an office a few doors down. The office is used by Hussein Masimbi and Amani Taramo, who work with the NOTA documentation project, which aims to collect and document traditional dance and music from all parts of Tanzania. Their video tapes are neatly marked and stored in a cabinet, along with some books and equipment. They take turns on Hussein's laptop, entering detailed information from their videos into a database.

As they attentively watch the dances they have captured on the laptop screen, the sound of traditional music drifts through the room. Their data gathering is a form of ethnographic fieldwork, as they travel around to villages to capture traditional dance and music performances by local groups on video. The idea is to cover all ethnic groups in the country, to build a national archive of traditional dance and music. Since we share an office, the ways in which Hussein and Taramo use digital technology become a backdrop for my daily fieldwork activities, complemented with informal chats and in-depth interviews. The material is so rich that I decide to write about it elsewhere.

In the afternoon, I meander over to the main theater, to check what the animation and documentary teams are up to. Their multimedia room in the interior of the theater building is hot and stuffy, the state-of-the-art iMac cooled with an old rusty table fan. Assisted by students from HKU, David Estomihi works quietly, painting backgrounds and cutting out figures in paper. A student is editing his video on the iMac, using headphones so as not to disturb the animation team, who prefer working in silence. I take some photos and video clips, chat with David and the instructor for a while, before leaving the room.

The hallmark of ethnographic fieldwork, participant observation offers a wealth of ethnographic data, which can be used to provide the thick description anthropology is known for (Geertz 1973). The level and scope of participation and observation vary tremendously, depending on the nature of the study. In my case, participant observation has essentially meant following daily activities as an observer rather than as an active participant. If I had been set to examine learning in greater detail, I could have enrolled in some courses, or I could have offered to teach some classes to gain a deeper understanding of teaching. I could also have volunteered in a managerial position, or assisted with administrative tasks, although my previous consultancies at the college already gave me some valuable insight into these bureaucratic practices. I was keen to take some dance classes, to use my own body as a research instrument as other anthropologists of dance have done (Wulff 2001), but my back problems put an end to such ambitions. Since I was set on capturing as much as possible of the institutional setting in which digital media are embedded, I chose to roam around instead, to cover as many activities as possible, based on the topics I have been investigating.

In selecting what activities, events, and places to focus on, the materiality of digital technology has been a helpful marker. Early on I made a mental inventory of computers, who used them and for what purposes. This allowed me to focus on specific locations, such as the Internet room and the multimedia room described above. Since these locations are quite public, access was easy, while the spare desk in the documentation room meant that I even had an office space of my own in the ICT building. In addition to following everyday activities in these technology-equipped locations, I paid attention to the use of digital technology in other contexts.

The presence of *mzungu* has served as another means of delineating my field, informed by my interest in intercultural interaction. Here I have mainly focused on activities taking place within two projects, the NOTA project with Norway and the HKU multimedia project with Holland. In addition to reviewing documentation from each project, I have also participated in classes with Dutch and Norwegian teachers as well as the program of performances initiated by the Norwegian theater manager. Since the Dutch project has largely focused on multimedia, I have been more actively following this project, covering the activities of two batches of students, in the spring and autumn of 2009. Forming part of a longer period of cooperation, and with a broader focus on institution building, the Norwegian project has given me additional insights into institutional transformation. Having interacted with NOTA project staff in my previous capacity as ICT consultant, I also have a longer history of ethnographic material to build upon. Since the NOTA and HKU projects are mainly carried out in English they have provided further insights into the linguistic and cultural aspects of intercultural interaction, while facilitating my own data gathering.

In order to appreciate the institutional context of TaSUBa, I have also carried out participant observation in settings where digital media and intercultural interaction were not at the center of my attention. Administrative offices were not so suitable for participant observation, staff being quite busy, while my access to management offices was limited to meetings on specific topics. Even so, I made a daily habit out of passing by the administration building, greeting the staff, checking the notice board and chatting for a while in the teachers' office. Sometimes I chatted with tutors under the shady trees nearby, or at adjacent cafeterias after office hours. I also sat in on classes, exams and auditions, and the occasional staff or project meeting. Whenever there was an event at the TaSUBa Theater, be it a music performance, beauty competition, or dance evening, I was present and a few times I also went to the Friday night disco. Whether of direct or indirect relevance to my inquiry, I have participated in these activities to get a deeper understanding of everyday life at TaSUBa.

The ways in which I have delineated my research field and carried out participant observation build on the rather traditional approach advocated by Miller and Slater (2000). They argue that "an ethnographic approach to the Internet is one that sees it as embedded in a specific place, which it also transforms" (ibid., 21). In order to capture the dynamics of Internet use, they advocate a variety of ethnographic methods, "based on a long-term and multifaceted engagement with a social setting" (ibid.). In my case, TaSUBa has offered such a place in which to contextualize the Internet within a specific social setting, which in turn is embedded in broader social and cultural patterns and processes. And it is in order to understand these layers of embeddedness and interconnectedness that I have carried out participant observation in the manner described above. Nonetheless, in order to appraise the translocal and transnational aspects of Internet development and use, not to mention the spatial and temporal dimensions of this social setting, I have combined participant observation with digital, visual, and sensory research methods, as well as interviews and document reviews.

My decision to carry out this rather traditional form of fieldwork differs from my earlier Internet ethnography. In my PhD research, I carried out "multi-sited fieldwork" among Internet pioneers in different countries, relying more on interviews and online communication than participant observation (Hannerz 2003, Marcus 1995, Uimonen 2001). Similar to Kelty's research on free software, my ethnographic object was the Internet itself and my research was aimed at studying distributed phenomena through a variety of online and offline methods (Kelty 2008, 19–20). At TaSUBa, I have made a point of staying put in one place, spending more time in the field, and gathering more varied forms of data. Being the only person at TaSUBa with a PhD and a Swedish national, I have enjoyed a more privileged social position vis-à-vis my informants than in my earlier research. In both projects, I have used the Internet for data gathering. With the Internet pioneers, I followed mailing lists by and for Internet professionals as well as websites of individuals and organizations, and I used email to initiate and maintain contacts with informants. Like Kelty, I benefitted from the self-documenting history of Internet developers (2008, 21). In my TaSUBa research, the Internet has not played an equally dominant role, which in itself is indicative of global variations in access and use. The TaSUBa website is not updated very often and email communication tends to be sporadic.

If I compare these two types of ethnographic fieldwork, the strengths and weaknesses of each become quite apparent, while their cross-fertilization is worth recognizing. My TaSUBa material has more ethnographic depth than my earlier work, but it does not provide the comparative perspective that I gained from moving between different field sites. It was by virtue of detecting common patterns in the visions and activities of Internet pioneers in such different places as San Jose in California, Geneva in Switzerland, Vientiane in Laos, and Kuala Lumpur in Malaysia that I felt empirically justified to draw conclusions about the very social and cultural essence of the Internet. On the other hand, since my engagements at TaSUBa cover an extended period of time, I have a better grasp of the dynamics of social change that I only glimpsed in the stories of the Internet pioneers. Even so, I would perhaps not have been as acutely aware of specific forms of social transformation at TaSUBa had I not come across similar trends among Internet pioneers in other social settings. And it is undoubtedly because of my earlier experiences of doing macro-anthropology that I have chosen to focus on digital media in relation to the broader processes of globalization and modernization at TaSUBa, this time from the perspectives of artists and art students in a more local and bounded social setting.

## Reflexive Video Narratives

"I really thought I should start in this room, because this is my office,"[5] Hussein narrates as he switches on the video camera. He films the interior of his office, while recounting that it used to be shared by three people, but one has left, so now they are two. He opens the doors of the wooden cupboard where he stores video tapes and books, while explaining his work with the TaSUBa dance and music archive. "I am actually really proud of this room," he notes, clarifying "maybe not the room itself, but what we have here … it's a lot of materials. If we get the opportunity to use them well, it will be a lot of resources." After filming some of his "visual material for teaching," Hussein underlines the importance of having a "place" where he can also tutor students. He films his desk, zooming in on the cable attached to his laptop: "another good thing also it is connected to the Internet, as you can see the Internet cable there." He proceeds with telling a story of how he actually managed to apply for a job by being able to submit his application on time through the Internet. After filming his office, we proceed to the Mwembe theater behind the ICT building, then the simple house where Hussein grew up, narrated with fond memories of the privilege of living in an artistic environment, the music room where he first learned to play the drum kit, the beach that inspires many students and where people come to have fun, the classrooms he studied in and where he now teaches, and the administrative block that used to host boys' dormitories. Holding my digital video camera, Hussein has been free to decide what to film and narrate, as we walk around campus to capture buildings and places that he finds important.

As exemplified by Hussein's video,[6] in this project I have explored what could be described as *reflexive video narratives*, produced by informants as we have walked through the TaSUBa campus and its surroundings with a video camera. This method combines walking with video (Pink 2007) with more participatory forms of media collaboration (Banks 2001). Pink used walking with video to capture the sensorial elements of place-making, filming her ten-minute walks with informants through a community garden site. The "walk around the garden was an exercise in experiencing and imagining," providing insights into the "sensory embodied experiences of the garden" for her research on the slow city movement (Pink 2007, 240). I have used walking with video in a more participatory manner, to create collaborative visual products, my role being that of a mediator or facilitator rather than film director (Banks 2001, 122–124).

In short, I have asked research participants to walk with me through campus and film what they consider to be important or interesting aspects of their surroundings for their everyday life at TaSUBa. Apart from my initial guidelines, I have mostly stayed quiet, observing the filming and listening to the accompanying narration. The production of reflexive video narratives has been a lot of fun, for all of us involved. Research participants have been inspired by the opportunity to reflect on their surroundings, not to mention the sense of empowerment stemming from mastering a video camera and directing a research process, while I have enjoyed the wealth of data thus gathered, research insights unfolding with every step taken and each video narrative produced.

Putting the video camera in the hands of informants to produce reflexive video narratives has added significant theoretical and methodological insights. For one, as Hussein interlaced the filming of buildings and places with recollections of his childhood, upbringing, and student life, he produced his life history in the form of a video narrative. If I had interviewed him instead, as I had originally planned, I would not have gotten the embodied history Hussein captured on film, since his narrative would have been more textual than audiovisual, delivered through static words rather than moving images. The recording process itself stimulated his memory, while capturing his recollections in real time. Second, the insistence of research participants to film outside campus[7] added a new dimension to the spatial distribution of campus life. After walking around campus, students expressed their desire to film in town and I gave them the camera so they could film whatever they wanted. When I later watched their video clips, I noted with great interest that they had walked to the bus station to film local buses, the road leading to Dar es Salaam, the post office and a church that they had passed on the way, places of great social significance to their student lives, as explained through their narratives.

As they stopped for dinner at the college canteen, they also filmed each other eating with their hands, before returning the camera. These video narratives broadened my appraisal of TaSUBa as a social aesthetic field, adding sensory and spatial dimensions that I had not gleaned from interviews, observations, or informal conversations. Third, the production of reflexive video narratives was circumscribed by sensory elements. It was simply too hot to walk around during the day, so we produced the videos in the morning or late afternoon. On one occasion, we had to interrupt the filming and seek cover from the abrupt torrential rainfall characteristic of the short rain season.

Sensory expressions are tied to cultural understandings of selfhood and society, which is why reflexive video narratives offer a wealth of information on the material, spatial, and temporal dimensions of social life. Everyday life takes place in physical environments, the particularities of which shape social life in the most intrinsic ways, even though much of it is taken for granted, something we simply adjust to without giving all that much thought to it. Yet it is through our corporeal existence in material environments that we experience the world, along with memories of past experiences. By activating social agency, especially reflexivity, a video camera can help visualize and record social data embodied in the physical, material environment. In this respect, the video camera becomes an actor or mediator (Latour 2005). The camera performs through the logic of filmmaking, recording a single perspective at a time, so the filmmaker must "proceed analytically, constructing a new reality out of fragments" (MacDougall 2006, 34). In this case, the fragments constitute memories and reflections triggered by the physical environment.

Reflexive video narratives are produced with an audience in mind, adding yet another dimension to digital mediations, capturing their interactive performativity (Schieffelin 1998). Performativity has an expressive dimension, it "reveals something (and accomplishes something) about the actor and the situation," since it "is 'read' by other participants" (ibid., 197). Similarly, "through the performance of narratives, we continue to write and rewrite the story of our selves" (Rapport 1998, 180). The tutors and students were familiar with my research project and their narratives were influenced by my presence.

So my being there certainly influenced the process; I was an audience and a participant. But my research collaborators also had other audiences in mind. As indicated by their use of English I was but one of the *mzungu* they were addressing. In my walk with the Chief Executive of TaSUBa (Chapter 7), it was clear that the video served as a carefully staged narrative for an audience of donors and other influential external partners. When I walked around with Nina[8] (Chapter 3), she made sure to introduce herself in front of the camera, posing by the fine art building, pointing to its painted image of Kilimanjaro, explaining it is the place she comes from and what it means to be a Chagga. For her, the audience was even broader, an unknown international crowd she was welcoming to her home country, the imagined presence of which influenced her narrative performance and with it the construction of her cultural identity.

## Sensory Expressions of Institutional Transformation

The sound is so unusual that I immediately grab my camera to capture it, while my nostrils fill with the smell of freshly cut grass, a smell so familiar and yet so out of place. Some staff members are hanging around watching the lawn mower[9] in action and they probably wonder why on earth I am filming the laborer as he carefully cuts a patch of grass. To me, the lawn mower adds yet another angle to institutional transformations, complementing the uniformed workers manually cutting the grass around the ICT building. There is nothing peculiar about these activities; they are just mundane efforts to maintain the campus grounds. But the sounds, sights, and smells alert me to activities that embody a social process of some significance, namely the replacement of student labor with a commercial company charged with the maintenance of the physical environment of TaSUBa. It is but one aspect of the changes taking place in the transformation to an executive agency, capturing highly significant aesthetic transformations (Chapter 4).

As we are walking around campus with video, several interlocutors remark on the lushness of the grass in front of the administration building. I have noted how often the sprinklers are turned on, spraying water across the neatly lined lawns to maintain their greenness. Yet another sign of the modernization process that the institutional transformation forms part of, in this case the use of modern technology to maintain a garden, which in itself is a rather modern construct, since the garden serves no practical function other than its aesthetic appeal. During water shortages, I have wryly noted that the sprinklers are still running, and I am not sure if it is advisable to water grass in the hot, blazing midday sun. But there are power dimensions to this seemingly innocuous labor of gardening that need to be recognized, a visual manifestation of which is the framed Master Plan posted amidst the greenery, expressing the visions of modernity espoused by management and development partners (Chapters 3 and 7).

My interest in air-conditioning (A/C) units[10] ▓ is not altogether unrelated to the fact that I suffer from the heat during much of my fieldwork. I am not alone in this sense of discomfort; most of my research interlocutors also complain about the heat during the hottest periods of the year. Students who originate from cooler parts of the country find it difficult to cope with the coastal climate and their level of activity decreases as the temperature rises. Although many of them have lived in Bagamoyo for years, teachers also find the heat quite unbearable. Fatigue, listlessness, and headache or nausea are common bodily reactions to the heat, as temperatures soar to around 40° Celsius, not that any of us are measuring it. It is just hot, sometimes unbearably so. But some people enjoy the chilled environment of air-conditioned space, and since A/C is so exclusive, so highly restricted to the spaces of a privileged few, it offers a good entry point for an analysis of power structures, a tactile rendering of social hierarchies and power relations[11] ▓ (Chapter 3).

This sensory orientation reflects a field site that is multisensory in several respects, from the materiality of its physical location to audio-visual and tactile forms of artistic production. If anything, I would argue that it is only by paying attention to the sensory manifestations of cultural production that I have been able to comprehend the complexities of institutional transformation. None of my informants have mentioned, let alone discussed, the lawn mower or water sprinklers and while they have commented on the company hired to maintain the campus and conveyed how A/C is talked about in reference to TaSUBa management, my decision to focus on such sensory details stems from my use of the analytical concept of social aesthetics. In some cases, I have actively looked for visual, auditory, or tactile data, the framed Master Plan being one of the visual manifestations of social change that I have photographed on several occasions. In other instances, sensory details have opened my eyes and mind to transformations that I have been unaware of, a poignant example of which is the lawn mower, the sound of which alerted me to further data gathering on the arrangements for campus maintenance.

The weather is of overriding significance to everyday life at TaSUBa, the experience of which is multisensory, combining auditory, haptic, olfactory, and visual modalities (Ingold 2005, 97). At TaSUBa the weather is rather typical of the equatorial, tropical climate, with high temperatures and high levels of humidity year round. There are seasonal rains, the short rains in November/December and the long rains of April/May, although climate changes seem to have had an effect on these over the last few years, with less rain falling more irregularly. Even so, during the rainy season, torrential downpours tend to curb most outdoor activity, while bringing down temperatures. After the rains, the sun tends to feel even hotter, while the air gets even more dusty as the ground dries up, no doubt amplified by the use of charcoal for cooking, the burning of garbage, as well as people, cattle, and vehicles stirring up unpaved sandy roads. The heat also decreases somewhat during the cool season, from June to August, and although temperatures rarely drop below 20° Celsius, some people find the weather cold enough to wear sweaters and jackets at night.

The weather is also related to institutional transformations. As argued by Ingold (ibid., 102–103), the weather is a medium of perception, occupying a conceptual space between the materiality of nature and the agency of human beings, thus functioning as "the generative current of a world-in-formation." This world-in-formation mediated by the weather is subject to human agency, not least through efforts to alter climatic conditions, as exemplified by the introduction of A/C to create an artificially cooler climate or sprinklers to offset the lack of rainfall. These technologies are in turn related to notions of modernity, the replication of climatic conditions of the rich North in the poor South expressing cultural aspirations for social inclusion in world society. Far from expressing a natural given order of things, the weather is thus firmly embedded in culturally informed understandings of social life and an important aspect of social transformations aimed at institutionalizing different forms of modernity.

A closer look at the weather can also reveal the social distribution of culture, since this medium of perception means different things to different people, thus exemplifying global culture as a network of perspectives. Visiting *mzungu* collaborators tend to appreciate the tropical sun and heat, which provides a sense of being on an exotic holiday, a feeling amplified by the landscape of the beach. Meanwhile, in a proud display of their cosmopolitan familiarity with other climates, TaSUBa staff and students often engage in discussions about the weather with visiting *mzungu*. For instance, when I show up at TaSUBa, those who have been to Scandinavia often ask me how cold it was in Sweden when I left, while recalling their own experiences of coping with freezing climates. The weather can thus be seen as a multisensory medium of perception that also mediates intercultural interaction, not least by offering a frame of reference for shared experiences.

### Facebooking and Networking

When I am in Sweden, I log into Facebook almost every day, and when I am in Tanzania, a few times per week. I joined Facebook in February 2008, after a South African friend, Shafika Isaacs, joked about her new "pixellated identity." She was one of my first Facebook friends, along with some of my more Internet-savvy friends in Tanzania and Sweden and I should mention that Simbo Ntiro was the first person to write on my wall. Initially, I did not use Facebook all that much, but as more and more of my friends joined, I logged in more often. In 2009, I noted a rapid growth in activity, and realized that Facebook was more than a passing fad. In Sweden, the number of users reached 2 million, or a remarkable 16 percent of the population, and Facebook was frequently mentioned in popular media. Meanwhile, I was getting more and more

Facebook friends in Tanzania, students and younger staff at TaSUBa, and friends in Dar es Salaam I had known for years. Reflecting the gap in Internet access, the Tanzanian Facebook population remains quite marginal, especially when compared with countries like Sweden. Even so, Facebook has grown into a global phenomenon of social significance. As I revise this text (May 2011), Facebook has an estimated 500 million active users, which corresponds to 25 percent of the world's Internet users and almost 8 percent of the total world population.

Having observed TaSUBa students using Facebook in the Internet room, I made further inquiries into their user patterns during group discussions. These sessions were held in the computer room, organized with the help of the ICT instructor. To get a sufficient representation of students, I held discussions with one group from each year. Altogether I got feedback from 43 students out of the student population of 120, covering 17 first-year students, 11 second-year students and 15 third-year students. I circulated a form to each group, where they filled in personal details and I asked each group similar questions. I filmed the discussions, mainly to help me record the responses, the video camera hoisted on a tripod at the back of the room. The questions focused on what kind of equipment they had, applications they were using, frequency of use, and perceptions of the Internet.

The growing popularity of Facebook was evident in the user patterns I gathered, the number of users rising with each year of admission. While only 4 out of 15 students in the third year used Facebook (27 percent), the figure grew to 4 out of 11 in the second year (36 percent) and 8 out of 17 in the first year (47 percent). A few students also used Tagged, hi5, MySpace and Netlog. Most of the students who used Facebook started using it while at TaSUBa, following recommendations from fellow students. In some cases, this meant that their introduction to the Internet in general coincided with their introduction to Facebook, a rather rapid shift from digital exclusion to Facebooking. Among the first-year students, 7 had used the Internet before joining TaSUBa (42 percent), among the third-year students only 3 had previous experience (20 percent), and none of the second-year students had used the Internet before joining the college (0 percent). Although students were not familiar with the concepts of social networking sites or social media, they were intuitively using Facebook to stay in touch with friends in Tanzania and overseas and to make new friends (see Chapter 6).

Generally defined as a social networking site, Facebook is anthropologically interesting in many respects.[12] From a digital anthropology perspective, one could argue that Facebook embodies the social and cultural essence of the Internet, its "culture of networking" (Uimonen 2001). If anything, Facebook brings forth some of the most salient features of the Internet, the origins of which predate the emergence of what has become known as social media, thus shaping the web into a more interactive interface than its more broadcast-like original design.[13]

In this project, Facebook has constituted a virtual field site, a social meeting place that can be studied ethnographically, while offering certain linkages and interconnections typical of "translocal" field sites (Hannerz 2003). In practical terms, Facebook has allowed me to stay in touch with informants between onsite fieldwork periods, thus giving me a chance to maintain a form of virtual interaction. Through Facebook I have also been able to observe how informants express themselves through digital media, both through text and images. In this regard, Facebook has constituted a translocal field site offering analytical linkages, especially with regard to translocal and transnational interconnectedness.

Since I have been particularly interested in Facebook use in relation to intercultural networking, I have paid extra attention to what language informants have communicated in. I have noted a preference to communicate in mother tongues, be it Kiswahili, Norwegian, Finnish, or Dutch. While this language preference offers interesting analytical insights into matters related to intercultural interaction (see Chapter 6), it has also raised some methodological challenges. To circumvent my limited language skills, I have sometimes used Google's online translation service. Computer generated as they are, these translations are of course not altogether accurate, and the misspellings, acronyms, and play on words so common in online communication tend to get lost in translation. Nonetheless, they have given me at least some idea of what users have been communicating about.

The visual interface of Facebook has lent itself quite readily to visual research methods. In Facebook, networks are visually represented in individuals' user profiles, denoting the user's entire network through names and profile pictures. This visual interface is clearly suited to anthropological network analysis, offering a visible means with which to map the social connections of individual users and groups. In doing so, I have drawn on visual anthropology, which traces social relations and cultural practices through visual cultural forms, especially images and photographs (Banks 2001, Banks and Morphy 1997, Ruby 2005). In addition to paying attention to what profile photos my informants have posted on different occasions, I have also been able to browse the profile photos of their networks of friends, thus conceptualizing photographs as systems of visual representation, which in the case of Facebook quite literally "act as sites for human interaction as well as providing the means for understanding our environmental, political and social worlds" (Wright 2008, 5). I have also used photo-elicitation techniques in interviews with a few informants (Banks 2001), asking them to comment on their profile photos as well as other photos they have posted on Facebook.

Doing participant observation in Facebook resembles the role of a participant-experiencer in ethnographic research on online communities (Garcia et al. 2009, 58). In my case, observations of informants' activities have been interwoven with my own use of Facebook, their experiences of online social networking being quite similar to mine. To complement my participant observation in Facebook, I have used it as a basis for offline interviews, going through their Facebook profile pages with some informants. These interviews have allowed me to ask both general and specific questions about their motivations and experiences of using Facebook, adding more depth to my online material. Had I not met my research interlocutors outside Facebook, I am sure my results would have been somewhat different. But that is a different research project altogether.

Perhaps the most rewarding aspect of Facebook in this project has been my ability to break the social isolation of writing this book.

During all those hours in front of the computer, I never had to feel lonely. In countries like Sweden, Facebook is reinvigorating a sense of community. In countries like Tanzania, that sense of community was never lost, but nowawadays it is even more global. Through Facebook, these communities are increasingly interconnected.

To my Facebook friends:

*Asanteni! Thank you! Tack! Takk! Kiitos! Bedankt!*

# NOTES

## Chapter 1

1  http://innovativeethnographies.net/digitaldrama/tuwaenzi-wakonge
2  http://innovativeethnographies.net/digitaldrama/tuwaenzi-wakonge#1
3  http://www.tasuba.ac.tz/
4  http://innovativeethnographies.net/digitaldrama/tuwaenzi-wakonge#15
5  http://innovativeethnographies.net/digitaldrama/research-methods#10
6  http://innovativeethnographies.net/digitaldrama/tuwaenzi-wakonge
7  http://innovativeethnographies.net/digitaldrama/karibu-tasuba#12
8  http://innovativeethnographies.net/digitaldrama/tuwaenzi-wakonge#2
9  http://innovativeethnographies.net/digitaldrama/tuwaenzi-wakonge#4
10  http://innovativeethnographies.net/digitaldrama/tuwaenzi-wakonge#6
11  http://innovativeethnographies.net/digitaldrama/tuwaenzi-wakonge#8
12  http://innovativeethnographies.net/digitaldrama/tuwaenzi-wakonge#10
13  http://innovativeethnographies.net/digitaldrama/tuwaenzi-wakonge#9
14  http://innovativeethnographies.net/digitaldrama/tuwaenzi-wakonge#11
15  http://innovativeethnographies.net/digitaldrama/tuwaenzi-wakonge#14
16  http://innovativeethnographies.net/digitaldrama

## Chapter 2

1  http://innovativeethnographies.net/digitaldrama/karibu-tasuba
2  http://innovativeethnographies.net/digitaldrama/karibu-tasuba#3
3  http://innovativeethnographies.net/digitaldrama/karibu-tasuba#12
4  http://innovativeethnographies.net/digitaldrama/karibu-tasuba#2
5  http://innovativeethnographies.net/digitaldrama/karibu-tasuba#27
6  When the open source operating system Linux was localized into Kiswahili as Kilinux a few years ago, I was surprised that the project was completed in just a few months. This speedy translation was accomplished by allocating only one minute for each word to be translated by distinguished Kiswahili professors. Unfortunately, when I tried to encourage the ICT staff at *Chuo Cha Sanaa* to adopt the Jambo Open Office application of the Kilinux project, they complained that the Kiswahili was difficult to understand, indicating that the language experts were not altogether familiar with computer speak.
7  http://innovativeethnographies.net/digitaldrama/digital-anthropology

8   http://innovativeethnographies.net/digitaldrama/digital-anthropology#2

9   http://innovativeethnographies.net/digitaldrama/digital-anthropology#1

10  Before it was converted into an Internet room, the computer room was used for dance classes, while the smaller adjacent rooms were used for storage of drums and acrobatics equipment. During some festivals, the dance room was also used to exhibit fine arts objects.

11  In 2008, I started a graduate course in digital anthropology at the Department of Social Anthropology at Stockholm University, see www.socant.su.se. In 2009, the University College of London (UCL) launched an MSc program in digital anthropology; see http://www.ucl.ac.uk/anthropology/digital-anthropology/. Kansas State University has a digital ethnography working group led by Dr. Michael Wesch; see http://mediated-cultures.net/. Christopher Kelty teaches a variety of courses about the Internet at University of California, Los Angeles, see http://kelty.org/classes/. Tom Boellstorff teaches courses in virtual anthropology at the University of California, Irvine; see http://anthrocyber2.blogspot.com/.

    A workshop in digital anthropology was organized at the biennial conference of the European Association of Social Anthropologists, EASA 2010, in Maynooth, Ireland 24–27 August 2010. The first of its kind at EASA, the workshop was convened by Daniel Miller and Heather Horst; see http://www.nomadit.co.uk/easa/easa2010/panels.php5?PanelID=599. At EASA 1998, I was the only anthropologist presenting a paper about the Internet (Uimonen 1998). Digital anthropology has also been discussed in the Media-Anthro mailing list for EASA's Media Anthropology Network, http://www.media-anthropology.net/, and there is a digital anthropology group in the Open Anthropology Cooperative, http://openanthcoop.ning.com/.

12  Estimates for 2010, prepared by the International Telecommunication Union (ITU). Out of the 2.0 billion Internet users, 1.2 billion are in developing countries. For mobile telephony, out of the total of 5.3 billion, the number in developing countries is estimated to be 73 percent, or 3.8 billion.

13  http://twobits.net/

14  http://www.youtube.com/watch?v=6gmP4nk0EOE&feature=channel

15  http://www.youtube.com/watch?v=TPAO-1Z4_hU&feature=channel

16  The broker is similar to Latour's (2005) "mediator," while Castells (2004) uses the more technical term "switcher."

17  http://innovativeethnographies.net/digitaldrama/digital-anthropology#22

18  Statistics by the International Telecommunication Union (ITU), http://www.itu.int/ITU-D/icteye/Indicators/Indicators.aspx#.

19  Statistics by Tanzania Communication Regulatory Authority (TCRA), http://www.tcra.go.tz/publications/broadcast.html.

20  DStv is the largest satellite TV provider in Tanzania, operated by MultiChoice Africa Incorporated. See http://www.dstvafrica.com.

21  Femina Hip is a multimedia platform and civil society initiative aiming to "promote healthy lifestyles, sexual health, HIV/AIDS prevention, gender equality and citizen engagement"; see http://www.feminahip.or.tz. It was established in 1999 and is directed by Minou Fuglesang, who wrote the first ethnography of media consumption among young women in East Africa (Fuglesang 1994). The Femina Hip website, www.chezasalama.com, is one of the most popular sites in Tanzania.

22  Dar es Salaam was connected to the fiber optic cable initiative Eastern Africa Submarine Cable System (EASSy) on 27 July 2009, but access rates have yet to be reduced by local operators.

23  Tanzania was one of the first countries in Africa to formulate a national ICT policy (Ministry of Communications and Transport 2003). Online at http://www.tanzania.go.tz/pdf/ictpolicy.pdf. Early ICT developments in Tanzania are analyzed in various

development reports (e.g. Esselaar et al. 2001; see also Ekström 2010). A group of Tanzanian ICT professionals set up the online community eThinkTankTz in 2000, to stimulate knowledge sharing and networking among professionals involved in ICT development, including the Tanzanian diaspora and foreign collaborators. The group still maintains a mailing list, with over 1,200 subscribers.

24 http://innovativeethnographies.net/digitaldrama/tasuba-theatre
25 http://innovativeethnographies.net/digitaldrama/liminality-creolization
26 http://innovativeethnographies.net/digitaldrama/liminality-creolization#1
27 http://innovativeethnographies.net/digitaldrama/liminality-creolization#2
28 http://innovativeethnographies.net/digitaldrama/liminality-creolization#3
29 Fredskorpset is a Norwegian program for professional exchange between Norway, Africa, Asia, and Latin America; see http://www.fredskorpset.no/en/.
30 http://www.nota-project.org/history.htm
31 http://www.nota-project.org/nota.htm
32 http://www.youtube.com/watch?v=MXpfDhgDKks
33 http://en.wikipedia.org/wiki/Ujamaa
34 http://en.wikipedia.org/wiki/Julius_Nyerere
35 Millennial capitalism refers to "capitalism at the millennium and capitalism in its messianic, salvific, even magical manifestations" (Comaroff and Comaroff 2000, 293).
36 On a personal note, 12 July 2004 also marked the first anniversary of my younger brother Jouko's unexpected death on 12 July 2003.
37 Simbo was one of the founders of eThinkTankTz. The community's website, which unfortunately has expired, had a condolence page for him after the accident on 13 July 2008. My personal tribute is available at www.net4dev.se/simbo.
38 Simbo, who among other things was a Wikipedia editor, and his brother Joseph, who has an encyclopaedic memory, posted a summary text about their late father in Wikipedia in 2006. See http://en.wikipedia.org/wiki/Sam_Joseph_Ntiro.
39 The film deals with the introduction of the Nile perch into Lake Victoria, and the effects of global trade on the local fishing industry. It was made by Hubert Sauper, released in 2004, and has received various awards. It was banned in Tanzania but widely circulated. http://www.darwinsnightmare.com/

## Chapter 3

1 http://innovativeethnographies.net/digitaldrama/karibu-tasuba#6
2 http://innovativeethnographies.net/digitaldrama/karibu-tasuba#2
3 Both Lange (2002) and Askew (2002) take note of this pamphlet, but it is questionable to what extent it was circulated or adapted. My material corroborates a recent analysis of Touré's cultural program in Guinea, where "the cultural revolution does not seem to have signified any real change in cultural, political or economic policy" (Dave 2009, 464). None of my interlocutors at TaSUBa/BCA has ever mentioned the cultural revolution, indicating that the concept was not particularly well established among the state's cultural actors, even though Tanzania had close ties with China, where the idea originated. Forced settlement into *ujamaa* villages in some rural areas has been recognized as one of the more negative and failed attempts at social engineering in Tanzania, yet this is not associated with a cultural revolution (e.g. Holmqvist 2010, Mwakikagile 2006). Understandably unpopular among many peasants, the creation of *ujamaa* villages in Tanzania can be contrasted with the forced resettlement of all urban populations into rural areas and the attempted ideological indoctrination of the peasantry during the Pol Pot regime in Cambodia, the inhumane brutality of which stands out in the social memory of Khmer peasants (Uimonen 1996).

4   http://innovativeethnographies.net/digitaldrama/tasuba-theatre
5   http://innovativeethnographies.net/digitaldrama/tasuba-theatre#1
6   In parallel, a more informal process of redressive action was taking place at the college, through the circulation of rumors about the causes of the fire. When I first started working at BCA, I was told that the fire was a result of an attempt to conceal the theft of music equipment that had been donated by Japan. It has been noted that for rumors and gossip to be harmful they need to be "spoken in contexts of ideology that are congenial to them" (Stewart and Strathern 2004, 30). In this case, the accusation of corruption, material destruction, and incompetence was well tuned to the ideals of transparency and good governance guiding the work of donors and other agencies in pursuit of neoliberal public sector reform (West and Sanders 2003). In this ideological context of institutional reform, the rumor complex served as a kind of weapon, which similarly to gossip acted as a catalyst of a social process, while advancing the status of the gossiper (Stewart and Strathern 2004, 37–49). For a different version of what actually caused the fire, see Chapter 7.
7   http://innovativeethnographies.net/digitaldrama/karibu-tasuba#12
8   http://innovativeethnographies.net/digitaldrama/karibu-tasuba#7
9   To clarify, culture is produced through "the interaction of perspectives," the perspective (cf. Bourdieau's habitus) denoting "the individual's portion of culture," which "exists in a tension zone between culture and social structure" (Hannerz 1992b, 64–68). In other words, while people are surrounded by flows of external meaning, they are not just passive recipients, but manage meanings in different ways, depending on their culturally shaped perspectives and their positioning in the social structure. Although the cultural flow concept is often misinterpreted, Hannerz himself has underlined that it does not refer to "unimpeded transportation," but rather "the infinite and problematic occurrence of transformation between internal and external loci" (ibid., 4).
10  Pathological readings of modern forms of governance are not exclusive to Africa. In his analysis of neoliberal reforms in New Zealand, Shore (2010) discusses the shifting roles of universities in terms of schizophrenia.
11  "Allowances and perdiems in public service: new form of corruption?" published on the online Tanzania Corruption Tracker System, based on Policy Forum Policy Brief 9.09, Budget Books. Recovered on 13 June 2010 from http://www.corruptiontracker.or.tz.
12  Having spotted a billboard outside Bagamoyo on a recent trip, advertising the services of a healer (*mganga*) who could help get a seat in parliament (*anasaidia kupata ubunge*), one journalist suggested that witchdoctors in Bagamoyo were "busy concocting spells to help the politicians win votes" (*Daily News*, 28 March 2010). Predicting that Members of Parliament "will be making trips to Bagamoyo and other places to consult the oracles of black magic and witchcraft," another journalist considered getting an octopus, which could also be used to "sniff out witches," thus addressing the witchcraft that "every conceivable failure" is blamed on in Bongo (*Citizen*, 17 July 2010). While exemplifying the commonality of witchcraft accusations, the *Citizen* article illustrates that the tendency to blame all kinds of social ills on witchcraft is quite problematic, not least since it diverts attention from underlying social causes (cf. Green 2005).
13  http://innovativeethnographies.net/digitaldrama/research-methods#2
14  http://innovativeethnographies.net/digitaldrama/karibu-tasuba#4
15  http://innovativeethnographies.net/digitaldrama/karibu-tasuba#5
16  Witchcraft is often associated with individual greed and jealousy and used to explain growing social inequalities (Green 2005, Sanders 2003). Accusations of witchcraft and rumours of possessing the power of witchcraft can be manipulated in various ways (Stewart and Strathern 2004). While successful people are often considered to be great

witches, and thus to be feared for their occult powers, for the elite it is often enough that ordinary people think that they have access to such special powers (Green 2005, 252–253).

17  Contrary to its ideals of transparency, the neoliberal world order is rife with occult cosmologies, from conspiracy theories and urban myths to beliefs in occult power like witchcraft (West and Sanders 2003).

18  http://innovativeethnographies.net/digitaldrama/liminality-creolization

19  http://innovativeethnographies.net/digitaldrama/liminality-creolization#5

20  http://innovativeethnographies.net/digitaldrama/liminality-creolization#4

21  The state of creolization is not the same as Anderson's creole state, a concept he uses to describe the rise of nationalism in the new American states (1991, 47).

22  Benítez-Rojo (1998) uses the concept of state of creolization to describe the instability of Caribbean cultural objects. While he argues that creolization is a product of the plantation, I find his postulations to be valid not only for Cuba and the Caribbean, but other cultural contexts as well. The notions of discontinuous series and cultural fragments are also compatible with the concept of culture as flow of meaning, distributed as a network of perspectives that I use in this book.

23  Often handled with the same discretion expected of extramarital affairs, the *nyumba ndogo* (little house) can range from a kept mistress to a second family. A modern polygamous practice, it is instructive of hybrid conceptions of morality in African cities such as Dar es Salaam (Lewinson 2006).

# Chapter 4

1  http://innovativeethnographies.net/digitaldrama/art-training

2  http://innovativeethnographies.net/digitaldrama/research-methods#7

3  Dramatool was an online platform for East African theater practitioners.

4  Greater equality between men and women was of course one of the aims of Tanzanian socialism, but women's active role in public life was not prioritized, nor was it necessarily put into practice (cf. Lange 2002). This is not to say that women have been altogether silent; they have for instance played a key role in Tanganyika's nationalist struggle for independence, as chronicled by Geiger (1997).

5  During *ujamaa*, even schools in urban areas combined theoretical teaching with manual labor, and Mwakikagile (2006, 123) recalls how as a student in Dar es Salaam he had to walk to a nearby farm, carrying agricultural tools, a "reminder that we were no better than ordinary peasants and workers simply because we had acquired some education and were destined to become part of the nation's elite." At BCA manual labor formed part of everyday student life until the college was transformed into TaSUBa, after which campus maintenance was outsourced to a commercial company.

6  http://innovativeethnographies.net/digitaldrama/art-training#19

7  http://innovativeethnographies.net/digitaldrama/art-training#20

8  http://innovativeethnographies.net/digitaldrama/art-training#21

9  http://innovativeethnographies.net/digitaldrama/art-training#23

10  In addition to the tuition fees, students are advised to budget an equivalent amount for other expenses, such as stationery, books and research, bringing their annual cost of study to almost TSH 2 million.

11  The financial strains of school fees is one of the most devastating social costs of structural adjustment in Tanzania and other African countries, along with the costs for healthcare, forcing households to adopt all kinds of strategies to raise extra money, including bribes (cf. Ferguson 2006, Kamat 2008, Mwakikagile 2006, Smith 2007). Throughout my years of engagement in Tanzania, I have found the payment of school

fees to be the most common source of financial stress among people from all walks of life and the primary reason for why many have not been able to study.

12  http://innovativeethnographies.net/digitaldrama/art-training#1
13  http://innovativeethnographies.net/digitaldrama/art-training#12
14  Mathilda, who wrote her exam work on "The effect of African dance on non Africans," runs Furaha Culture & Art centre in Stockholm, Sweden, offering workshops and courses in East African dance, along with cultural safari trips to Tanzania.
15  http://innovativeethnographies.net/digitaldrama/art-training#2
16  http://innovativeethnographies.net/digitaldrama/digital-anthropology#8
17  http://innovativeethnographies.net/digitaldrama/art-training#13
18  http://innovativeethnographies.net/digitaldrama/art-training#16
19  http://innovativeethnographies.net/digitaldrama/digital-anthropology#12
20  http://innovativeethnographies.net/digitaldrama/digital-anthropology#13
21  The term "banking system of education" echoes the thinking of Paulo Freire who criticized the modern education system in his famous book *Pedagogy of the Oppressed*.
22  Having heard several students compare TaSUBa with ADEM I decided to pay a visit to the Agency for the Development of Educational Management. One of my former colleagues from the Ministry of Education showed me around the impressive compound, with air-conditioned, computer-equipped classrooms and covered walkways. While I couldn't but agree with the superior quality of the facilities, I also realized that I felt quite awkward in this environment. The clothes I was wearing, which had felt just right at TaSUBa, felt out of place at ADEM, my white linen trousers and loose white blouse making me feel rather bohemian compared with the suits and tailored batik dresses of this agency's executive-looking staff. It became quite clear that the students who evoked ADEM as a model did not care much for the artistic field in their comparison of educational facilities. The School of Library Archives and Documentation Studies (SLADS), which I visited while working for the Ministry of Education, has been rapidly modernized by the energetic Director of the Tanzania Library Services Board (TLSB). Although it has a more relaxed atmosphere than ADEM, SLADS is by no means artistic in its orientation and I recall with some amusement how shocked the Director was to find me staying in a non-air-conditioned house next to TaSUBa, a place I felt privileged to be in since it was the residence of the late Mzee Kaduma.

## Chapter 5

1  http://innovativeethnographies.net/digitaldrama/mastering-marimba
2  http://innovativeethnographies.net/digitaldrama/mastering-marimba#5
3  http://innovativeethnographies.net/digitaldrama/mastering-marimba
4  http://innovativeethnographies.net/digitaldrama/mastering-marimba#4
5  http://innovativeethnographies.net/digitaldrama/mastering-marimba#8
6  In telling me his life history, Matitu also told me the story of his instrument, which I would like to reproduce here, out of respect for his knowledge and in humble recognition of unequal relations between European scholars and African musicians (Agawu 2007). When telling me the story of the *marimba*, as told to him by his grandfather, Matitu focused on social relations and morality. The *marimba* is played by several tribes in Tanzania. Among the *wazaramo*, it dates back to the early twentieth century, when it was known as *ulengela*. Inspired by children drumming with banana leaves to fend off birds in the *shamba* (farm), a young village boy constructed a box out of rough wood. When playing it in the village, people said he was beating it, "*Mwaneno, kulimba ulengela*" in their tribal language (this son is beating ulengela). After some time, the name *ulengela* was forgotten, and the instrument came to be known as *marimba*

(beating). The boy's name was Kabudika, which in Kizaramo means someone who is lazy and does not like hard work. But this lazy boy created an instrument that proved to be very popular and his way of being lazy even earned him some money. The boy formed a group, complementing the *marimba* with different drums they crafted from tree trunks and corrugated iron. The group was very popular, especially among women who invited them to play for traditional celebrations and community parties. Over time, other groups formed. Subject to jealous beatings by groups who saw them as rivals, one of the later groups developed a special dance, *mkwaju ngoma* (stick dance), from dancing with sticks to defend themselves. Matitu's brother was a member of this group.

7   I appreciate and acknowledge John Sagatti's help in identifying the most popular music genres in contemporary Tanzania, kindly updating me via Facebook while I was writing this chapter.

8   http://nota-project.org/tramo.htm

9   Born (2005, 8) defines musical assemblage as "a particular combination of mediations (sonic, discursive, visual, artefactual, technological, social, temporal) characteristic of a certain musical culture and historical period." I am grateful to Georgina Born for sharing her excellent work on music and cultural production during her visit at Stockholm University in March 2009 and our subsequent email correspondence. I also appreciate her use of Gell's theories, which encouraged me to make the effort to understand and use them in my own work.

10  http://innovativeethnographies.net/digitaldrama/recording-masamva

11  http://innovativeethnographies.net/digitaldrama/recording-masamva#2

12  http://innovativeethnographies.net/digitaldrama/recording-masamva#7

13  http://innovativeethnographies.net/digitaldrama/recording-masamva#7

14  http://innovativeethnographies.net/digitaldrama/recording-masamva#6

15  http://innovativeethnographies.net/digitaldrama/recording-masamva#1

16  Gell (1998, 235) explains protention in terms of prospective or future-oriented relations and retention as retrospective or past-oriented relations. While his theoretical extrapolations are based on the oeuvres of individual artists, he later extends this argument to distributed objects in general, which is also how he categorizes the totality of an individual's art work.

17  See COSOTA, Copyright Society of Tanzania, at http://cosota-tz.org.

18  http://innovativeethnographies.net/digitaldrama/recording-masamva#4

19  http://innovativeethnographies.net/digitaldrama/recording-masamva#5

20  http://innovativeethnographies.net/digitaldrama/nakupenda-afrika

21  http://innovativeethnographies.net/digitaldrama/nakupenda-afrika#10

22  TaSUBa and Utrecht School of the Arts (HKU). Development of an Artistic Portfolio. Project Proposal, n.d.

23  For the 2008 projects, there is a wiki at http://www.arjenklaverstijn.com/wiki/index. php?title=The_projects_of_2008.

24  http://www.virtualstudionetwork.com/

25  http://marlynspaaij.blogspot.com/

26  http://innovativeethnographies.net/digitaldrama/nakupenda-afrika#7

27  http://innovativeethnographies.net/digitaldrama/nakupenda-afrika#8

28  http://innovativeethnographies.net/digitaldrama/nakupenda-afrika#9

29  http://innovativeethnographies.net/digitaldrama/nakupenda-afrika#11

30  http://innovativeethnographies.net/digitaldrama/karibu-tasuba#25

31  Cultural improvisation is also found in artistic productions that straddle different art forms, as exemplified by William Forsythe and his ballet company Ballett Frankfurt, that "operate at the intersection of neoclassical and contemporary traditions" (Wulff 1998, 45).

32  The cosmopolitan perspective can even be traced to the Swahili civilization preceding the modern formation of Tanganyika. Indeed, if the world is conceptualized as a global ecumene, from oikoumene the entire inhabited world as the ancient Greeks understood it (Hannerz 1996, 7) then it is quite clear that even the Swahili oikumene (Middleton 1992) reached well beyond the shores of the Indian Ocean. Researchers have validated the existence of "cosmopolitan cities and seaports" along the Swahili coast "as early as the first century A.D." (Askew 2002, 32).

33  Recursive publics build on the openness of the technical protocols of the Internet (TCP/IP), which, in the words of its codesigner Dr Vint Cerf, was "a tool to overcome disparities, allowing different systems to connect to one another, to interwork. It was egalitarian, it was non-proprietary" (Uimonen 2001, 38).

34  Helena Wulff should be credited for making this observation and kindly sharing it with me.

# Chapter 6

1   http://innovativeethnographies.net/digitaldrama/tuwaenzi-wakonge#8
2   http://innovativeethnographies.net/digitaldrama/art-training#7
3   http://innovativeethnographies.net/digitaldrama/art-training#8
4   http://innovativeethnographies.net/digitaldrama/nakupenda-afrika
5   http://innovativeethnographies.net/digitaldrama/nakupenda-afrika#1
6   http://innovativeethnographies.net/digitaldrama/nakupenda-afrika#2
7   http://innovativeethnographies.net/digitaldrama/nakupenda-afrika#6
8   http://innovativeethnographies.net/digitaldrama/facebook-pamoja
9   http://sanaasana.weebly.com/
10  David's blog is at http://sanaasana.weebly.com/.
11  http://innovativeethnographies.net/digitaldrama/facebook-pamoja#7
12  http://innovativeethnographies.net/digitaldrama/facebook-pamoja#1
13  http://innovativeethnographies.net/digitaldrama/facebook-pamoja#4
14  http://innovativeethnographies.net/digitaldrama/facebook-pamoja#5
15  The term "networked publics" is used to capture the "active participation of a distributed social network in the production and circulation of culture and knowledge," thus capturing young people's media engagements on and offline (Ito 2010, 19). Since Facebook is not really public (access requires membership and users determine the accessibility of their content in the privacy settings of their individual accounts), I prefer the term "networked place." I differ from Miller's (2011) reading of Facebook as a community, which fails to recognize the social intricacies of the culture of networking that I have always associated with the Internet (Uimonen 2001).

16  Gershon (2010) focuses on romantic relationships between young Americans, more precisely how such relationships are ended in new media, rather than friendship.

17  This holds especially true for women, who play such a pivotal role in the constitution of social relations around the world. In Tanzania, a mother is named after her firstborn as Mama [name of firstborn]. If she hasn't borne children yet, a woman is referred to as the mother of her husband, who is jokingly referred to as her firstborn, which is why some friends used to call me Mama Simbo.

18  One of my favorite uses of *pole* is *pole na kazi* (sorry for your work), expressing sympathy for and recognition of someone's labor.

# Chapter 7

1   http://innovativeethnographies.net/digitaldrama/tasuba-theatre#14
2   http://innovativeethnographies.net/digitaldrama/tasuba-theatre#10

3  http://innovativeethnographies.net/digitaldrama/tasuba-theatre#16
4  http://innovativeethnographies.net/digitaldrama/tasuba-theatre#15
5  http://www.swedenabroad.com/Page____83747.aspx
6  http://innovativeethnographies.net/digitaldrama/tasuba-theatre#17
7  Lange (2001, 156) notes that the state institutions of the Drama Department of the University of Dar es Salaam and the College of Arts in Bagamoyo have sought to "revive traditional performance modes" through the development of a genre called African theatre, which is often performed at the College's annual arts festival. While often focusing on local historical themes, the genre has more in common with European classical drama than with popular theatre, which tends to be "comical, over-acted and burlesque," with a strong dose of humor (ibid.).
8  http://innovativeethnographies.net/digitaldrama/tasuba-theatre#20
9  http://innovativeethnographies.net/digitaldrama/tasuba-theatre#21
10  http://innovativeethnographies.net/digitaldrama/tasuba-theatre#11
11  http://innovativeethnographies.net/digitaldrama/tasuba-theatre#18
12  Originally a film festival, ZIFF has evolved into a major arts festival attracting artists and visitors from around the world, now claiming to be East Africa's largest film and arts festival. More information at http://www.ziff.or.tz/.
13  Edmondson (2007, 65) discusses the popularity of *kukata kiuno* (to cut the waist), erotic dance moves that have become "virtually synonymous with the concept of *ngoma* [here, dance] in the cultural imagination." This hip-swaying movement originates in initiation rituals for young women. She notes that the Bagamoyo College of Arts has excluded such erotic dances in its repertoire of traditional dances, which she compares to a literary canon, limited to eight dances "sanctioned by the authority of the state" (ibid. 69). Although it is true that TaSUBa tutors dislike the public performance of erotic dances from initiation rituals, especially in commercial venues, the fact that such dances are allowed at the annual festival demonstrates that the state is not that hegemonic a force. Moreover, the college's meager repertoire of eight to ten dances is largely a result of a lack of teachers and a lack of resources for teachers to acquire new dances.
14  http://innovativeethnographies.net/digitaldrama/tasuba-theatre#19
15  http://www.swedenabroad.com/Page____83747.aspx
16  http://innovativeethnographies.net/digitaldrama/research-methods#9
17  http://innovativeethnographies.net/digitaldrama/kamambe
18  http://innovativeethnographies.net/digitaldrama/kamambe#7
19  http://innovativeethnographies.net/digitaldrama/kamambe#8
20  http://innovativeethnographies.net/digitaldrama/kamambe#1
21  http://innovativeethnographies.net/digitaldrama/liminality-creolization#6
22  http://innovativeethnographies.net/digitaldrama/kamambe#17
23  http://innovativeethnographies.net/digitaldrama/kamambe#18
24  http://innovativeethnographies.net/digitaldrama/kamambe#10
25  http://innovativeethnographies.net/digitaldrama/kamambe#13
26  The Tanzania Education Authority (TEA), an executive agency under the Ministry of Education and Vocational Training (MoEVT), offers grants to institutes of higher education for the procurement of ICT facilities from its Education Fund. See http://www.tea.or.tz.
27  http://innovativeethnographies.net/digitaldrama/karibu-tasuba#7

## Chapter 8

1  These include the African Development Bank, Canada, Denmark, the European Commission, Finland, Germany, Ireland, Japan, the Netherlands, Norway, Sweden, Switzerland, Britain and the World Bank (Reuters 14 May 2010).

2 http://af.reuters.com/article/topNews/idAFJOE64D0FI20100514?pageNumber=2&virtualBrandChannel=0&sp=true

3 Kitchen parties are usually organized shortly before a bride's wedding, often at restaurants or similar venues. This social function is a hybrid between traditional initiation rituals and modern bachelorette parties, popular among urban middle classes. Kitchen parties are organized by women, for women, and no men are allowed to participate. In addition to advising the bride-to-be on various aspects of married life, the bride is showered with gifts, ranging from *khanga* to modern kitchen ware. Kitchen parties are often followed by send-off parties, in which both bride and groom participate. Guests are expected to give cash contributions to subsidize these social events, which can be rather costly, followed by a wedding ceremony that tends to be as lavish as people can possibly afford.

4 http://www.pambazuka.org/en/category/panafrican/60700/print

5 http://innovativeethnographies.net/digitaldrama/tuwaenzi-wakonge#12

6 http://vitalimaembe.wordpress.com/

## Chapter 9

1 http://innovativeethnographies.net/digitaldrama/research-methods

2 Interesting work is for instance taking place at the Sensory Ethnography Lab at Harvard University, see http://sel.fas.harvard.edu/.

3 http://innovativeethnographies.net/digitaldrama/research-methods#5

4 http://innovativeethnographies.net/digitaldrama/research-methods#6

5 http://innovativeethnographies.net/digitaldrama/research-methods#8

6 http://innovativeethnographies.net/digitaldrama/research-methods#9

7 http://innovativeethnographies.net/digitaldrama/karibu-tasuba#27

8 http://innovativeethnographies.net/digitaldrama/karibu-tasuba#2

9 http://innovativeethnographies.net/digitaldrama/research-methods#3

10 http://innovativeethnographies.net/digitaldrama/research-methods#1

11 http://innovativeethnographies.net/digitaldrama/research-methods#2

12 For a discussion of terminology, see Beer 2008, boyd and Ellison 2007.

13 In critical respects, such as user-generated multimedia content, individual and collective communication, and reconfiguration of private/public boundaries, the so-called Web 2.0 is but a continuation of technological developments that can be traced back to the early days of ARPANET and the "networking culture" characterizing the working style of its early developers, which constituted the original "ethos of the Net" (Hafner and Lyon 1996, 145, Naughton 2000, 138).

# BIBLIOGRAPHY

Abu-Lughod, Lila. 2005. *Dramas of nationhood: the politics of television in Egypt.* Chicago, Ill.: University of Chicago Press

Agawu, Kofi. 2007. "To cite or not to cite? confronting the legacy of (European) writing on African music." *Fontes Artis Musicae,* 54, no. 3: 254–262

Aguilar, Mario I. 1999. "Localized kin and globalized friends: religious modernity and the 'educated self' in East Africa." In *The anthropology of friendship,* edited by Sandra M. Bell and Simon Coleman, 169–184. Oxford: Berg

Anderson, Benedict. 1991. *Imagined communities: reflections on the origin and spread of nationalism.* London: Verso

Appadurai, Arjun. 1996. *Modernity at large: cultural dimensions of globalization.* Minneapolis: University of Minnesota Press

Appiah, Kwame Anthony. 1998. "Cosmopolitan patriots." In *Cosmopolitics: thinking and feeling beyond the nation,* edited by Pheng Cheah and Bruce Robbins, 91–114. Minneapolis: University of Minnesota Press

Apter, Andrew H. 2005. *The Pan-African nation: oil and the spectacle of culture in Nigeria.* Chicago: University of Chicago Press

Askew, Kelly M. 2002. *Performing the nation: Swahili music and cultural politics in Tanzania.* Chicago: University of Chicago Press

—— 2004. "Jack-of-all-arts or *ustadhi*? The poetics of cultural production in Tanzania." In *In search of a nation: histories of authority and dissidence in Tanzania,* edited by Gregory Maddox and James L. Giblin, 304–327. Oxford: James Currey

Bakari, Juma. 1998. "Satires in theatre for development practice in Tanzania." In *African theatre for development: art for self-determination,* edited by Kamal Salhi, 115–133. Exeter: Intellect Books

Banks, Marcus. 2001. *Visual methods in social research.* London: SAGE

Banks, Marcus and Howard Morphy, eds. 1997. *Rethinking visual anthropology.* New Haven: Yale University Press

Barcellos Rezende, Claudia. 1999. "Building affinity through friendship." In *The anthropology of friendship,* edited by Sandra M. Bell and Simon Coleman, 79–97. Oxford: Berg

Barendregt, Bart. 2008. "Sex, cannibals, and the language of cool: Indonesian tales of the phone and modernity." *Information Society,* 24, no. 3: 160–170

Bartlett, Lesley, Marla Frederick, Thaddeus Gulbrandsen, and Enrique Murillo. 2002. "The marketization of education: public schools for private ends." *Anthropology & Education Quarterly,* 33, no. 1: 5–29

Bayart, Jean-François. 2009. *The state in Africa: the politics of the belly*. 2nd ed. Cambridge: Polity

Beck, Ulrich, Scott Lash, and Anthony Giddens. 1994. *Reflexive modernization: politics, tradition and aesthetics in the modern social order*. Oxford: Polity

Beer, David. 2008. "Social network(ing) sites ... revisiting the story so far: a response to danah boyd & Nicole Ellison." *Journal of Computer-Mediated Communication*, 13, no. 2, 516–529

Bell, Sandra M. and Simon Coleman, eds. 1999. *The anthropology of friendship*. Oxford: Berg

Benítez-Rojo, Antonio. 1998. "Three words towards creolization." In *Caribbean creolization: reflections on the cultural dynamics of language, literature, and identity*, edited by Kathleen M. Balutansky and Marie-Agnès Sourieau, 53–61. University Press of Florida

Bodley, John H. 1990. *Victims of progress*. Mountain View, Calif.: Mayfield

Boellstorff, Tom. 2008. *Coming of age in second life: an anthropologist explores the virtually human*. Princeton: Princeton University Press

Born, Georgina. 2005. "On musical mediation: ontology, technology and creativity." *Twentieth-century music*, 2, no. 1: 7–36

—— 2009. "Afterword: recording: from reproduction to representation to remediation." In *Cambridge companion to recorded music*, edited by Nicholas Cook. Cambridge: Cambridge University Press

—— 2010. "The social and the aesthetic: for a post-Bourdieuian theory of cultural production. *Cultural Sociology*, 4, no. 2: 171–208

Bourdieu, Pierre. 1977. *Outline of a theory of practice*. Cambridge: Cambridge University Press

—— 1993. *The field of cultural production: essays on art and literature*. New York: Columbia University Press

boyd, danah. 2010. "Friendship." In *Hanging out, messing around, and geeking out: kids living and learning with new media*, edited by Mizuko Ito, 79–115. Cambridge, Mass.: MIT Press

boyd, danah and Nicole Ellison. 2007. "Social network sites: definition, history, and scholarship." *Journal of Computer-Mediated Communication*, 13, no. 1: 210–230

Boyer, Dominic and Elizabeth Rata. 2010. "What is driving university reform in the age of globalization?" *Social Anthropology/Anthropologie sociale*, special issue: *Anthropologies of university reform*, 18, no. 1: 74–82

Brusila, Johannes. 2001. "Musical otherness and the Bhundu Boys: the construction of the 'west' and the 'rest' in the discourse of 'world music'." In *Same and other: negotiating African identity in cultural production*, edited by Maria Eriksson Baaz and Mai Palmberg, 39–56. Uppsala: Nordic Africa Institute

Carrier, James G. 1999. "People who can be friends: selves and social relationships." In *The anthropology of friendship*, edited by Sandra M. Bell and Simon Coleman, 21–38. Oxford: Berg

Castells, Manuel. 1996. *The information age: economy, society and culture. Vol. 1, The rise of the network society*. Malden, Mass.: Blackwell

—— 1997. *The information age: economy, society and culture. Vol. 2, The power of identity*. Malden, Mass.: Blackwell

—— 1998. *The information age: economy, society and culture. Vol. 3, End of millennium*. Malden, Mass.: Blackwell

—— 2001. *The Internet galaxy: reflections on the Internet, business, and society*. Oxford: Oxford University Press

—— 2004. "Informationalism, networks, and the network society: a theoretical blueprint." In *The network society: a cross-cultural perspective*, edited by Manuel Castells, 3–45. Northampton, Mass.: Edward Elgar Publishing

Caulfield, Janice. 2002. "Executive agencies in Tanzania: liberalization and Third World debt." *Public Administration and Development*, 22: 209–220

Chernoff, John Miller. 1979. *African rhythm and African sensibility: aesthetics and social action in African musical idioms*. Chicago: University of Chicago Press

Cohen, Julie E. 2007. "Creativity and culture in copyright theory." *University of California Davis Law Review*, 40: 1151–1204

Coleman, Gabriella. 2010. Ethnographic approaches to digital media. *Annual Review of Anthropology*, 39: 1–16

Comaroff, Jean and John L. Comaroff. 2000. "Millenial capitalism: first thoughts on a second coming." In *Public Culture*, 12, no. 2: 291–343

——, eds. 2006. *Law and disorder in the postcolony*. Chicago: University of Chicago Press

COWI. 2002. *Review of Bagamoyo College of Arts*. Report prepared for Swedish Embassy in Dar es Salaam

Dahl, Gudrun. 2001. *Responsibility and partnership in Swedish aid discourse*. Uppsala: Nordic Africa Institute

—— 2007. "Words as moral badges: a flow of buzzwords in development aid." In *Sustainable development in a globalized world: studies in development, security and culture, volume 1*, edited by Björn Hettne, 172–199. Palgrave Macmillan

Dave, Nomi. 2009. "Une nouvelle révolution permanente: the making of African modernity in Sékou Touré's Guinea." *Forum for Modern Language Studies*, 45, no. 4: 455–471

Dowden, Richard. 2009. *Africa: altered states, ordinary miracles*. London: Portobello

—— 2010. "Corruption is the killer that we all ignore." *TimesOnline*, 8 February

Edmondson, Laura. 2007. *Performance and politics in Tanzania: the nation on stage*. Bloomington: Indiana University Press

Ekström, Ylva. 2010. *"We are like chameleons!": changing mediascapes, cultural identities and city sisters in Dar es Salaam*. Diss. Uppsala : Uppsala universitet

Eriksson Baaz, Maria. 2001. "Introduction-African identity and the postcolonial." In *Same and other: negotiating African identity in cultural production*, edited by Maria Eriksson Baaz and Mai Palmberg, 5–21. Uppsala: Nordic Africa Institute

Escobar, Arturo. 1994. "Welcome to Cyberia. Notes on the anthropology of cyberculture." *Current Anthropology*, 35, no. 3: 211–231

—— 1995. *Encountering development: the making and unmaking of the third world*. Princeton: Princeton University Press

Esselaar, Miller and Associates. 2001. *A country ICT survey for Tanzania*. Report prepared for Sida/SAREC

Favero, Paolo. 2007. "'What a wonderful world': on the 'touristic ways of seeing,' the knowledge and the politics of the 'culture industry of otherness'." *Tourist Studies*, 7, no. 1: 51–81

Feld, Steven. 1990. *Sound and sentiment: birds, weeping, poetics, and song in Kaluli expression*. 2nd ed. Philadelphia: University of Pennsylvania Press

Ferguson, James. 1994. *The anti-politics machine: "development," depoliticization, and bureaucratic power in Lesotho*. Minneapolis: University of Minnesota Press

—— 1999. *Expectations of modernity: myths and meanings of urban life on the Zambian Copperbelt*. Berkeley, Calif.: University of California Press

—— 2006. *Global shadows: Africa in the neoliberal world order*. Durham, NC: Duke University Press

—— and Akhil Gupta. 2002. "Spatializing states: toward an ethnography of neoliberal governmentality." *American Ethnologist*, 29, no. 4: 981–1002

Fillitz, Thomas. 2009. "Contemporary art in Africa: coevalness in the global world." In *The global art world: audiences, markets, and museums*, edited by Hans Belting and Andrea Buddensieg, 116–134. Ostfildern. Hatje Cantz

Finnström, Sverker. 2007. "Panafrikanism 3000." *Tidskriften Arena*, 2: 30–33

—— 2008. *Living with bad surroundings: war, history, and everyday moments in northern Uganda.* Durham: Duke University Press

Foucault, Michel. 1980. *Power/knowledge: selected interviews and other writings 1972–1977.* Brighton: Harvester P

—— 1991. "Governmentality." In *The Foucault effect: studies in governmentality,* edited by Graham Burchell, Colin Gordon, and Peter Miller, 87–104. Chicago: University of Chicago Press

Friedson, Steven M. 2009. *Remains of ritual: northern gods in a southern land.* Chicago, Ill.: University of Chicago Press

Fuglesang, Minou. 1994. *Veils and videos: female youth culture on the Kenyan coast.* Diss. Stockholm University

Garcia, Angela Cora, Alecea I. Standlee, Jennifer Bechkoff, and Yan Cui. 2009. "Ethnographic approaches to the Internet and computer-mediated communication." *Journal of Contemporary Ethnography,* 38, no. 1: 52–82

Garsten, Christina and Helena Wulff, eds. 2003. *New technologies at work: people, screens and social virtuality.* Oxford: Berg

Geertz, Clifford. 1960. "The Javanese Kijaji: the changing role of a cultural broker." *Comparative Studies in Society and History,* 2, no. 2: 228–249

—— 1973. *The interpretation of cultures: selected essays.* New York: Basic Books

Geiger, Susan. 1997. *TANU women: gender and culture in the making of Tanganyikan nationalism, 1955–1965.* Portsmouth, NH: Heinemann

Gell, Alfred. 1998. *Art and agency: an anthropological theory.* Oxford: Clarendon

Gershon, Ilana. 2010. *The breakup 2.0: disconnecting over new media.* Ithaca, NY: Cornell University Press

Geurts, Kathryn Linn, 2002. *Culture and the senses: bodily ways of knowing in an African community.* Berkeley: University of California Press

Gingrich, André and Marcus Banks, eds. 2006. *Neo-nationalism in Europe and beyond: perspectives from social anthropology.* New York: Berghahn Books

Goffman, Erving. 1990 [1959]. *The presentation of self in everyday life.* London: Penguin

Gould, Jeremy and Julia Ojanen. 2003. *"Merging in the circle": the politics of Tanzania's poverty reduction strategy.* Helsinki: University of Helsinki

Green, Maia. 2005. "Discourses on inequality." *Anthropological Theory,* 5, no. 3: 247–266

—— 2006. "International development, social analysis, … and anthropology? Applying anthropology in and to development." In *Applied anthropology: domains of application,* edited by Satish Kedia and John van Willigen, 110–129. Westport: Praeger

Green, Maia and Simeon Mesaki. 2005. "The birth of the 'salon': poverty, 'modernization,' and dealing with witchcraft in southern Tanzania." *American Ethnologist,* 32, no. 3: 371–388

Gupta, Akhil. 1995. "Blurred boundaries: the discourse of corruption, the culture of politics, and the imagined state." *American Ethnologist,* 22, no. 2: 375–402

—— and Aradhana Sharma. 2006. "Globalization and postcolonial states." *Current Anthropology* 47, no. 2: 277–307

Hafner, Katie and Matthew Lyon. 1996. *Where wizards stay up late: the origins of the Internet.* New York: Simon & Schuster

Hallam, Elizabeth and Tim Ingold, eds. 2007. *Creativity and cultural improvisation.* New York, NY: Berg

Haller, Dieter and Cris Shore, eds. 2005. *Corruption: anthropological perspectives.* London: Pluto

Hancock, Graham. 1989. *Lords of poverty: the power, prestige, and corruption of the international aid business.* New York: Atlantic Monthly Press

Hannerz, Ulf. 1980. *Exploring the city: inquiries toward an urban anthropology.* New York: Columbia University Press

—— 1987. "The world in creolisation." *Africa*, 57, 546–560

—— 1992a. "The global ecumene as a network of networks." In *Conceptualizing society*, edited by Adam Kuper, 34–56. London: Routledge

—— 1992b. *Cultural complexity: studies in the social organization of meaning.* New York: Columbia University Press

—— 1996. *Transnational connections: culture, people, places.* London: Routledge

—— 2003. "Being there ... and there ... and there!" *Ethnography*, 4, no. 2: 201–216

—— 2004. *Foreign news: exploring the world of foreign correspondents.* Chicago: University of Chicago Press

—— 2006. "Theorizing through the new world? Not really." *American Ethnologist*, 33, no. 4: 563–565

—— 2010. *Anthropology's world: life in a twenty-first-century discipline.* London: Pluto Press

Hart, Keith. 2000. *The memory bank: money in an unequal world.* London: Profile Books

Hastrup, Kirsten. 1998. "Theatre as a site of passage: some reflections on the magic of acting." In *Ritual, performance, media*, edited by Felicia Hughes-Freeland, 29–45. London: Routledge

Hasty, Jennifer. 2005. "The pleasures of corruption: desire and discipline in Ghanaian political culture." *Cultural Anthropology*, 20, no. 2: 271–301

Havnevik, Kjell. 2010. "A historical framework for analysing current Tanzanian transitions: the post-independence model, Nyerere's ideas and some interpretations." In *Tanzania in transition: from Nyerere to Mkapa*, edited by Kjell Havnevik and Aida C. Isinika, 19–56. Dar es Salaam: Mkuki na Nyota Publishers

Heilman, Bruce and Laurean Ndumbaro. 2002. "Corruption, politics, and societal values in Tanzania: an evaluation of the Mkapa administration's anti-corruption efforts." *African Journal of Political Science*, 7, no 1: 1–19

Herzfeld, Michael. 2007. "Senses." In *Ethnographic fieldwork: an anthropological reader*, edited by Antonius C. G. M. Robben and A. Jeffrey, 431–441. Malden, MA: Blackwell Pub

Hine, Christine. 2000. *Virtual ethnography.* London: SAGE

Holmqvist, Stig. 2010. *På väg till presidenten.* Stockholm: Carlsson

Horst, Heather A. and Daniel Miller. 2006. *The cell phone: an anthropology of communication.* New York, NY: Berg

Hylland Eriksen, Thomas. 2003. "Creolization and creativity." *Global Networks, special issue: Globalization, creolization, and cultural complexity: essays in honour of Ulf Hannerz*, 3, no. 3: 223–237

Ingold, Tim. 2005. "The eye of the storm: visual perception and the weather." *Visual Studies*, 20, no. 2: 97–104

Ito, Mizuko, ed. 2010. *Hanging out, messing around, and geeking out: kids living and learning with new media.* Cambridge, Mass.: MIT Press

ITU. 2011. Measuring the information society 2011. Geneva: International Telecommunication Union

Kamat, Vinay. 2008. "This is not our culture! Discourse of nostalgia and narratives of health concerns in post-socialist Tanzania." *Africa: The Journal of the International African Institute*, 78, no. 3: 359–383

Kapferer, Bruce. 1973. "Social network and conjugal role in urban Zambia: towards a reformulation of the Bott hypothesis." In *Network analysis: studies in human interaction*, edited by Jeremy Boissevain and J. Clyde Mitchell. The Hague: Mouton

Kaplan, Danny. 2007. "What can the concept of friendship contribute to the study of national identity?" *Nations and Nationalism*, 13, no. 2: 225–244

Kedia, Satish and John van Willigen, eds. 2005. *Applied anthropology: domains of application.* Westport: Praeger

Kelty, Christopher M. 2008. *Two bits: the cultural significance of free software.* Durham: Duke University Press

Kipnis, Andrew B. 2008. "Audit cultures: neoliberal governmentality, socialist legacy, or technologies of governing?" *American Ethnologist*, 35, no. 2: 275–289

Kirkegaard, Annemette. 2001. "Tourism industry and local music culture in contemporary Zanzibar." In *Same and other: negotiating African identity in cultural production*, edited by Maria Eriksson Baaz and Mai Palmberg, 59–76. Uppsala: Nordic Africa Institute

Lange, Siri. 2001. "'The shame of money': criticism of modernity in Swahili popular drama." In *Same and other: negotiating African identity in cultural production*, edited by Maria Eriksson Baaz and Mai Palmberg, 143–157. Uppsala: Nordic Africa Institute

—— 2002. *Managing modernity: gender, state, and nation in the popular drama of Dar es Salaam, Tanzania*. Diss. Bergen University

Latour, Bruno. 1993. *We have never been modern*. Cambridge, Mass.: Harvard University Press

—— 2005. *Reassembling the social: an introduction to actor-network-theory*. Oxford: Oxford University Press

Lévi-Strauss, Claude. 1966. *The savage mind*. Chicago: University of Chicago Press

Lewinson, Anne. 2006. "Love in the city: navigating multiple relationships in Dar es Salaam, Tanzania." *City & Society*, 18: 90–115

Liep, John, ed. 2001. *Locating cultural creativity*. London: Pluto Press

Lindquist, Johan. 2010. "Labor recruitment, circuits of capital and gendered mobility: reconceptualizing the Indonesian migration industry." *Pacific Affairs*, 83, no. 1: 115–132

Little, Peter D. 2005. "Anthropology and development." In *Applied anthropology: domains of application*, edited by Satish Kedia and John van Willigen, 33–59. Westport: Praeger

MacDougall, David. 1997. "The visual in anthropology." In *Rethinking visual anthropology*, edited by Marcus Banks and Howard Morphy, 276–295. New Haven: Yale University Press

—— 1999. "Social aesthetics and the Doon school." *Visual Anthropology Review*, 15, no. 1: 3–20

—— 2006. *The corporeal image: film, ethnography, and the senses*. Princeton, NJ: Princeton University Press

Malcomson, Scott L. 1998. "The varieties of cosmopolitan experience." In *Cosmopolitics: thinking and feeling beyond the nation*, edited by Pheng Cheah and Bruce Robbins, 233–245. Minneapolis: University of Minnesota Press

Mandela, Nelson. 1995. *Long walk to freedom*. London: Abacus

Marcus, George. 1995. "Ethnography in/of the world system: the emergence of multi-sited ethnography." *Annual Review of Anthropology*, 24: 95–117

Mauss, Marcel. 1967. *The gift: forms and functions of exchange in archaic societies*. New York: W.W. Norton & Company Inc

Mbembe, Achille. 2001. *On the postcolony*. Berkeley, Calif.: University of California Press

McLaren, Peter. 1986. *Schooling as a ritual performance: towards a political economy of educational symbols and gestures*. London: Routledge & Kegan Paul

Mercer, Graham. 2007. *Bagamoyo: town of palms*. Dar es Salaam: Graham Mercer

Middleton, John. 1992. *The world of the Swahili: an African mercantile civilization*. New Haven, CT: Yale University Press

Miller, Daniel. 2010. *An extreme reading of Facebook*. Open Anthropology Cooperative Press. www.openanthcoop.net/press

—— 2011. *Tales from Facebook*. Cambridge: Polity Press

Miller, Daniel and Don Slater. 2000. *The Internet: an ethnographic approach*. Oxford: Berg

Mirzoeff, Nicholas. 2009. *An introduction to visual culture*. 2nd ed. London: Routledge

Mitchell, J.Clyde, ed. 1969. *Social networks in urban situations*. Manchester: Manchester University Press

MoCT. 2003. *National information and communications technologies policy*. Ministry of Communications and Transport, The United Republic of Tanzania

MoEC/BCA. 2003. *Strategic plan for the development of the Bagamoyo College of Arts 2003–2006*. Ministry of Education and Culture/Bagamoyo College of Arts, The United Republic of Tanzania

MoEVT. 2007. *ICT policy for basic education*. Ministry of Education and Vocational Training, The United Republic of Tanzania

Molony, Thomas, Lisa Ann Richey and Stefano Ponte. 2007. "'Darwin's nightmare': a critical assessment." *Review of African Political Economy*, 13: 598–608

Mwakikagile, Godfrey. 2006. *Life under Nyerere*. Dar es Salaam: New Africa Press

Narayan, Kirin and Kenneth M. George. 2001. "Interviewing for folk and personal narrative." In *Handbook of interview research: methods and context*, edited by Jay Gubrium and James Holstein, 815–831. New York: Sage

Naughton, John. 2000. *A brief history of the future: the origins of the Internet*. London: Phoenix

NOTA. 2006. *Application for the continuation of the NOTA-project autumn 2006–spring 2011*. Bagamoyo/Stavanger: Bagamoyo College of Arts (BCA), University of Stavanger (UiS) Department of Music and Dance, Stavanger School of Culture (SSC). Online at http://nota-project.org

Ntarangwi, Mwenda, ed. 2006. *African anthropologies: history, critique and practice*. London: Zed Books in association with Codesria

Ntiro, Simbo and Paula Uimonen. 2006. "The impact of WSIS on Tanzania's ICT4D landscape." In *Beyond Tunis: flightplan*. Kuala Lumpur: Global Knowledge Partnership (GKP)

Nyerere, Julius K. 1979. "Unity for a new order." *Challenge*. Article taken from Nyerere's address to the Ministerial Conference of the Group of 77 in Arusha, Tanzania, February 12, 1979

Ong, Aihwa and Stephen J. Collier, eds. 2005. *Global assemblages: technology, politics, and ethics as anthropological problems*. Malden, MA: Blackwell Publishing

Paine, Robert. 1999. "Friendships: the hazards of an ideal relationship." In *The anthropology of friendship*, edited by Sandra M. Bell and Simon Coleman, 39–58. Oxford: Berg

Palmberg, Mai. 2001. "A continent without culture?" In *Same and other: negotiating African identity in cultural production*, edited by Maria Eriksson Baaz and Mai Palmberg, 197–208. Uppsala: Nordic Africa Institute

Peek, Philip M. 1994. "The sounds of silence: cross-world communication and the auditory arts in African societies." *American Ethnologist*, 21, no. 3: 474–494

Perullo, Alex. 2005. "Hooligans and heroes: youth identity and hip-hop in Dar es Salaam, Tanzania." *Africa Today*, 51, no. 4: 74–101

Pink, Sarah, ed. 2006. *Applications of anthropology: professional anthropology in the twenty-first century*. New York: Berghahn

—— 2007. "Walking with video." *Visual Studies*, 22, no. 3: 240–252

—— and David Howes. 2010. "The future of sensory anthropology/the anthropology of the senses." *Social Anthropology/Anthropologie sociale*, 18, no. 3: 331–340

Piot, Charles. 2010. *Nostalgia for the future: West Africa after the cold war*. Chicago: University of Chicago Press

PO–PSM. 2006. *The Executive Agencies Programme: implementation workbook*. President's Office–Public Service Management, The United Republic of Tanzania

PO–PSM. 2008. *Public Service Reform Programme II booklet*. President's Office–Public Service Management, The United Republic of Tanzania

Rapport, Nigel. 1998. "Hard sell: commercial performance and the narration of the self." In *Ritual, performance, media*, edited by Felicia Hughes-Freeland, 177–193. London: Routledge

Robbins, Bruce. 1998. "Introduction: part I: actually existing cosmopolitanism." In *Cosmopolitics: thinking and feeling beyond the nation*, edited by Pheng Cheah and Bruce Robbins, 1–19. Minneapolis: University of Minnesota Press

Ruby, Jay. 2005. "The last 20 years of visual anthropology: a critical review." *Visual Studies*, 20, no. 2: 159–170

Sanders, Todd. 2003. "Reconsidering witchcraft: postcolonial Africa and analytic (un)certainties." *American Anthropologist*, 105, no. 2: 338–352

Schieffelin, Edward L. 1998. "Problematizing performance." In *Ritual, performance, media*, edited by Felicia Hughes-Freeland, 194–207. London: Routledge

Shivji, Issa G. 2006. *Let the people speak: Tanzania down the road to neo-liberalism*. Dakar, Senegal: Codesria

—— 2009. "Nyerere's nationalist legacy." *Pambazuka News*, Issue 460. Online at http://www.pambazuka.org/en/category/panafrican/60700/print

Shore, Cris. 2010. "Beyond the multiversity: neoliberalism and the rise of the schizophrenic university." *Social Anthropology*, 18: 15–29

Shore, Cris and Susan Wright, eds. 1997. *Anthropology of policy: critical perspectives on governance and power*. London: Routledge

—— 1999. "Audit culture and anthropology: neo-liberalism in British higher education." *Journal of the Royal Anthropological Institute*, 5, no. 4: 557–575

—— 2000. "Coercive accountability: the rise of audit culture in higher education." In *Audit cultures: anthropological studies in accountability, ethics and the academy*, edited by Marilyn Strathern, 57–89. New York: Routledge

Simensen, Jarle. 2010. "The Norwegian-Tanzanian aid relationship: a historical perspective." In *Tanzania in transition: from Nyerere to Mkapa*, edited by Kjell Havnevik and Aida C. Isinika, 57–70. Dar es Salaam: Mkuki na Nyota Publishers

Smart, Alan. 1999. "Expressions of interest: friendship and *guanxi* in Chinese societies." In *The anthropology of friendship*, edited by Sandra M. Bell and Simon Coleman, 119–136. Oxford: Berg

Smith, Anthony D. 1988 [1986]. *The ethnic origins of nations*. Oxford: Basil Blackwell

Smith, Daniel Jordan. 2007. *A culture of corruption: everyday deception popular discontent in Nigeria*. Princeton, NJ: Princeton University Press

Spear, Thomas. 2004. "Indirect rule, the politics of neo-traditionalism and the limits of invention in Tanzania." In *In search of a nation: histories of authority and dissidence in Tanzania*, edited by Gregory Maddox and James L. Giblin, 70–85. Oxford: James Currey

Stewart, Pamela J. and Andrew Strathern. 2004. *Witchcraft, sorcery, rumors, and gossip*. Cambridge: Cambridge University Press

Stokes, Martin. 2004. "Music and the global order." *Annual Review of Anthropology*, 33, no. 1: 47–72

Stoller, Paul. 1989. *The taste of ethnographic things: the senses in anthropology*. Philadelphia: University of Pennsylvania Press

—— 1997. *Sensuous scholarship*. Philadelphia: University of Pennsylvania Press

—— 2006. "Circuits of African art/paths of wood: exploring an anthropological trail. In *Exploring world art*, edited by Eric Venbrux, Pamela Sheffield Rosi, and Robert L. Wesch, 87–110. Long Grove, Ill.: Waveland Press Inc.

—— 2009. *The power of the between: an anthropological odyssey*. Chicago: University of Chicago Press

Strathern, Marilyn. 1995. *The relation: issues in complexity and scale*. Cambridge: Prickly Pear Press

—— 2000. "Introduction: new accountabilities." In *Audit cultures: anthropological studies in accountability, ethics and the academy*, edited by Marilyn Strathern, 1–18. New York: Routledge

Swantz, Marja-Liisa and Aili Mari Tripp, eds. 1996. *What went right in Tanzania: people's response to directed development*. Dar es Salaam: Dar es Salaam University Press

TaSUBa. 2006. *Review of Curriculum.*
—— 2007. *Taasisi ya Sanaa na Utamaduni Bagamoyo (TaSUBa): framework document.* Ministry of Information, Culture and Sports, The United Republic of Tanzania
—— 2008. *Taasisi ya Sanaa na Utamaduni Bagamoyo (TaSUBa): strategic plan* (2008–2011). Ministry of Information, Culture and Sports, The United Republic of Tanzania
—— and Utrecht School of the Arts (HKU). n.d. *Development of an artistic portfolio: project proposal*
Tenhunen, Sirpa. 2008. "Mobile technology in the village: ICTs, culture, and social logistics in India." *Journal of the Royal Anthropological Institute*, 14, no. 3: 515–534
Thompson, Katrina Daly. 2008. "Keeping it real: reality and representation in Maasai Hip-Hop." *Journal of African Cultural Studies*, 20, no. 1: 33–44
Turner, Victor Witter. 1969. *The ritual process: structure and anti-structure.* London: Routledge & Kegan Paul
—— 1987. *The anthropology of performance.* New York: PAJ
—— 1996 [1957]. *Schism and continuity in an African society: a study of Ndembu village life.* Oxford: Berg
Uimonen, Paula. 1996. "Responses to revolutionary change: a study of social memory in a Khmer village." *Folk*, 38: 31–52
—— 1998. "Inter-national and intra-national boundaries in cyberspace." Paper presented at the biennial meeting of the European Association of Social Anthropologists (EASA), Frankfurt am Main, 4–7 September
—— 2001. *Transnational.dynamics@development.net: Internet, modernization and globalization.* Diss. Stockholm University
—— 2003a. "Networks of global interaction." *Cambridge Review of International Affairs*, 16, no. 2: 273–286
—— 2003b. *Digital empowerment – a strategy for ICT for development (ICT4D) for DESO.* Stockholm: Sida/DESO
—— 2004. *Information and communication technology (ICT) strategy for Bagamoyo College of Arts.* Bagamoyo College of Arts/Embassy of Sweden in Tanzania
—— 2006. *ICT user study at Bagamoyo College of Arts.* Bagamoyo College of Arts and Sida/ Embassy of Sweden Dar es Salaam
—— 2009a. "Internet, arts and translocality in Tanzania." *Social Anthropology/Anthropologie sociale*, 17, no. 3: 276–290
—— 2009b. "Lärande i en digitaliserad värld". In *Didaktisk design i digital miljö: nya möjligheter för lärande*, edited by Staffan Selander and Eva Svärdemo Åberg, 54–69. Stockholm: Liber
—— 2011. "African art students and digital learning." In *Interactive media use and youth: learning, knowledge exchange and behavior*, edited by Elza Dunkels, Gun-Marie Frånberg, and Camilla Hällgren 222–239. Hershey, PA: Information Science Reference
Varenne, Hervé. 2007. "On NCATE standards and culture at work: conversations, hegemony, and (dis-)abling consequences." *Anthropology & Education Quarterly*, 38, no. 1: 16–23
Weiss, Brad. 2002. "Thug realism: inhabiting fantasy in urban Tanzania." *Cultural Anthropology*, 17, no. 1: 93–124
Werbner, Pnina, ed. 2008. *Anthropology and the new cosmopolitanism: rooted, feminist and vernacular perspectives.* Oxford: Berg
Wesch 2007. Web 2.0 … the machine is us/ing us. Online at http://www.youtube.com/wat ch?v=6gmP4nk0EOE&feature=channel
—— 2008. An anthropological introduction to YouTube. Online at http://www.youtube. com/watch?v=TPAO-1Z4_hU&feature=channel
West, Harry G. and Todd Sanders, eds. 2003. *Transparency and conspiracy: ethnographies of suspicion in the new world order.* Durham: Duke University Press

Wilf, Eitan. 2010. "Swinging within the iron cage: modernity, creativity, and embodied practice in American postsecondary jazz education." *American Ethnologist*, 37, no. 3: 563–582

Winders, James. A. 2006. "Mobility and cultural identity: African music and musicians in late-twentieth-century Paris." *French Historical Studies*, 29, no. 3: 483–508

Wolf, Eric. 1956. "Aspects of group relations in a complex society: Mexico." *American Anthropologist*, 58, no. 6: 1065–1078

—— 2001 [1966]. "Kinship, friendship and patron-client relations in complex societies." In *Pathways of power: building an anthropology of the modern world*. Berkeley: University of California Press

Wright, Susan and Annika Rabo. 2010. "Introduction: anthropologies of university reform." *Social Anthropology/Anthropologie sociale*, special issue: *Anthropologies of university reform*, 18, no. 1: 1–14

Wright, Terence. 2008. *Visual impact: culture and the meaning of images*. Oxford: Berg

Wrong, Michela. 2009. *It's our turn to eat: the story of a Kenyan whistleblower*. London: Fourth Estate

Wulff, Helena. 1998. *Ballet across borders: career and culture in the world of dancers*. Oxford: Berg

—— 2001. "Dance, anthropology of," *International Encyclopedia of the Social and Behavioral Sciences*, 3209–3212. Oxford: Elsevier

—— 2005. "'High arts' and the market: an uneasy partnership in the transnational world of ballet." In *The sociology of art: ways of seeing*, edited by David Inglis and John Hughson, 171–182. Basingstoke: Palgrave

——, ed. 2007. *The emotions: a cultural reader*. Oxford, UK: Berg

# INDEX

DATE DUE